Praise for
Paradise Lost, Paradise Regained

"For fifty years I have been reading theological works, and this work by Jacob Zighelboim now ranks at the top. He has written an extraordinary, mature, and compelling account not only of the unique human condition but also of the origin, evolution, and role of a 'designer being or God' in human self-consciousness. As perhaps only a physician/scientist could, Zighelboim describes the impact of human suffering on the way humankind has come to understand, describe, and cope with the challenging reality of their world. In doing so, the perspective he offers is simple but powerful and ultimately full of hope for how the human species may yet reach its most glorious potential. I place *Paradise Lost, Paradise Regained* among the three most important books I have read."

> —*The Reverend Jeremy Campbell, PhD, former President of Claremont School of Theology and Claremont Lincoln University*

"*Paradise Lost, Paradise Regained* is an insightful and remarkable book. It should be read by anyone who hungers to taste the deeper meaning of the 'forbidden fruit' of the Garden of Eden in our lives and who also wants to have a broader understanding of human consciousness and how it shaped our Jewish ancestors' millenary struggle to overcome suffering."

> —*Rabbi Stan Levy, cofounder of the Academy for Jewish Religion California*

"A rich revelation of the history, myths, and attempts by the Hebrews to conquer the suffering that has afflicted humanity since time began. Zighelboim artfully engages us in a profound contemplation of our interconnectedness with God and all life and proposes a new Genesis myth that re-envisions humanity as integrative, realistic, and humane."

> —*Carolyn Conger, PhD, consultant, spiritual teacher, and author*

Paradise Lost, Paradise Regained

Jacob Zighelboim, MD

CJP PRESS

CJP Press
9663 Santa Monica Blvd, # 1430
Beverly Hills, CA 90210

Ordering Information
Quantity sales. Special discounts are available on quantity purchases by cor-
porations, associations, and others. For details, contact the "Special Sales
Department" at the address above.

Printed in the United States of America

ISBN: 978-0-9990400-4-1 (pbk)

First Edition

21 20 19 18 17   10 9 8 7 6 5 4 3 2 1

In recognition of our Hebrew ancestors
who imbued their stories with divine wisdom

To my wife, children, grandchildren and all their loved ones.
May the wisdom of our ancestors illuminate your lives.

"For He who wounds is He who soothes the sore,
and the hand that hurts is the hand that heals."
—*Job 5:18*

Contents

Preface

REGARDLESS OF WHERE OR when we are born, the kind of parents we have, the god or gods we worship, or the cultural values we espouse, we all share the same yearning: to live a life in which suffering is either nonexistent or rare.

Suffering, however, is a physiological and psychological given, the price we pay for the many remarkable privileges we have as self-conscious, reflective human beings. Accepting it as an irrevocable part of our experience has been and remains difficult. As a result, a great deal of our energy has been spent trying to control, ameliorate, and, if possible, eliminate this burdensome foe.

These millenary efforts have promoted, at least in part, the development of our sciences and technologies as well as a rich religious mythology aimed at explaining our suffering while also offering us guidance as to how to attain a better, happier life. An example of this mythology can be found in the pages of the Hebrew Bible. There, we encounter detailed descriptions of the stories that emanated from the soul of our Israelite ancestors in response to their distressing and frightening experiences and their developing awareness of the ruthless world in which they lived.

In reviewing the underlying meaning of these powerful stories with a lessening of suffering in mind we will be better able to comprehend why they took the form they did, what they intended to accomplish, their unintended consequences, their successes in reducing individual and collective suffering, and, ultimately, their inability to provide sustainable relief from the innately heavy burden that comes with self-reflection.

My intention in writing this book is to provide a coherent and cohesive account of the struggle of our forebears to recover the paradisiacal life they had seemingly lost as well as to sketch out a path that offers new possibilities for the successful resolution of the distress that has afflicted humanity from the beginning of time, a distress born from our difficulty in accepting all that being human entails.

The book is divided into four parts, each one describing a particular stage in the evolution of our Hebrew ancestors' millenary effort to conquer suffering. Part I, chapter 1, describes the many benefits that the dawn of self-reflective consciousness brought us as well as the suffering implicit in being sentient beings—our primordial wound. Chapter 2 investigates the different approaches man has taken to overcome this consequence and chapter 3 examines the myth of man's fall from grace in Eden as a result of transgressing God's injunction not to eat from the tree of the knowledge of good and bad. In response, God curses man's life, expulsing him from Eden. What was originally man's primordial—*unavoidable*—wound became now his primordial—*avoidable*—illness, a condition resulting from an encrusted belief in our innate badness.

Part II analyzes the mythical developments following man's banishment from Eden. These myths are aimed at helping man recover his standing with God as well as the self-esteem and self-worth he lost as a result of the curse God levied on him. They speak of a sacred covenant between God and man, first through the person of Noah and several generations later with Abraham, a more mature, self-reliant, self-affirming, and self-realizing person, whom God called to establish a new way of life, one based on ethical principles and moral values (chapter 4). Abraham's experiment in righteous living, consolidated through the life of his son Isaac and grandson Jacob as well as their respective wives, led to the betterment of man's existence; his life became more harmonious, resourceful, and balanced. But such progress would have had little social, political, and psychological significance if it could not be extended to the lives of a much larger community of people, a whole nation.

So in chapter 5 the book looks at the conjoint efforts of a community of six hundred thousand souls who, after experiencing enslavement for centuries, witnessed the emergence of a redeemer/liberator figure in their midst: Moses, a charismatic, spiritually heightened leader, ready to free his people from slavery and deliver them into a life of prosperity and happiness—the land of milk and honey God had promised their ancestors. Having succeeded in freeing his people, Moses understood that after living in bondage for so long they would have great difficulty living a free, ethically principled, moral life. Hence, from the depth of his soul, new mythical ideas emanated; God, the Bible tells us, revealed to Moses the Ten Commandments along with 613 precepts to live by; with these, they could hope to attain the peacefulness and happiness for which they so yearned.

Once in possession of this guiding Instruction, the people of Israel were able to enter the Promised Land and establish themselves as a sovereign nation comprised of twelve tribes. During the initial period of nationhood, they enjoyed goodness and well-being, but the honeymoon did not last too long. Surrounded by powerful enemies that coveted their lands and possessions, the nation's safety was often threatened and compromised. Something needed to be done to secure sovereignty. Something that a land divided into independent tribal enclaves ruled by tribal chieftains, as they had decided to do in order to accommodate the desires of the returning tribes, could not accomplish.

Chapters 6 and 7 reveal a growing tension building up in the Israelite community as a result of the opposing needs of its citizenry: the need for respect of civil rights secured by them after much struggle and the need for safety and stability for the community and the nation as a whole. New figures appeared on the Israelite landscape to help them address this burgeoning crisis: the monarch, responsible for securing the nation's sovereignty and maintaining order and peace, and the Prophet, whose job was to serve as the nation's alter ego, ensuring that the ethical principles and the moral values espoused by their tradition were respected and sustained.

Unfortunately, the establishment of a monarchy in Israel did not bode well for the health of the nation. This lengthy period of Israelite history was marred by strife and a progressive loss of the important gains they had made when they reconquered the land. In the end, the Assyrians managed to subjugate the kingdom of Israel; its people dispersed, never to return. The kingdom of Judea, on the other hand, was able to survive for a few more centuries but in the end also fell first to the Babylonians and later to other empires, never quite regaining its independence.

The pain and misery these developments evoked in the population added to their inability, despite multiple efforts, to recapture their freedom and sustain it for a significant period, which led to the appearance of two novel responses aimed at helping the people overcome their existential distress. These responses are discussed in part III. The first is captured in the pages of the Books of Job and Koheleth (chapters 8 and 10); it offers a new explanation for why man suffered so much and what he needed to do to reduce and hopefully eliminate his suffering. This new explanation was revolutionary and potentially resolving—it still is—but unfortunately it was too demanding to be integrated into the fabric of Israel's collective life at that time. The second response, which took place during the middle of the fifth century BCE (before the Common Era), consisted of the appearance of the sacred Torah—the five books of Moses—in written form and is described in chapter 9. Up until then, Moses's Instruction to the people of Israel had been passed on orally.

The binding of the commandments, the laws, the rules, and the precepts in books constituted an important development in the life of the Israelite community, for it allowed its citizens to have an authoritative, reliable, and unchanging set of precepts and commandments by which to guide their lives. It also freed them from the influence of the Prophets and priests who until then had been indispensable for passing on of God's Law. Unfortunately, while having the Torah in written form did help to improve the livelihood of the community in Canaan, in the end, it did not solve their underlying problem; they continued to suffer. This despairing situation created the social and psycho-spiritual conditions for the emergence of two mythical novelties never before seen in Israel.

The first is examined in part IV, chapter 11; it involves the appearance during the last two centuries BCE of apocalyptic literature in the form of the Book of Daniel. This book presaged the dawn of an era of everlasting happiness and goodness for Israel and humanity at the end of time. This futuristic vision must have afforded our forebears much comfort, raising their hopes for a better tomorrow.

The second development, discussed in chapter 12, involved the arrival in Israelite society of men like Hillel the Elder and Jeshua of Nazareth, men who embodied the energy of healing and compassion that was sorely needed to balance the more legalistic, severe, judgmental aspects of the religious tradition.

Despite the remarkable ingenuity, beauty, and sustainable power of the myths that our Israelite forebears produced over more than a thousand years, they were only partially effective in redeeming their suffering. Hence, in chapter 13, a renewed iteration of the Eden myth is offered, one that intends to correct the misunderstanding incurred by our ancestors when framing the dawn of human consciousness in condemnatory terms. The new version of the Eden myth sees consciousness as the greatest development in human history and as a gift to be cherished and appreciated. Grounded in present-day knowledge and understanding of human experience afforded by science and our evolving culture—a knowledge which, parenthetically, is in continuous flux—this new myth aims at restoring us to our rightful place in the Creation, a place from which we can willfully embrace our role as custodians of life and as people who cherish our humanity in the fullness of its complexity, people able to rejoice in the privilege of being alive in the world we imagine God created for us.

A Note on the Language

You may notice that I often use the term "man" to refer to all people or an individual person and that masculine pronouns (he, him, and his) are therefore used as well. This was done for a variety of reasons. I often refer to biblical translations that use masculine terms to refer to all humans or an individual (of any gender). So I chose to use terms that were consistent with those texts. I also wanted to avoid awkward "he or she" phrasing when referring to an individual.

PART I

The Primordial Wound /
The Primordial Illness

CHAPTER 1

The Human Condition

Self-Conscious Awareness

AS HUMAN BEINGS, WE are born into a world we neither created nor understand. Although we arrive unconscious of self or others and fully dependent on caretakers to supply us with nourishment, shelter, and protection, we do not appear as totally helpless creatures. Indeed, we come with many innate resources to deal with our physical and human environments. Our bodies possess such inborn abilities as breathing, crying, swallowing, and digesting food. Moreover, we are wired to respond adaptively to hunger, thirst, wetness, and other uncomfortable body sensations. And while our immune system is still somewhat immature at birth, over a very short period it acquires the capacity to protect us from the noxious effects of a myriad of bacteria, viruses, parasites, and other foreign substances—even though it has never encountered these before and most assuredly never will.

The Paradisiacal Life: Our First Months

During our initial six months, we live guided by such natural impulses and adaptive responses that function primarily as undifferentiated parts of a larger whole. While in this state of being, our experiences are shrouded in darkness: much of what is happening to us is potentially knowable and often is known by those taking care of us (the infant is hungry, wet, hurting, and so forth). But we cannot accurately be said to "know" any of it. The preconscious existence of infancy is predictable and fairly orderly, even though chaotic episodes occur from time to time. In this kind of reality, neither the actions of living organisms nor those of nature as a whole are experienced as divided into such binary categories as good and bad, right and wrong, or into systems of reward and punishment. In this presubjective stage, ours is a world without time or space where there reigns no history—no beginning or ending. Here life flows as it did for billions of years, an endless unrolling of events, some routine and some massively transformative, but unknowable until consciousness first emerges and brings some of these events to the light of knowing.

Realizations such as these became reinforced some years ago when I began regularly visiting my newly born granddaughter. Whenever I walked in, she turned her head and looked at me, but I was sure she had no idea who I was. Though she had recently started to smile, this delightful expression, which reflects an emerging need to connect, was not willed or even conscious. Rather, it was an instinctive reaction, one of nature's ways to ensure she received proper attention and care. As I watched during these first months, her simple existence seemed by and large fulfilling. When hungry she cried for food, an automatic reaction she had been able to perform from the very beginning; and when feeling satiated she either fell asleep, exhausted from her efforts to feed, or lay placidly in her crib making soft lovable noises. Though she was, in fact, a most vulnerable being, totally dependent for her survival and well-being on her parents' care, she was ignorant of such facts and hence, did not experience the pain of knowing doubt, uncertainty, or even the awesome privilege of having to choose. Instinctually driven in all she did, neither self nor others being part of her awareness, her being was guided only by mental images of pleasant or unpleasant sensations. Though infants get sick, feel pain, and die, illness and death were not real for her—and in this sense did not exist.

As infants first begin maturing, they learn to crawl and stand up. They also demonstrate new interpersonal behaviors such as waving hands to say goodbye or turning the head when called. These bodily responses suggest they are beginning to emerge from the relatively undifferentiated, egoless state into which they were born. Now infants recognize familiar faces. But this initial recognition, as far as we know, does not seem to be made by a functioning ego. In other words, infants can be seen responding affectionately to their mothers, fathers, or nannies but do not yet know they are doing it, nor do they know who these people are. This kind of life seems paradisiacal to me—the pain of knowing still dormant in their budding souls.

The Emerging "I" and the Development of Self-Reflective Consciousness

Beginning usually during the latter part of the second year of life, the paradisiacal stage of the infant's life becomes gradually replaced by a new stage characterized by the appearance of powerfully adaptive mental and physical attributes. The capacity to walk, which typically emerges during this stage, enhances the child's ability to secure food, to secure water, and to handle his environment, all of which increase his chances to survive. During this same period, and a few months preceding the arrival of language, the appearance of the first evidence of a differentiated self comes about. Infants are able now to make the self/ nonself discrimination by pointing their fingers accurately when asked, "Where is Mommy, Daddy, Grandpa, Grandma," or toward themselves when their names are mentioned. They are transitioning from respond-ing to otherness with their bodies to willfully using parts of their bodies, in this case, their fingers, to express themselves. Additionally, and in a remarkable transformation of mind, children begin to manifest such unique human qualities as using words to designate specific objects in their immediate environment: mama, dada, paci, baba, moo (milk). As this is happening, human infants demonstrate not only their skill in recognizing objects but also in assigning meaning to them by represent-ing them symbolically by name. This process of assigning and later on searching for meaning will continue for the duration of their lives.

As linguistic capacity increases, children use it to illustrate an evolving "ownership" over objects in their environment and even over parts of their bodies. When referring to the pacifier they had enjoyed for months, they declare with newfound authority, "Mine!" Similarly, other things come into their stated possession: "My tummy, my toes, my bottle, my doggy, my book." I remember when my fourteen-month-old granddaughter pointed her finger toward her bruised big toe on her right foot saying, "Owee." When I asked her the next day, "Where is your owee?" she pointed to the correct foot and toe. Something in her was now able not only to understand words and respond to them appropriately but also to indicate what was happening to her internally. No longer was her discomfort generalized: she was conscious of the location of her pain. Now able to retrieve that knowledge from her memory bank, my granddaughter showed a capacity to establish links between events occurring at different times in her life. She was starting to bind time, chronological time. A few months later, as her linguistic capacity expanded and became more refined, she was able to articulate her awareness of the flow of time: the past, present, and future became part of her daily life.

All of this is possible because, at this stage, infants are now in possession of a psychic organ—the ego—that knows where their bodies begin and end, where different body parts are located and can say so.

The appearance of an objectifying self heralds an even more remarkable development: the appearance of a subject capable of saying *I*. "Where is my beautiful granddaughter," I asked as I walked into her bedroom pretending I could not see her. "I am here, Grandpa. Can't you see me? I am here." This was the first moment I heard her say "I," although her parents reported having heard it several times before. The emergence of an objectifying self is a critical event in ontogeny; it defines the moment in which the child completes his transition from living a life of images and sensory meanings to one punctuated by self-consciousness, self-reflection, and thoughtful actions. From here on, the child will be able to objectify the physical world in which he is embedded as well as the inner life of private feelings, images, and bodily sensations he alone can know.

The ego, the part of the psyche that initially said my and mine and now says I, has no specific physical form; it cannot be located in any part of the human brain, or for that matter the body, and cannot be dissected. And yet it is as real as anything we will ever know. In sleep, it seems to give up its vigilant attempt to direct the organism's perceptions and reactions, allowing aspects of the mysterious, unconscious life to come to the surface in the form of dreams. Nonetheless, upon awakening, this ego structure miraculously returns to function as the center of our being.

Language provides the developing child a way to articulate her thoughts, her desires and needs, her experiences, her perceptions, her values, her beliefs, and her theories of why things are the way they are. In brief, it gives children the means to create stories about themselves and the world they inhabit that will powerfully condition their realities, as well as provide them with the means to control these.

Our capacity to create narratives makes the world with all its grandeur and splendor come alive for us. An ancient Jewish teaching acknowledges this fact when asserting that God created the world with words. Taken at face value, the statement seems nonsensical. How could words give birth to the material world? But when the statement is understood as acknowledging the transcendental effect that the dawn of human consciousness had on the existing world, it makes perfect sense. Metaphorically speaking, it suggests that while the universe may have come into being eons before the appearance of the first human being, it became known only when conscious humans capable of communicating their experiences symbolically appeared on the planet. God may have created the universe, but it is man who made His Creation known. As a result, humans acquired the ability to intervene and influence its course in ways no other species ever had.

Perceived in this way, the assertion is accurate: worlds are indeed created with words. Many centuries later, John, a Jewish man living in the first century of the Common Era (CE) who authored the last of the Gospels, made allusion to this reality when stating, "In the beginning was the Word, and the Word was with God, and the Word was God" (John 1:1).[1] Whether the Word is God is a matter of belief and faith but what is indisputable and empirically based is that human history indeed started when words began to flow from the depth of humanity's imagination.

Each human narrative gives birth to a unique and irreplaceable reality with its beauty, mystery, challenges, triumphs, failings, and explanatory theories. In the case of my grandchildren, the emergence of their speaking-selves transformed them into subjects that

7

now owned all their bodies' sensations and actions, and their evolving voices enhanced their ability to relate to the rest of the world. Their feelings of joy, fear, excitement, shame, interest, or guilt in this new state were anchored on subjects they experienced personally. In essence, the moment their egos emerged from the silence of preverbal existence they became *persons* who owned everything that happened to them and were able to say so. Every sensation, mood, occurrence, and perception was now theirs, belonged to them, and would become part of their life history. From this point on, my grandchildren, as with other normal children, could assert themselves in the world: "I want milk; I will get the guitar, see a movie, play with the ball."

At this juncture, children also have become witnesses to the events happening in and around them: "My body is telling me it is hungry," "I love to play at the beach," "I don't like rainy days." Additionally, they have begun to experience themselves in control over significant parts of their outer and inner lives. But they are also emerging from the world of natural rhythms and flows to a world of values, of good and bad people, good and bad experiences, pleasant and unpleasant feelings, and, more importantly, to a world in which these very qualities will unavoidably define their lives and their persons.

As the ego-self takes shape, it becomes involved in regulating the child's bodily functions and innate impulses, moving him away from dwelling in perpetual reactivity to outer or inner environmental cues and toward a world that can be objectified. In this objective world, actions are often delayed to allow the individual to scan his accumulated experiences—his memory bank—and come up with the best solution to the problem faced. Children move from acting impetuously and reflexively—like when withdrawing a hand from a hot stove—to acting responsively. As an example, my grandson, at the age of four, referring to an area reserved for child's play asked, "Can I go in there?" Left to mere impulses he would have run straight into the playground, but his developing ego had wrested him in the hands of a powerful entity, one capable of restraining desires and adapting to circumstances with possibilities he was learning to decode. After I had assented to his request, his swift passage into the play area confirmed that the force restraining his urge had just released him. His newly acquired capacities will decrease the chance of him coming into conflict with his caring handlers, and later on, with the world at large.

In earliest infancy, our responses to stressful occurrences are automatic, governed by the same flight or fight response we share with our mammalian relatives. The emergence of our ego-self makes conscious the awareness of alternatives as well as the ability (and often need) to make choices. Some children, to give another example, are inclined to push aside other kids who cut in front of them either in school or on the playground. Their reactions do not seem hostile but rather a simple assertion of their presence and rights. Later on, however, they are taught to use words to stop an action they deem undesirable. From then on, when someone cuts in front of them they can assume a firm body posture and declare, "Sorry, no cutting." This tactic works for them often enough, and although they occasionally will revert to their old ways, increasingly they learn to depend more on reasoning and cooperative language, at least as the first response when attempting to stand up for their rights and interests. All these emerging skills give the developing child freedoms otherwise unknown in nature.

As the psyche continues to mature a further development is the appearance of a drive to self-sufficiency. Usually beginning in the months following a child's second birthday it asserts itself rather definitively: "No, no, no, I'll do it *solito*," my grandson, at the age of two and a half, demanded when I foolishly tried to help him climb the stairs to the second floor in my home (*solito* is Spanish for "by myself," a word his nanny had taught him). His vigorous rebuke made me understand he was entering a phase of psychological growth aimed at reducing his dependency on others and helping him acquire mastery over the world in which he lived. The inner urge toward autonomy continues growing in strength: "I'll pour the juice, feed myself, open the car door, climb into the car seat, push the market cart, play my CDs, turn the TV on, carry the bags." Such expressions are now part of children's linguistic repertoire, expressing their relentless pursuit of independence.

This drive is so strong in fact that woe to those who try to interfere with it, particularly when done in the name of efficiency. The cries of frustration and disappointment that follow such attempts can wrench the heart and make one regret such ill-timed and inappropriate acts. I had the misfortune of committing such an ignominy one Wednesday morning when I usually would take my grandson to a gymnastic class near his home. Because we had met with unexpectedly heavy traffic, the class had already started by the time we arrived. To enter the gym kids must remove their shoes and socks, and that day my grandson was adamant he was going to do it *solito*. He managed to take off his shoes without much difficulty, but when it came to removing his socks, he was unable to pull them over his ankle. Despite tremendous efforts, he had no success. Time kept passing, and I was concerned he was missing important parts of the class, so I tried to help him—and got a sharp rebuke: "No, no, no. I will do it myself." I backed off and let him try a few more times, but seeing it was going nowhere I proceeded to remove the socks without asking for his permission. Visibly frustrated, he got into an awful funk, even refusing to participate in class activities. After a great deal of persuasion, he agreed to join the class, but I was left feeling guilty and terribly sorry for having caused his heartache. I had learned my lesson, though. Later, whenever I saw him struggling with some difficulty, I first made sure he had exhausted all his options; only then would I softly say, "Do you want me to help you?" To which he often responded in the affirmative.

The Inquiring Mind

In tandem with self-sufficiency, one also notices the gradual emergence of an inquiring mind: "What does accident, emergency, fog, routine, tour mean?" "Are you going to watch TV with me?" "Where is Grandpa going?" "How are apples, yogurt, eggs, TVs made?" By asking about the appropriateness of certain actions and the meaning of words children are seeking both approval and clarity about how to live safely in the environments in which they exist.

At this stage, young children are adventurous and willing to try new things, but they also become progressively more aware of dangers and threats that have to be taken into consideration before deciding whether or not to venture into new territory. As has been said, this kind of ever-developing risk assessment and the choice of action following it is something only self-conscious beings can make.

The profound and transcendent transformations described before are dependent upon the expansion not only of our capacity for reflective consciousness but also of the emergence of an array of mental functions intimately associated with it. I am referring, of course, to complex language, reasoning, imagining, thinking, dreaming, and the parallel development of our locomotor and sensorial biological capabilities. In the case of my grandchildren, I was privileged to witness how each of these notable developments materialized. Some appeared gradually while others came on so suddenly as to seem miraculous. These new faculties included progressing from a state in which all they could do was lie flat on their backs making uncoordinated movements of arms and legs to that special day in which their gait became steady, allowing them to walk up and down stairs with abandon. Later on, and with a little coaching, they were able to competently stand on their two hands, do summersaults, walk unassisted on the balance beam, dance ballet, swim like a fish, and claim the world as their oyster. Simultaneously, their evolving linguistic proficiency allowed them to move from uttering isolated words to being able to use language with increasing dexterity; before long they were able to negotiate subtle interpersonal understandings and even a secret humor regarding the complex relationships of aspects of our physical nature we share with all animals. One day, as I was leaving my three-year-old granddaughter's dance class, I told her we were first going to her home to visit Mr. Blank (I meant Mr. Potty), and then we would go on to the Museum of Natural History.

"Who is Mr. Blank, Grandpa?"

"Someone you need to spend some time with before going to the museum."

"Would you give me a little hint?"

"Okay," I said. "Mr. Blank's name starts with a P."

"Oh, I know who it is," she said gleefully. "It is . . . "—and here she paused for emphasis seemingly having fun with it—"Mr. Potty!"

Within a short time, I witnessed how my grandchildren profited from their ever-growing ability to express feelings, concerns, and fantasies: "Today, I don't feel like going to soccer practice." "When you leave me alone at school I feel afraid." "When I grow up I will take all my family on a ride in my airplane. We will go all over the planet Earth and to the moon, too." All such developments exemplify the happy progression of a complex process of maturation, which takes place in all our bodies and minds.

The emergence of an individual child's self-reflective consciousness is indeed the crowning event of an evolutionary process that started with the development of the first living cell some four and a half billion years ago. Watching its rapid unfolding in children kindles profound appreciation for the wonders of our human nature.

This remarkable attribute of mind confers great benefits on a personal, collective, and even a planetary scale. In its absence, the wealth of our inner world, with its rich images, feelings, fantasies, and dreams, would be forever unreflected and unknown. Similarly, the external world, with its colossal beauty and mystery, would lack reality: nobody would speak of, care about, or be concerned with it. "I like the beach, trees, doggies, snowflakes, horses, flowers, the sun, the beautiful moon and stars that light up the night." These and similar statements are uttered daily by children, their joy of living growing as they mature and are able to encompass more and more of the grandness of the space into which they have been thrust. Progressively, they will learn to appreciate nature's marvels, including those associated with their human nature: the warmth and comfort of their parents' tender care, the concern of friends for their well-being, the compassion many demonstrate for those who suffer, the generous giving of time and energy to those in need, the spirit of cooperation that bursts forth when most required, and the perennial effort to be fair and just.

Additionally, the arising of reflective consciousness has introduced into nature's evolution a force that vastly accelerates change. Changes in our bodies, our minds, our society, and our relationship to the natural world, which may have taken millions of years to unfold, can now blossom in a single lifetime. Other animals, even fairly sophisticated ones, fracture bones but cannot develop means to enhance their repair: but thousands of years ago the first splints and bandages were conceived and made; centuries later, casts and antiseptic liquids, x-rays, and so on were developed. We survive such mishaps, gradually healing and regaining functionality, when other living creatures would merely become another's food.

In my case, as a cancer survivor, I would not be alive today if not for the medical treatments that our self-reflective consciousness made possible. Similarly, in full appreciation of the privilege he has received, a close friend has survived for more than two decades thanks to a kidney transplanted from a cadaver. In more general terms, our understanding of hygiene and nutrition has reduced the frequency of or wholly suppressed preventable terrible illnesses that formerly ravaged entire civilizations (and in some places of the world, sadly, still do). Such modern miracles would have been impossible without this quintessentially human attribute.

As self-conscious individual beings, we also learn to appreciate our unique constitution and temperament. Some of us like mangos while others prefer bananas. Some like to talk softly while others are vociferous. Some are inclined toward the sciences and others toward the arts. Some like classical music and others like pop.

Moreover, just as each young person learns to check childish impulsivity through self-reflection and also to correct and refine behavior, so does our species. Reflective self-awareness is the central means for increasing all adaptation to the presence, demands, and needs of other human beings around us.

From collective self-consciousness comes our gradual sorting out of what succeeds for village, nation, and eventually humankind: the quest for individual and social freedom, safety, and happiness. Morality, ethical principles, and laws develop: Don't steal; don't beat up your children; don't despise other races, religions, or cultures; respect people's autonomy and others' rights; and don't do to others what you wouldn't want to be done to yourself.

From self-consciousness also comes most of our pleasures—the meals we create to suit our cultivated tastes, ceremonies of delight in eating, the art of making love, the ability to engage ourselves intimately with the complexity of another. Through self-consciousness, we create ever more comfortable shelters; we travel far and return safely; we read books or write them; and we have symphonies, waltzes, perfumes, and clean socks. And as has been noted, without self-consciousness none of these fine things would be known or appreciated by us.

A Two-Edged Sword: The Problem of Human Suffering

This species-wide development of reflective self-consciousness, however, is not a teleological process. In other words, its appearance was not purposefully driven but rather the product of complex trials and errors of evolution. Its emergence, while highly beneficial, has imposed unintended consequences on us, its beneficiaries, and on the environment in which we live.

One such consequence was the introduction of suffering into the living world. Self-consciousness accomplished this by causing our private inner lives to be revealed to us. By this, I mean the uniquely human act of *knowing our unpleasant feelings*. Because suffering, as distinct from pain, results from our being self-conscious, it is unavoidable. Regardless of when or where we are born, the family we belong to, or the kind of upbringing we receive, as long as we are self-conscious beings we will suffer.

Though preconscious human infants experience pain and other unpleasant feelings, they lack an inner subject capable of knowing them. For them, unpleasant feelings are part of a sophisticated repertoire of emotional responses—joy, disgust, excitement, shame, guilt, and sadness, which evolution has expertly wired into their bodies. These emotions are part of an innate set of responses babies use to support themselves during the most vulnerable stage of human existence. Long before their cognitive faculties make themselves known, their affective apparatus—innate emotional states that express themselves primarily through smiling and crying—helps them communicate their needs and wants to others as they struggle to ensure that their fundamental life requirements are met. Even at this early stage of life, the more complex feelings, like guilt and shame, have essential survival benefits for them. By having the capacity to feel guilt and shame, they can more effectively regulate their infantile behaviors so as to ensure the goodwill of their caregivers.

Infants must have the ability to modulate their behavior in response to negative cues received from those on whom they are totally dependent. Responding to disapproval by caregivers with feelings of shame and guilt keeps them from pursuing behaviors that trigger such undesirable responses. Given what adults may see as undesirable behaviors by infants, the unpleasant emotions they feel can even play a life-saving role. Once the child becomes a knower of her feelings, though, she can report on the pain and consequent feelings, reflect on them, and imagine their future development or lack of it. Knowing one's unpleasant feelings is a preeminent instance of how reflective consciousness operates as a two-edged sword.

As consciousness expands, one also notices an attendant increase in emotional distress. Children begin to manifest discomfort in response to new places and people, anxiety when feeling unprotected, and embarrassment regarding the body. Just a few months after being toilet trained, young children begin to ask their parents and caretakers to leave the bathroom because they need privacy, thus revealing feelings of shame regarding a bodily function that previously had been natural and comfortable. During the first years of their lives, all my grandchildren were fairly unconcerned about doing the "big jump" from the top of a three-foot wall built on the shallow side of our home pool. A year later the place from which they used to jump with abandon was now too high for them. Their growing awareness of their vulnerability caused them to become more controlled and measured in their actions. They also started to manifest fear of dark places and loud noises. Why this was so, I do not know. I suspect it was triggering fears of loss or annihilation. On the other hand, they all became deeply attuned to my personal well-being, and so whenever I stumbled, coughed, or ached, they inquired with concern in their voices. I find these and other experiences that reveal children's enhanced awareness of environmental threats deeply moving. Part of me feels compelled to step in and protect my grandchildren from these ills, but another part knows to back off. Nonetheless, it is still distressing to see their discomfort and to know that the unpleasantness caused by their self-awareness of these discomforting feelings will be forever a part of their lives: all I can do is reassure them and give them my love.

Reflective self-consciousness also allows us the privilege of knowing the *reality of our circumstances*. By this, I include awareness of the inevitability of our death, the uncertainty surrounding our life, and the lack of control each of us exercises over important aspects of existence: we can get sick, die, be injured physically, sexually, emotionally, and so forth at any moment. Pondering this information often evokes fear, hurt, anger, and disillusionment. A few years ago, a good friend shared with me a moving experience. As he was driving his five-year-old grandson home, the boy began to talk about leaves falling from trees, the passing of the seasons, and why all this happened. He seemed quite intrigued by the subject and at one point asked my friend: "If I were to lose my hair, would that be like the trees losing their leaves?"

"Yes, sweetie, that is a good way to think of it," he said.

The boy kept quiet for a minute or so and then his eyes welled up with tears and in a soft, cracking voice, he said, "Grandpa, I don't want to die."

"But of course you don't, love, and you will not. Not now," answered my friend.

"But will I die when I get old?"

"Yes, love," he said, "everyone does."

"But I don't want to."

"I know. I don't want to either," his grandpa remarked, "but it is the way life is."

"But can't we do something, Grandpa? Can we place new batteries in the person's body and bring them back?"

"That sounds like a good idea," my much-relieved friend said. "Do you think it's a good idea?"

"Yes, Grandpa. I think it is a good idea."

In this short and poignant exchange, this man's grandson articulated, for the first time, an awareness of death as something undesirable and, more importantly, as something he was vulnerable to. And even though, at this juncture, death was something the boy could not comprehend rationally, the idea evoked hurt and sadness in him. Before becoming conscious of it, death, even though he had come in touch with it through the movies he watched on his DVD player and the lyrics of songs he liked to listen to, was not a concern. But from then on this was going to be something he was going to wrestle with for the rest of his life.

A different source of suffering arises from our ability to concern ourselves with what our unpleasant feelings may portend for the future ("What if the pain in my belly means I am dying?" "Yesterday I could not remember my friend's name. I'm sure I am losing my mind."). The conclusions we reach from exploring these thought exercises are sometimes rooted in fact but more often than not are the by-product of ignorance, fear, and prejudice. This type of suffering begins in early childhood but increases as we grow and become more aware of the world we live in and the dangers it contains. As we reach adolescence we discover, both through direct experience and through intellectual learning, that the grand planet on which we live, with all its glorious natural beauties, is also a ruthless, amoral theater full of natural disasters on a colossal scale, killing infinite numbers of organisms as well as bringing forth wholly new species.

Disasters aside, we recognize that British-born philosopher Alan Watts was right when, in reference to bacteria, worms, molds, birds, and ourselves, he wrote, "The living world is a mutual eating society." What we desire most—to live as well and as long as possible—will inevitably be denied us. Pleasant, healthy living may be crushed when least expected. Into such a reality, some people are born with congenital malformations or genetic disorders that profoundly damage the quality and the length of their lives. Others, not yet adults, will suffer from serious illnesses or accidents and die.

We arrive at adulthood knowing that for some people life entails calamities that burden their existence with unmitigated sorrow while others sail through it almost unscathed. These differing fates underscore nature's ruthless randomness. Nature's awesome powers, when unleashed—tornados, hurricanes, earthquakes, floods, torrential rains—may cause serious physical damage and injury to our loved ones and us. Many of us are indeed tormented by the knowledge that our desire to live a long life, to feel secure in our bodies, and to see our plans and expectations fulfilled may not be attained, or worse, cannot be attained.

Finally, consciousness endows us with the ability to imagine events that have not happened and may never happen; yet because our thoughts can evoke feelings, we experience such imaginings emotionally, as if they actually did happen. The torment we put ourselves through when one of our adolescent children does not return home on time is a good example. Growing up, I went through a period in which I panicked whenever my father was late from work. Several of my classmates' fathers had died from heart attacks during the preceding months, and this had impacted me deeply. During this time I would persistently go to the window to check whether any of the cars approaching my apartment building were his. I envisioned him having died on route and me and my mother being left alone and helpless. A similar type of suffering afflicts people who torment themselves with preoccupation regarding minor deviations of normal bodily functions. These people are afflicted by a condition called hypochondriasis, and while their physical afflictions are often trivial, their worries are all too real and so is their fear and persistent despair. Suffering that stems from the existence of a psychiatric disorder or distorted ideas arising from our upbringing, beliefs, cultural environment, religious persuasion, and personal experiences may often be overcome with dedication and effort.

Another unintended consequence of the dawn of self-reflective consciousness has been the emergence in us of a great potential for the constructive and the destructive, the two inexorably intertwined. From creatures whose responses were simply instinctual, reflexive, and stereotypical, consciousness transformed preconscious humanoids into creatures endowed with free will and choice: alternate ways to respond to events predicated not only on what they perceived but also on the way they interpreted their perceptions. Man's ability to process information gave rise to narratives and actions expressing the way he understood the information received, which at best has been—and always will be—an approximation of what is. This is so because all information humans receive is filtered through a processing system of restricted discriminatory capacity shared by all members of our species, although the capacity to discern this information varies between individuals. No matter how hard people may try, they will never be able to perceive the world identically. The degree of distortion each individual introduces into his or her perceptions is a by-product of each person's unique genetic makeup, familial background, religious and cultural upbringing, economic status, personal encounters, and the presence or absence of mental disorders. All these factors influence the way we translate the world of existence into that of human reality, which in turn affects the way we experience and respond to it. Clearly, the more accurate our interpretations of the information processed, the more meaningful and helpful our responses will be to us and to those with whom we interface regularly, and the better we will be able to take care of ourselves and suffer less.

Anyone who has observed children closely has experienced seeing innocent creatures dependent on their caretakers for survival transition into becoming autonomous beings making important decisions about their lives and the lives of others, decisions that neither their parents nor society at large can control or ensure that they will ultimately lead to positive outcomes. It is unquestionable that the environment in which we grow up, our personal experiences, and our genetic makeup will influence the kind of people we will become and the kind of lives we will live. So while most children grow up to become solid individuals who try to live a moral and principled life, others, the great minority, become outlaws and criminals, wreaking havoc in their communities and committing heinous crimes, promoting wars, and ethnic and racial cleansing and all forms of abuse—physical, sexual, political, economic, and more. These destructive acts stem from the same ability to use one's mental endowments and the self-reflective consciousness that we all possess but—for myriad reasons—these few have chosen to use it for evil rather than good.

Pain and Suffering

In common speech, "pain" and "suffering" are sometimes used inter-changeably. But just as often, they entail a distinction in meaning. For example, when we say "he is suffering greatly" we usually mean more than he is experiencing great bodily pain. By using the word "suffer-ing," we imply that in addition to the unpleasant physical sensation of pain the person is also distressed by experiencing many added unpleas-ant emotions: fear, shame, worry, anxiety, or guilt. These added dis-tressful feelings result primarily from the array of negative thoughts that being in pain usually evokes in us. Typical of such all-too-human thoughts are these: "Is this pain a harbinger of something really bad? Am I no longer good enough to deserve others' care? Will my pain become worse? Will I be able to work and support my family? Did I do something to deserve or cause my pain?"

Though pain is biologically ancient, suffering is a recent entry into evolutionary history, and the neural pathways responsible for its mani-festation are different from those involved in pain. People under the influence of an anesthetic, in a state of deep sleep, or in a coma, for example, will respond to painful stimuli in tangible ways, despite their not being consciously aware they are in pain. For example, they will grimace when pricked with a needle, thus acknowledging the painful nature of the stimulus; but we have no evidence they are suffering.

Given that the conscious self is not only the locus of our unpleas-ant feelings but also the condition capable of modulating their inten-sity—augmenting or diminishing them via the thoughts they evoke in us—it is reasonable to suggest that pain and suffering are potentially dissociable. In other words, though we may be in physical distress, if we can either avoid or contain the threatening thoughts that often follow unexpected and/or unexplained pain, then the inner distress invariably associated with the physical event will not escalate, and the experience will be better tolerated. Take for example a person who is afflicted with daily headaches that are relieved with over-the-counter analgesics. If she thinks these headaches are simply due to tension at work or home, she is likely to go on with her life without being tormented with worry and despair. If on the other hand, she convinces herself the headaches presage some imminent disaster, like a stroke, brain tumor, or infection, then in addition to the physical discomfort provoked by the headache, she will be overcome with anxiety and a sense of foreboding, all of which will tend to persist even after the headache has been resolved. Such negative amplification of distressing feelings that result in increased anguish is frequent in cancer patients, particularly among many who, ironically, after successful treatment show no evidence of persistent disease. Despite the favorable news regarding their illness they live in terror of recurrence and are often anxious, obsessively anticipating the return of the dreaded disease. In such cases, the cause of suffering is not the presence of illness or some physical symptom but a conviction that the disease will invariably recur and doom their lives.

A man I befriended years ago was afraid of needles and anesthesia. He detested how anesthesia made him feel and worried about the side effects doctors always warned him about. So he underwent many medical and dental interventions—colonoscopies, skin biopsies, root canal treatments—without availing himself of any general or local anesthetic. These choices did not reflect some hidden masochistic tendency, for although these procedures were somewhat painful and uncomfortable, they did not cause him to suffer, whereas his fear of needles and anesthesia did. When I asked him why he would put himself through such extreme discomfort when access to "the wonders of modern medicine" was so readily available, he explained how he had learned to process physical pain as an expression of his body's aliveness, an approach that evoked comforting feelings, balancing the uncomfortable ones, and thus making the experiences tolerable.

Regrettably, we live in a culture intent on avoiding pain at all cost and in which the biological meaning of pain has been perverted or lost. Pain perception, which appeared millions of years ago and has been sustained throughout evolution, did not emerge to make us (or other living creatures) miserable. Instead, it developed to enhance our chances of survival, and if displeasure is what it takes, so be it. For example, in the early 1970s, when training to become a physician, I was taught that when a patient came to the emergency room with pain suggestive of possible acute appendicitis it was critical to avoid blunting the pain until a definitive diagnosis was made. The pain, we were taught, was essential in helping us discern what was happening in the patient's abdomen; by blunting the pain with medications, we would endanger the patient.

Unfortunately, the current cultural climate has led to a loss of our appreciation of the value of pain as well as of our ability to separate physical pain from the experience of suffering. "You can rest assured," my friend revealed when queried, "that if any of the procedures I described to you before had engendered significant suffering in me, I would not have hesitated to take an anesthetic or painkiller." His ability to separate pain from suffering caused his tolerance for pain to rise, and while the medical or dental interventions were indeed uncomfortable, they did not require changing his approach. He was fortunate to have learned to raise his pain threshold by freeing himself from the kind of thoughts and beliefs that amplify distress and impel so many of us to grab a painkiller more out of fear of what we imagine might happen than for the pain and discomfort that is actually occurring. Additionally, by becoming less dependent on medication for pain control, he approached the pain-provoking experiences with more confidence and was thus exempted from the many side effects associated with taking drugs, which at times can be severe. My friend's clear elucidation helped me to see the wisdom of his approach and over the years has conferred many benefits upon me: I have learned to raise my ability to tolerate pain of all kinds, not just physical pain. Moreover, in my work as a physician, it made me less inclined to prescribe medication for minor ailments or functional disorders that could be handled with nonharmful remedies and psychological support.

There are rare instances, however, in which the suffering normally evoked by pain does not manifest. In a condition called pain asymbolia, afflicted people know they are experiencing pain and can even describe its sensory qualities—stabbing, burning, piercing—but they don't experience the pain as unpleasant. If pain is not perceived as something unpleasant the fear reaction that often follows is blunted. A similar situation may evolve in people who have consciously developed the habit of mentally reframing, swiftly and strongly, what for most of us are terribly upsetting events, in a different light. For example, Jewish Kabbalists believe that to effectively manage the world, God draws toward Him the most pious and righteous people first. Those holding such beliefs, when afflicted with an incurable illness early in life, may interpret this as signifying divine recognition of their piousness and righteousness and thus will look forward to their demise. By the same token, those who believe that by sacrificing their lives for some religious dogma they will be rewarded in heaven may go to their death feeling thrilled, especially if their life on earth has been miserable and empty.

The Primordial Wound

The suffering brought forth by self-reflective consciousness has produced an incurable *psychic wound* in the human soul. This wound, however, is no psychological defect or physiological aberration. Just as perceiving (and experiencing the disgust of) bad odors and tastes protects us from ingesting potentially harmful foods, so does our capacity for subjectivity and the suffering that goes along with it keep us alert to the many challenges we encounter during our daily living. Feelings are indeed the resources—the language—our bodies use to communicate inner states to our conscious, ego-centered selves, and while this may cause us suffering it also allows us to address inner disturbances in a caring and constructive way.

All this notwithstanding, humanity has had great difficulty in accepting that suffering is part of being human. The state of distress provoked by the reality of this condition is universal and independent of specific childhood psychopathologies, socioeconomic status, religious beliefs, or cultural mores. Only when self-reflective consciousness ceases—after we lose the part of our brain responsible for this function, for example—will this innate suffering end. The rest of the time, regardless of how successful, famous, or seemingly happy we become, some degree of despair, no matter how large or how small, will always lurk beneath our apparent calm. And it is this underlying despair that our human ancestors thousands of years ago and we now are trying to cope with and hopefully integrate into the fabric of our daily lives so that we will experience it with less negative amplification.

CHAPTER 2

Major Human Responses to Suffering

THROUGHOUT HUMAN EXISTENCE, SELF-CONSCIOUS man has attempted to respond to the suffering his very nature imposes on him. We cannot know the earliest forms these responses adopted because they would have long predated any written or even archeological record. But we can reasonably speculate about the form they took during the last three thousand years of humanity's psychosocial evolution.

Considering that suffering is an unavoidable by-product of the emergence of our self-conscious nature, we can say that it was an integral part of man's daily life from the very beginning and therefore a serious challenge to his emotional and physical well-being. On the other hand, early man naturally embraced the diversity of the *pleasant feelings* some life experiences elicited in him and his innate capacity to amplify them—also a result of being self-conscious. Thus, he enjoyed the accomplishments he made in the course of his life as well as the increase in pleasure caused by his ability to imagine being held in high esteem because of his triumphs, or by seeing himself as continuing to make similar accomplishments in the future, or even more important ones. He was able to use his self-awareness to promote positive feelings in other ways too, by devising methods for entering into altered states of consciousness through meditation or drugs, wherein he could experience feelings of calmness and elation at being alive and connected to the majestic universe of which he was a part. What's more, just as we do today, a person might have enhanced his pleasure then by imagining partnering with a wonderful other and living happily ever after.

But despite the agreeable maneuvers that consciousness allowed, awareness of unpleasant, disturbing feelings—present, past, and future, particularly when persistent—posed difficult problems for him, shading his life with anxiety and grief.

Just as he would have been driven to search for experiences yielding pleasurable feelings, so too would he have been driven to search desperately for ways to vanquish those that were unpleasant and persistent.

Environmental Modification and Control

A major pathway used in the effort to reduce existential angst was the application of the powers self-consciousness afforded man to transform and control his world physically. One can easily imagine a story of human development along such lines as the following: Knowing his vulnerability to nature's many destructive forces—physical, chemical, and biological—roused persistent consternation in man's heart. At any moment earthquakes, floods, or famines could take out his family; poisonous waters and mysterious diseases could decimate an entire population, as could war and human cruelty. Something needed to be done to alleviate his anguish. Using his powers of intelligence, reasoning, and logic, and his innovative spirit, he attempted, through trial and error, to first understand and then subjugate the inanimate and animate world in which he lived. His capacity to observe, experiment, and reason allowed him to follow this path, giving him hope that he would succeed in learning how to control the natural and psychical forces that caused his suffering. For example, having witnessed fire arising spontaneously in nature, and recognizing the potential benefits it could confer upon him and his tribe, he felt compelled to find a way to generate it at will. After many attempts, he succeeded in endowing himself with an invaluable resource in his struggle for survival and stability. The fire he could now create at will protected him from predators, warmed him in cold weather, and allowed him to cook his food, which increased the range of comestibles he could eat and digest. Over time he developed special gear and technologies that allowed him to ward off hostile attacks by other humans as well as initiate them when it seemed necessary to do so.

In spite of the important gains achieved by the trial and error approach to understanding and controlling nature, including human nature, they were insufficient to ameliorate man's persistent distress fundamentally. While making fire transformed his life in many positive ways, he still could not control most of nature's larger, invisible forces. Knowing his life was constantly threatened afflicted him to no end. He continued to pursue the path of trial and error and, gradually, as he progressed, acquired an increasingly more accurate understanding of the physical and human world in which he lived, enabling him to turn his world into a more hospitable one. But he still needed other, more immediate ways to relieve the concerns permeating his soul. And so, from the depths of his anxious heart, man created mental constructs to refashion his world in an imaginative, comforting, and reassuring way.

Mental Constructs

These aforementioned mental constructs expressed themselves outwardly by giving birth to narratives (myths, legends, heroic tales) and religious rituals and practices that together intended to explain man's experiences and, more specifically, why suffering was such an integral part of his human condition and how he could overcome it. These psychic emanations derived from the human capacity to process information and were built upon man's unique ability to express such constructs in words and images that could be shared with others. The reality they described, however, was fundamentally psychical—an interpretation of human experience conditioned by man's genetic makeup, his emotional responses and needs, his imaginings, and his hardcore beliefs—a reality often at odds with the empirically based reality his trial and error approach may have yielded or might still yield in the future. To be effective, though, these narratives had to be generated collectively. They had to be capable of spreading rapidly among the population, affecting the way people perceived reality either by evoking soothing, calming feelings that reduced suffering or by inadvertently creating distressing, unpleasant ones that amplified their suffering, which then motivated them to develop a new set of beliefs, rituals, and practices to, once again, reduce these unexpected exacerbations and thus hopefully eliminate suffering altogether.

Lacking identifiable ownership, it was easy to think of these stories as having otherworldly origins, which amplified their power to alter human behavior. Moreover, given the strong emotional responses they tended to evoke, it is not surprising that these myths became very real in the minds of men and, regardless of what their empirically derived knowledge implied, even proved, were difficult to dislodge.

Man's yearning for narratives that explain, justify, and help him address the invisible, mysterious, daunting, and awesome world surrounding him has always been—still is—an ever-present expression of his need to find meaning and purposefulness in all that happens to and around him. In fact, when his experiences lack such critical ingredients he is hard-pressed to engage his survival challenges successfully. People confronted with life-threatening, incurable illnesses, for example, when faced with the irreversibility associated with their medical condition, tend to search urgently for satisfying explanations of what is happening to them. The idea that their affliction was part of nature's randomness—the luck of the draw—and that there was nothing they could have done to avoid it or, now that it was established in them to reverse its course, is simply too distressing for many to accept. Accordingly, one often sees such patients creating and adopting mythical ideas that explain their fatal disease as the result of divine or karmic retribution for ignorance, past misdeeds, or some known or unknown character flaw. These mythical ideas have personal value, and while they may burden the individual with guilt and responsibility, they also offer actionable alternatives for a way out: "If I become a better person and seek redemption, I will be able to heal my body and restore myself to health."

Similar mythological constructs arise after collective tragedies—for example, the devastating attack perpetrated by Islamic terrorists on American soil on September 11, 2001. The collective vulnerability this event exposed and the uncertainty it created regarding possible future attacks motivated the emergence of a variety of narratives that attempted to explain it in more reassuring ways: God's punishment for Americans' lack of piousness, a secret plot by the government, the work of a foreign spy agency, a by-product of America's imperialistic tendencies, and so forth.

The stories invented by those who seek powerful, reassuring explanations for serious illness or psychic traumas serve as "origin myths," stories humanity has collectively created from the beginning of time to try to relieve the suffering provoked by existential threats. Origin myths attempting to explain how man and his unique physical and mental constitution came into being are found throughout recorded history and all over the world. The bulk of these myths attribute the existence of the universe and humanity to the creative acts of a supernatural being or beings or forces whose nature is completely different from that of man. That this idea of an extrahuman originator is ubiquitous makes perfect sense once we consider that each one of us is born into a preexistent and preconfigured world governed by laws and principles long predating our arrival. Accepting that neither our predecessors nor we could have created this world may have led man to the inevitable conclusion that some transcendent force, a designer Being or God, created the universe in which he lives. The theistic interpretation of man's origins and the birth of religion and religious ritual and practice were probably unavoidable consequences of humanity's arrival on the planetary scene. It appears there is present in the genetic matrix of man an inclination to the spiritual, the transcendental: an innate feeling of being part of something larger than he, something he cannot fathom but can sense is there. We know, for example, based on the rituals uncovered in burial sites, that already some thirty thousand years ago primitive man had developed a belief in the existence of an afterlife.[1]

As his consciousness expanded and the realities of his unique human condition became better known to him, man's theistic mythology provided a powerful antidote to his feelings of foreboding and angst. Explanatory systems such as these allowed him to identify possible causes of his suffering—for example, the unpredictability of the behavior of the gods, ancestral misdeeds, the perennial struggle between the forces of good and evil, or human fallibility. They allowed him to devise redemptive stories and practices, such as making offerings (including animal and human sacrifice), rituals of invocation, incantation, drinking of special potions, and abiding by complex systems of prohibited actions (taboos). All these inventions were intended to pacify gods and shield man from harm, restore him to health, enhance his chances for remaining alive, and, primarily, relieve the underlying torment wielded on him by the unpleasant feelings evoked by knowing his circumstances.

Though man's mythological constructs have been effective in assuaging some of his unease, they also probably hindered, at times for centuries, his efforts to understand the world empirically. Witnessing the power that natural forces exerted on his life, he deified and worshiped them. Thus, for thousands of years, polytheistic religions offered man a diversity of nature gods—the sun, the moon, the planets, mother earth, the oceans, the wind, fire—to which he could dedicate his prayers, chants, and offerings. As the objects of his persistent reverence and devotion, he felt no immediate need to investigate them experimentally; thus he deprived himself of the opportunity to learn how to harness their power and make them work for his benefit.

Once the transition to a monotheistic creed—belief in a singular, supernatural God, Creator, and Ruler of the All—was made, man gradually became freer to use his creativity and imagination to explore the natural phenomena he had previously revered. Having lost their imagined sacredness, they gradually came under the perspective of his curiosity and his capacity for reasoning and practical invention. Under a monotheistic mythological formulation, man's intellectual capacities were now free to examine nature. Centuries later the result of this transition burst forth in a plethora of discoveries in science and technology. Along with this new knowledge came an ever-expanding body of evidence-based, rational, reproducible information that has been of great help to humankind.

Altered States of Consciousness

In addition to his narrative-based approaches to the resolution of his individual and collective suffering, man also tried to transcend his primordial wound by developing special mental techniques to control his inner world. Realizing that what made him suffer was his consciousness of unpleasant feelings, regardless of how and why they had originated, and discovering his innate ability to enter into an altered state of consciousness, he embarked on a path to develop better ways to harness this resource and thus vanquish his nervousness and misgivings. By using his mental abilities, he was able to calm down feelings of unpleasantness and even make them disappear altogether, if only for a brief period. His intention here was neither to understand what caused his suffering—animate or inanimate forces of nature— nor to appeal to some extraneous entity—a god or spirit capable of neutralizing it—but rather to use his innate mental faculties to overcome the oppressive effects that consciousness of unpleasant feelings arose in him.

Meditation and trance states have been used by many cultures and traditions in the past, usually for the sole purpose of influencing the gods or spirits responsible for causing man's ills, and hence for reversing them and for guiding him on his path to recovery. An example of this is shamanism, a practice based on the belief that certain members of the community could act as intermediaries between their fellow men and the spirit world. These wise men—shamans—presumably had the ability to access supernatural realms and draw from them solutions to problems afflicting individuals and communities. To accomplish their aim shamans would enter into an ecstatic trance: they might use mental techniques or consciousness-altering drugs or actions such as dancing, singing, and playing or emitting rhythmic, repetitive music or sounds. The trance state allowed the sages to draw information from the spirit world about the cause of an individual's or a community's ills and the way to cure them. In India, for thousands of years, the yoga tradition has used special postures, breathing techniques, and meditation to foster detachment from pain and the promotion of emotional calm and physical well-being without appealing to or communicating with the supernatural.

Notwithstanding these age-old efforts on many fronts, it was not until the advent of Buddhism, five centuries before the Common Era (BCE), that suffering was explicitly identified as the quintessential human ill and a practice was set up for the declared purpose of overcoming it. According to legend, Siddhartha Gautama spent years searching for ways to overcome his suffering. He did so by addressing the painful feelings induced in him by events in his life in a variety of ways, from fasting to meditating. After a number of unsuccessful attempts, he was finally able to attain nirvana, a state of awakened enlightenment that relieved him from the anguish that had oppressed him for so long. Following this transcendental achievement Siddhartha, now the Buddha (the Awakened One), began to teach others the path to this wonderful state. He based his teachings and practices on Four Noble Truths, the first one being that "life is suffering."

To Buddhists, the source of suffering is man's attachment to anything evoking unpleasant feelings in him. And while a similar awareness may have underpinned older religious and spiritual traditions, it was only with Buddhism that it became an explicit and sole concern. The focus of Buddhist practice is to transcend man's despair not by altering human nature (man's hard-wired unpleasant feelings) or sensorial reality but rather by helping people overcome their tendency to become attached to unpleasant feelings, or to that which provokes them, and thus find their way to a state of enlightened detachment. Buddhist tradition has evolved over the centuries to include much more than just mindful meditation: following ethical precepts, becoming a monastic by renouncing conventional living, cultivating wisdom and discernment, studying scriptures, and participating in devotional practices are, to name but a few, all pathways to salvation from suffering. But it is this entering into a state of detached enlightenment that makes it unique and distinguishes it from other religious and spiritual traditions.

A path founded on meditation, nature retreats, fasting and silence, and other techniques or approaches to calming the inner world works best for people living a contemplative life, those who are able to abstract themselves from many of the trials and tribulations of ordinary living. However, those engaged in marriage, raising children, working for a living, and competing in the world are not as able as the contemplative to sustain detachment. While the effort is important, its effects do not last long enough for the ordinary citizen and thus do not resolve effectively the suffering provoked by humanity's primordial wound and illness. Moreover, by portraying disagreeable feelings as something we need to transcend, part of what is inborn is defined as undesirable: this is not an effective way to integrate our humanity and resolve our existential challenges. Being in opposition to what is innate in us is a recipe for disillusionment and frustration. Moreover, disagreeable feelings are protective, part of the armor we wear to overcome our many trials effectively.

The Scientific Understanding of Life and World

Religions of every kind, with their narratives and mind-altering practices, have characterized human history as far back as we can trace it. But given the recent developments in science and technology they have come under a new questioning. Over the last four hundred years scientifically derived knowledge has grown exponentially. This has led to the progressive development of a body of empirically derived knowledge and techniques, all of which have improved considerably man's capacity to prepare for and overcome natural disasters, diseases, and other conditions that threaten his survival and foster pain and misery. Nowadays, many illnesses that once ravaged the human community have been fully eradicated. Longevity has increased by several decades since the discovery of antibiotics and the institution of principles of sanitation in our cities and homes. Droughts, famines, and natural disasters still occur, but their lethality has been significantly curtailed. The development of psychotropic drugs has also helped shape the feelings and perceptions of those afflicted with mental illnesses, thus considerably improving the quality of their lives.

These successes have caused many to question the versions of reality advanced by religious narratives. And yet, despite this questioning, religion continues to thrive alongside modern science. The many remarkable contributions science has made to man's physical comfort and longevity notwithstanding, scientifically derived knowledge, its methodologies, and its tools have not, as many had predicted, quelled humanity's thirst for religious mythology or practices. On the contrary, during the last few decades in the United States, for example, man's participation in religious observance has increased.

In seeking to understand why this is so it is necessary to see that an explanatory system affirming that man's worst afflictions are by-products of randomness, that his life has no transcendent meaning (i.e., we live in a godless world), that his rights are not inalienable, that suffering is inevitable and death irreversible, and that upon dying he becomes food for worms leaves man wanting. It is an inadequate substitute for the soothing effect that religious mythologies can and do offer—for example, the comforting effect of the idea of a fatherlike God whom we will join in the afterlife, a just God who rewards the righteous and condemns the wicked, or a practice that promises freedom from pain and grief in the afterlife. Such promises have profound effects on the human soul. For some, scientifically derived information is reassuring enough to relieve a good part of their anxiety and distress, but this is certainly not the case for most. And as long as the scientific explanations of life fail to ameliorate the suffering provoked by man's deepest concerns and needs—the meaning and purpose of his life, how to overcome despair, what happens after he dies, how life came into being—stories and practices regarding his origin and circumstance that are rooted in nontestable beliefs rather than on reasoning and logical thinking will endure. Why? For the simple reason that they help him maintain hope, and hope is something he cannot live without.

The fact is that each of the pathways undertaken by man to reduce his suffering has been partially successful, but none of them, either alone or in combination, has been able to resolve it fully. For the millions of Jews and over a billion Christians who follow the Judeo-Christian tradition, the more than one billion followers of both the Islamic and the Hindu traditions, and the more than half a billion Buddhists, religious myth and religious practice—prayer, penitence, abstinence and asceticism, performance of duties and good deeds, and otherwise trying to fulfill God's will—has been and still is a core approach to dealing with the universal problem of why we suffer and how we can heal our affliction.

In my own way, I have found new meaning in the sacred stories the Jewish tradition offers. As a modern man and scientist who has spent a good part of his life seeking to understand and integrate the reality of his primordial wound and place it within the framework of his biological and psychological understanding of life and the world, the narratives of the Hebrew Bible have provided me with the clues, the inspiration, the guidance, and the support I needed to better understand how the primordial wound (our innate, incurable suffering) afflicting me, as well as the rest of my fellow humans, came into being, and how it became a primordial illness. More importantly, it has led me to comprehend what is required to incorporate the fact of suffering into a positive, self-affirming understanding of my human condition.

Read as man's evolving attempt to deal with the bewildering complexity of his human reality—more concretely, his inescapable suffering—the Jewish Bible provides solutions that worked for a time but in the end were insufficient to overcome his constitutional angst. Taken together, the stories depict a struggle for positive meaning, for a comforting view of human life, and for a way to make suffering comprehensible and manageable. We can learn much about humanity's efforts to deal with the uniquely human experience of suffering by reviewing the evolution of that struggle through the mixture of myth and history, fact and imagination that we find in its challenging stories and proclamations. And if read rightly, the climax of that millenary effort as depicted in the Books of Ecclesiastes and Job points toward a thoughtful, enlightened resolution that affirms man as he is, complete with his suffering and his ability to mitigate both its personal and collective expression, at least a good part of it. This is a resolution that we can accept, embrace, and delight in.

Let us begin this revisioning of the Hebrew Bible at the beginning, with Genesis. In the end, however, we will find a way to an answer to the beliefs encoded in the myth of the Garden of Eden and The Fall.

This response will be a new Genesis one that gives man his proper dignity and acknowledges the wonder of his nature and that of the God his unbridled imagination gave shape to.

CHAPTER 3

The Eden Myth of Creation

An Attempt to Explain the Mystery
of Innate Suffering

AS WE SHALL PRESENTLY see, the Book of Genesis offers a narrative that is an advance on earlier ones invented by humanity to assuage its existential distress. These earlier narratives, emerging from the depths of man's imagination, depicted humanity as ruled by emotionally unstable deities (e.g., the ancient Pagan Pantheon). The unpredictable behavior of these deities made them seem uncaring of the needs and yearnings of ordinary people, reflecting accurately the ways in which the physical and the animate world behaved toward them. As a result, man's conscious life was filled with images of impulsive, primitive gods, their sudden favors, and their unpredictable punishments. Because any disaster might suddenly be visited upon man, he was fearful: he felt naked and exposed to capricious heavenly rulers who, without warning, could transform his life and the world around him into chaos.

Knowing they were blameless recipients of the gods' aggressions must have been of little solace to our suffering forebears, but it may have exempted them from feeling any sense of individual or collective responsibility. For them, life was fate—an unalterable destiny. But though knowing themselves to be victims of this fate, they could look to heroic figures and their magic rituals to try to ward off their fears, misfortunes, and sorrows with occasional success. These imagined heroes possessed physical strength, a sharp wit, virtue, and a sense of honor, and they were often conceived as having divine ancestry.

The Plaything of Fate

Such an archaic understanding of nature and human life is on full display during the initial stages of a child's conscious life and is given contemporary expression through the large number of superheroes children worship. It has been approximately one month since my four-year-old grandson began to wear a Superman costume and express fascination for this godlike character. He is excited by and pleased with Superman's ability to fly, see through physical barriers, and move mountains, as well as his dedication to fighting evil. Whenever we get together nowadays, betraying a devious smile, the first thing he does is ask, "Grandpa, do you know who I really am?" "Yes," I tell him in a voice quieted to ensure his secret is not revealed, "you are Superman." My response invariably evokes great satisfaction in him and propels us into interesting adventures in which he, as Superman, guides me to Metropolis, his adopted city, in search of opportunities to rescue those in dire need. Moreover, his world has become populated with many other heroic figures: Super Why! Super Readers, Diego the Animal Rescuer, Dora the Explorer, Batman, Spiderman, and Aquaman. Such imagined beings offer hope and reassurance to many contemporary children who perceive themselves as living in a world where exposure to natural and supernatural forces can threaten their survival and general healthfulness.

Through their offerings to the gods, ancestral humans created the illusion that they could appease them and keep them happy and thus live protected from their irrational impulsiveness. Their interactions with the gods, however, were nonrelational: They did not involve mutual allegiance and responsibilities. Seldom did the gods speak to humans, encouraging them to follow a particular path. Instead, they acted upon them and their world rather erratically. On occasion, they may have seemed responsive to man's offerings, but they never acknowledged responsibility for securing his happiness. This dynamic was reflective of an early stage of collective psychological functioning in which man's ego was fragile and vulnerable, and he had no sense of being in relationship with the archetypal dimensions of his psyche operating in the unconscious realms of his soul.

Fortunately, such primitive level of functioning and the understanding it fostered of our natural and human world could not persist indefinitely. In time, human minds evolved—albeit slowly. As internal pressures within ancestral man's psychic depths mounted, demanding a more accurately reassuring view of the world's workings, new myths arose from the largely unconscious domain of his mind. These were narratives that provided a somewhat more mature and accurate account of his experiences and observations and therefore more substantial hope that an enduring resolution of his anguish was possible.

The Eden Myth I: "And God Created Man in His Image"

The opening chapters of Genesis exemplify this evolution in human thinking with the Creation of Adam and Eve. It is amazing that humankind took so long to make this important step forward. This new myth imagined the world ruled by a single omnipotent God, Creator of the All, who introduced order into the unformed, chaotic universe. He crowned His efforts by making man in His own image. Depicted as being endowed with vaguely defined divine attributes, man, like God, was also superior to all other creatures: "Be fertile and increase and fill the earth and master it; and rule the fish of the sea, the birds of the sky, and all the living things that creep on earth" (Gen. 1:28).

Understanding the myth as the by-product of man's conscious and unconscious drive for mastery of the world he lived in, we should view this part of the myth as the affirmation of powers he had already experienced when exerting his intelligence, imagination, and creativity on less well-endowed creatures and other parts of the environment. The myth was also designed to relieve man of some of his apprehension, for it clearly implies that God the Creator was not only the source of human superiority but was also a moral God that cared for him: "It is not good for man to be alone; I will make a fitting helper for him" (Gen. 2:18). This caring, however, was not unconditional: as we shall see later, it was predicated on man's unqualified obedience to God's commands.

By entrusting the totality of Creation into the hands of a singular deity, the newly monotheistic man acknowledged his belief in a God responsible for everything happening under the sun, a God capable of provoking as well as preventing whatever most afflicted him. This supernatural being, he surmised, had given birth to the natural forces his forebears worshiped as nature gods and was not only a protector of man but also a guide directing man as to how to live his life.

This version of reality was a tremendous change from earlier polytheistic narratives, which viewed the phenomenal world as underpinned by multiple, confusing, and even conflicting forces. Metaphorically, these forces were imagined as many separate divinities that from time to time wreaked havoc on the world. While polytheism did justice to the complexities of phenomenal reality, it also institutionalized human uncertainty and vulnerability, given the apparent arbitrariness of events. Reality, while ostensibly cyclical and predictable, an eternal repetition of events—day and night, the seasons, the phases of the moon, the cycles of women's bodies, birth and death—also exhibited nature's uncharted ways, and these were symbolized by the unpredictability of the actions of the many gods. They were capricious and competing gods, deities that could only be placated with regular and complicated rituals performed by man to avoid being the recipient of the gods' humanlike fickleness and wrath. Not knowing how much devotion to a particular god might be enough to ward off its fury or secure its favors was only one source of additional distress. Worshippers also had to be afraid of enraging one deity while trying to serve another.

Aware of the envy he frequently carried in his own heart as well as the outrage he experienced at perceived wrongdoings by others, man could not help but conceive his gods as driven by motives and sensibilities identical to his own. Given that uncertainty was an unavoidable part of his daily life, one can easily imagine how early man might have felt at such times when his well-being was compromised by unexpected droughts, floods, or volcanic eruptions or by attacks from other stronger or better-equipped animals or men. Even his occasional failure to reproduce despite his persistent effort, as will be discussed in further chapters, was a mystery and heartache. All these serious afflictions would be perceived and explained as punishments.

The new monotheistic creed did not exempt him from such painful experiences but did offer a centralized authority man could appeal to and please and who would ultimately offer forgiveness. Having to serve a single master, man could conceivably break once and for all the chain of inevitability that hung over his soul and begin to relate to that which was greater than he, making favorable results potentially more achievable.

While polytheism was freighted with incomprehensible and unpredictable divine rivalries in which gods vying for power had often seemed to cause serious damage to an individual, tribe, or Earth itself, such disturbing possibilities were eliminated once man could concentrate his worship on a singular God. The new creed further comforted its inventors by specifically implying that they could know or learn to know what the singular God wanted (God's Will), so that by following His wishes and demands they could assure their own and their families' welfare.

Similar mythical constructs underlie part of children's relationships with their parents, whom they often experience as powerful, godlike beings capable of protecting them from all harm. Like many people, I can still vividly remember running into my parents' bedroom some nights, frightened by what seemed like threatening shadows or unusual noises in my dark room. The moment I cuddled with them in their warm bed, however, I felt protected and secure. I came to realize, as I grew older, that my parents could have done little to shelter me had an intruder gotten into our home. But as a child, slipping into bed with them had taken away my distress. Just as children learn to follow parental dictates in return for safety, support, and love, so our ancestors attempted to do the same.

But from the very beginning, aspects of his nature—man's innate drive for autonomy, his need to be his own person and follow his own inclinations—interfered with this submissive effort. Just recently, a friend shared with me the woes his adult daughter experienced in trying to persuade her seven-year-old daughter, his granddaughter, to wear the dress she had chosen for her little munchkin to wear for an upcoming family celebration and the fierce resistance the little girl had demonstrated; she was going to wear the outfit she had found to her liking and nothing else!

The Eden Myth II: Disobedience of the Divine Command Wreaks Suffering

While some aspects of the Eden myth have brought comfort to man's soul, other features seem ill designed to soothe his angst. Rather, one may think them intentionally designed to increase it. These derive from details of the story that imagine man committing a primal misdeed for which he will have to suffer grievously for his entire life.

Though God permitted man to eat from every tree planted in the Garden of Eden, He prohibited him from eating from the tree of the knowledge of good and bad, threatening death were he to disobey. This seems to imply God's opposition to man becoming a self-aware, free, and moral being. Indeed, in its further details, the myth essentially states that it was man becoming conscious of himself and of the choices such consciousness allowed him that introduced death, toil, and many kinds of pain into his life.

Many modern people raised in the scientific, cultural atmosphere of the last few centuries have been understandably puzzled by this part of the Eden myth. Why would human beings invent a myth that imagined pain and death to result from their acquiring self-knowledge and free will? Modern science shows us that death is a biological inevitability: every creature, from the simplest to the most complex, will naturally die. Why would earlier humanity devise a myth so contrary to what we now know is nature's law? Moreover, why would it formulate a myth in which the quintessential human attribute—the ability to discriminate between good and bad (that which pleases or displeases, helps or hinders, fosters our survival or hastens our end)—is viewed so negatively?

To answer these puzzling questions one must suppose that in creating this aspect of the Eden myth man was giving voice to one of his deepest contradictions. And that contradiction, which we all have personally experienced, is rooted in our feeling ambivalent about the very quality that defines our human essence. Early man knew (if not consciously then at least intuitively) that the same self-awareness that gave him a godlike ability to survive and prosper also condemned him to live in anguish. "All those subtle demonisms of life and thought," as Herman Melville expressed so beautifully in his famous book Moby-Dick,[1] were directly related to being self-conscious. Bearing witness to the relative innocence and happiness that characterizes the life of unconscious human infants with their lack of concern and worry and then contrasting it with the disheartenment felt as an adult, man yearns to return to that original state of carefree, blissful living he imagined some earlier ancestors once enjoyed in some place like the Garden of Eden. Given the enormous ignorance about nature and human nature prevalent at the time the myth emerged, it is difficult for us moderns to imagine man interpreting his angst in a more accurate, constructive way. Convinced that an all-loving, merciful, and just God created him, man could not countenance the idea that this God would have wanted him to suffer. It, therefore, followed logically that self-consciousness and its unwelcomed consequences were not what his compassionate Creator intended. Some other cause must be adduced for this unfortunate occurrence, and if it couldn't be attributed to the omnipotent Almighty, it must by necessity reside in man himself, not now but rather in the misty past, an ancestral wrongdoing.

Additionally, when attempting to understand why our forebears formulated the dawn of consciousness in such negative terms, we must also recall that earlier human beings were much more vulnerable to life's vicissitudes than modern man. They lived under threats of injury and annihilation from all sorts of natural events, many of which we have been able to overcome, albeit only very recently. In those early times, there were no dams to protect settlements from floods, no antibiotics to ward off diseases, and no fire departments to contain conflagrations. Infant deaths were common, famines regular, and war and other plagues were aspects of seemingly unremitting cycles. The terrifying *awareness* that such dangers might come at any time was part of the life of no other creature. And it would not have been part of man's either had he stayed in Eden living the paradisiacal existence God had intended for him.

On the other hand, there was no use bemoaning the obvious: like it or not, man was a self-conscious and self-reflective creature afflicted by the anxieties, fears, worries, sadness, guilt, shame, and other unpleasant feelings some life experiences evoked in him. To mitigate the misery associated with such common occurrences he needed to imagine a way out of his unfortunate condition. Attributing responsibility for pain and suffering to a good fatherlike God was impossible. On the other hand, to countenance the idea that suffering and the conditions that caused it was an inevitable part of human existence raised feelings of such heightened despondency and depression, they were too much to bear. A psychic conundrum was engendered and to resolve it man's myth creator—which can also be conceived as his primordial artist—gave form to a narrative that posited self-reflective consciousness as arising from an *avoidable event*, rather than from his human nature. Death and misery thereby became by-products of his disobedience to God's command, which his capacity for free will allows, rather than the results of God's actions or intention. Within such a mythical construct, the comforting benevolent role of God was to create the *potential* for man to become a self-conscious being. By endowing him with the gift of free will, the responsibility for the torments that accompanied self-consciousness needed a scapegoat, and so was born the myth of the first couple.

This mythical maneuver achieved two important goals. First, it allowed man to sustain his comforting belief in God's ultimate fairness and redemptive power; though God created the conditions for consciousness to appear, He Himself did not make the grief-laden faculty materialize nor was He responsible for the choices man made thereafter. Second, man could retain the fantasy that God's intentions were to provide him a life free of injury, illness, death, and the suffering these occurrences provoked. Given the view of this new God as also having a fundamentally compassionate nature, it was an easy next step for early humans (and later ones, too) to convince themselves that, eventually, He would forgive their previous misdeeds and in the end help them recapture the paradisiacal life they had unfortunately lost but had never stopped yearning to regain.

A more contemporary analysis of the myth suggests, however, that our ancestors knew instinctively that pleasant and unpleasant (good and bad) experiences were part of God's world long before humans appeared on the planetary stage. What had been missing, though, was an agent capable of knowing these experiences *consciously*. After all, pleasant and unpleasant experiences are integral parts of the lives of many living creatures but at no point in time do they comprehend this or understand how their bodies respond to them. Man, however, by eating from the forbidden tree, introduced into nature the capacity of knowing pleasure and displeasure—later subjectively turned into good and bad. Consequently, he knows joyfulness as well as suffering. His need to exempt God from responsibility for this kind of knowing, rather than reflecting the truth about how this came about and why, gives testimony to his deep-seated need for a ruling God of justice and morality and for a life where there is real potential for achieving enduring happiness. In short, ancestral man might have reasoned as follows: "Yes, we suffer—we know anxiety, we know we hurt and will hurt, and all the rest of it. Nonetheless, even though suffering is our fault (and if not ours, then whose?), God will save us." At a deeper level, though, man may have already intuited that morality and justice were qualities only self-conscious beings endowed with free will could manifest; hence, the responsibility for bringing them forth was ultimately going to be his and not his Creator's.

The power of this myth, enduring even to our own day, also arises from its success in expressing abiding human impulses, thoughts, feelings, and actions. We know we are vulnerable to seduction, so it is easy for us to identify with our ancestral parents' susceptibility to the enticing promises of the Garden serpent. Furthermore, the deep feelings of fear and shame that Adam and Eve experienced after disobeying God's injunction are bred into our bones. Despite its many merits, the Judeo-Christian tradition still rests on a binary system of reward and punishment meant to guide our actions. This system of behavioral control and its inevitable consequences for our self-concept and sense of worth is so deeply ingrained in us that it feels almost innate, as though it were inescapable.

Which of us is not haunted by early childhood conditioning of fear, shame, or guilt? I still remember with trepidation the childhood day when I threw a stone that inadvertently shattered the rear window of a car belonging to a friend's father. Though I was only eleven years old at the time, I at once felt an acute certainty that I would somehow be compelled to pay a grave price for my terrible act. My certainty clothed itself in images of my father bursting into a fit of anger and punishing me severely. Conspiring with my mother for how best to ease the blow—for she too was concerned about my father's reaction—we decided I should go to bed early so that when he came home from work, I would already be sleeping (or pretending to be). In this way, the fateful confrontation could be delayed and hopefully defused. Father succumbed to my mother's persuasive powers and forgave my misdeed, and I escaped unscathed—but the fear of retribution, like faded fears from other forgotten events, remained with me and even today sometimes resurfaces into my mind, incited by who knows what current events.

All of us can remember one or more such occurrences, the surface outcroppings of otherwise buried childhood moments when we were brought to feel shame and guilt and to fear retribution for our faults. These conditioned behaviors are part of our training to becoming social adults and from that perspective are beneficial and necessary. But we need to decondition some of these once we reach adulthood if we are to avoid living in persistent fear and unhappiness.

The Eden Myth III: Man's Expulsion from Eden— The Primordial Illness

Though we can analyze and understand the motives that led ancient man to the Eden myth, some still present in us today, we must view its message as highly flawed. Perceiving that great development in humanity's history as an act of disobedience to a just and loving God clearly denigrates the dawn of self-reflective consciousness. Though

He had wanted paradise for Adam and Eve, their waywardness cursed man's future existence forever. After this transgression, God's tone became harsh, and He said to Adam: "Because you did as your wife said and ate of the tree about which I commanded you, 'You shall not eat of it,' cursed be the ground because of you. By toil shall you eat of it all the days of your life, thorns and thistles shall it sprout for you, but your food shall be the grasses of the field. By the sweat of your brow shall you get bread to eat until your return to the ground for from it you were taken. For dust you are, and to dust you shall return" (Gen. 3:17–19). To Eve He said, "I will make most severe your pangs in childbearing; in pain shall you bear children" (Gen. 3:16). Even the curse placed on the serpent can be seen as underscoring the myth's negative view of consciousness (Gen. 3:14, 15).

God's punishing words and the long-term implications of the curse levied on Adam and Eve attest to the depth of despair our ancestors must have felt regarding their persistent state of suffering. By envisioning Adam and Eve as being guilty for their condition, the original purpose of the myth—to relieve human suffering—was undercut. Instead, it increased human despair by transforming what until then was humanity's primordial wound into humanity's *primordial*—and until now, incurable—*illness* (a state of suffering provoked by man being divinely condemned). Man's innate suffering derived from his self-knowledge of hard-wired unpleasant feelings became hugely amplified by our ancestors' misguided interpretation that it was caused by our imagined base and evil nature.

Man was henceforth asked to see his self-conscious nature as bad: bad in how it originated—disobedience—and bad in its results. As Milton famously summarized, it was "the fruit of that forbidden tree whose mortal taste/Brought death into the world, and all our woe/with loss of Eden."[2] Man was hereafter required to accept that death and disease (ranging from colds and broken bones to diabetes, arthritis, heart disease, and cancer), far from being natural inevitabilities, were by-products of his doings. Likewise, the anxieties about such unavoidable events also arose from his constitutional gullibility, immorality, and evil inclinations. Whereas modern psychology makes much of the need for self-esteem as essential for our health and well-being, the Eden myth fundamentally undercuts any self-esteem that people might reasonably feel. So this aspect of the myth gave birth to a state of persistent unwellness—man's primordial illness—by institutionalizing notions such as these: that each individual is fundamentally flawed and condemned to endure suffering; that he must engage in a ceaseless effort of acknowledging his flaws; that he must use every possible means to undo his inclination to wickedness and corruption, if such means can be found. Otherwise, he can never expect to find enduring happiness in his lifetime.

The most precise articulation of this unfortunate complex of ideas is found in the Christian doctrine of original sin, particularly as articulated by Saint Augustine (354–430 CE). According to this canon, Adam and Eve, by sinning, lost the original state of holiness and perfect ease into which they had been originally born not only for themselves but also for all generations to come. Moreover, their offense perverted the human soul, transforming man into a depraved creature subject to perennial suffering. This perversion was passed on to their children, and from them, it continued to be passed from parent to child through the generations. In Saint Augustine's view, all humanity was contained in the original couple, and therefore all humanity sinned together with Adam and Eve.³ Man, therefore, is a blemished creature who lacks the freedom to obey the will of his God on a consistent basis, earning him divine wrath. The resultant of all this is a life of misery, which is fundamentally unredeemable on earth.

Despite it being a misguided and harmful explanation of man's innate suffering, the doctrine of original sin encapsulates deep truths: the birth of human consciousness did provoke an irreparable wound in man's soul, and because it is part of his nature, this wound is often experienced as a congenital, inherited condition.

Man suffers, however, not for having transgressed God's injunction or for the irreversible perversion of his soul that this caused. No, this part of suffering, as we have seen in chapter 1, is a direct consequence of the appearance of our kind. But our inability to accept this irrevocable truth has saddled us with much additional and unnecessary suffering. The long-echoing resonance of the myth of the Fall has filled us with a damning interpretation of ourselves and of the human condition, one that cements the idea that we suffer not because we are human but *because we are bad*.

The Submission of the Feminine Principle: An Additional Ill

Not only did the Eden myth attribute culpability for humanity's suffering to the primordial couple but it made it clear it was Eve, the first woman, who bore the greatest responsibility. After all, it was she who succumbed to the instigation of the Garden serpent; it was she who seduced Adam to eat from the forbidden tree; and finally, it was she who received the harshest punishment, even though she, unlike Adam, had never heard about the prohibition directly from God. Not surprisingly, after the Fall, God said to the woman, "In pain shall you bear children. Yet your urge shall be for your husband, and he shall *rule over you*" (Gen. 3:16). With the swift stroke of a short sentence, "and he shall rule over you," the fate of women, and more precisely of the feminine principle living and manifesting naturally in them (although present in men as well), was sealed for centuries to come. The feminine principle and the women who express it naturally were to remain under the control of the masculine principle in men and women. That one short sentence resulted in millennia of subjugation and submissiveness. It was up to man to see to it that Pandora's box would remain closed, thus preventing woman from bringing further misery into his life.

The myth demonstrates that man feared woman from the beginning of time. He feared what he perceived as her unpredictability, her irrationality, her capriciousness, her emotionality, and the mystery of her fertility and procreative powers. As a result of all this, he felt compelled to keep her on a short leash. After all, she was a seductress, a demon of the night who could easily cause him to lose control of his body and his actions and thus bring further suffering into his soul. For the next few thousand years it would be primarily the masculine principle in the archetypal soul/psyche of our forebears that would define mythically, socially, and politically the nature of man's relationship with God and with each other, as well as the nature of his efforts to overcome suffering.

Nonetheless, a transordinary feminine presence, which found expression in his world, lived in the unconscious of man from the very beginning of time. In the Hebrew tradition, it was not until some five hundred years BCE when this force emerged full-blown in the life of exemplary Job. We also hear about her in the Book of Proverbs, written around the third or fourth century BCE, when she says to man "I, wisdom; live with Prudence; I attain knowledge and foresight," intimating she was part of the Lord's Creation "from the very beginning of His course, as the first of His works of old" (Prov. 8:12, 22).

Acquired Suffering

As mentioned earlier, the suffering provoked by humanity's primordial wound and its ubiquitous primordial illness is further amplified, sometimes considerably, during childhood and adolescence through the relentless process of *socialization*, to which all of us have been subjected. This process, applied for the purpose of making us fit for social living, deepens the individual's conviction of being a deviant creature inclined to badness. Inevitably, this process of persistent correction, which reflects parental disapproval of our actions and its implicit threat of rejection and abandonment—either by our Father in heaven or His representatives on earth—further injures our self-esteem.

And even though caring parents and others will dedicate efforts to affirm them, young children already harbor bad feelings about themselves. Unable to understand why the noise and the mess they create could bother anyone, confused by their parents' occasional fights and their unavailability when needed, and living a self-centered life appropriate for their young age, they have begun to learn that their actions are sometimes viewed as reprehensible and unwelcome. Little by little their innocence becomes tarnished.

One of my cousins recently told me how, while driving his grandson to a class, his best friend Robert called. At some point in the conversation, he asked his munchkin to say hello to him.

"I don't want to," the boy answered.

After hanging up, my cousin turned to his grandson and said, "You know, you don't have to do what you don't want to."

The boy did not respond immediately but a few minutes later said, "Grandpa, sometimes I feel very sad."

"Why is that so, sweetie?"

"Because mommy and daddy force me to do things I don't want to."

Taken aback by his disclosure, my cousin asked, "Why would mommy and daddy do that?"

"Because sometimes I do *bad* things to my younger brother, and they send me up to my room for a time out, and I don't want to go, but they force me, and I cry and cry until my time is up."

In these few candid words, my cousin's grandson revealed how he had internalized the idea of having an inclination to do bad things. When he reaches adulthood, like other children, he will carry in his soul the conviction that something bad and twisted dwells within. I remember my mother emphasizing over and again that I (and for that matter all other children) was like a young tree needing careful supervision and shaping if I was to "grow up right" or "grow up well." Otherwise, left to my own designs, I would surely "grow up wrong" or "bad"—*twisted*.

Such culturally conditioned suffering increases over time as we keep bumping up against social, religious, and other cultural norms and rules we are not naturally inclined to accept. Furthermore, this kind of suffering is often exacerbated by individual childhood traumas caused by psychopathologies in our parents, family members, teachers, and even neighbors.

The result is that we often grow up feeling guilty of having wronged our parents and our God, and fearing the terrible consequences that must await us. Gradually, by the many moments of parental disapproval we have experienced, we become convinced that there is something inherently wrong with us; otherwise, why would we need so much correcting? Not surprisingly, we inevitably enter adolescence and then our adult years saddled with feelings of insecurity, inadequacy, self-doubt, guilt, fear of life, and an internalized parental image that is strict, severe, judgmental, and irascible. One that repeatedly affirms these truths by inflicting sovereign self-beatings that, while experienced and known only by us, are all too real. Of course, not everyone experiences these feelings consciously or with the same intensity. And while some people may claim persuasively that childhood and adolescence were good, even very good, when probed and examined more deeply, these feelings and concerns are likely to be discovered.

To deconstruct the acquired layers of suffering mentioned above one must address them diligently in early adulthood and beyond, whether with the help of mental health professionals, spiritual counselors, or self-analysis and purposeful change of harmful habits of thought and action. With hard work and much determination, our ability to be self-reflective and self-conscious allows us to overcome the low self-esteem resulting from much of the cultural indoctrination to which all of us are subject.

Another Aspect of Eden Myth Ambivalence

Man's ambivalence toward the rise of self-consciousness, clearly the most significant event in evolutionary history, is only partly rooted in the pervasive Eden myth. An even more basic cause is the terrible conflict that reflective self-consciousness brought into his formerly subhuman life. As we all know, each of us is endowed with an instinctual, physical drive to preserve our life at all costs. Strictly speaking, this ancestral instinct is unconcerned with whether its actions evoke pleasant or unpleasant consequences. In people with incurable illnesses, this drive to live as long as possible is often displayed in the fullness of its strength. Despite the dire situation they face, something within propels them forward with relentless vigor toward extending their lives, even if they were to gain only a few days. These people are willing to endure the most taxing treatments and suffer terrible side effects for the iffy possibility of a few more days, weeks, perhaps months of life. Other living creatures—a bird, a mouse, a bee—will do everything possible to evade being captured, and for what reason if not to preserve their lives? Unconscious of self as they are, their bodies seem to have an inborn understanding that being caught is undesirable, and therefore they mobilize all their resourcefulness and determination to escape.

The emergence of consciousness, however, brought forth a complement of unique abilities that have powerfully enhanced man's capacity to create favorable survival conditions. Abilities like foresight ("This will happen again"), planning ("So I must prepare"), learning from repeated experiences ("I can take better steps next time it happens"), remembering the lessons of such experiences ("Some steps worked well and others did not; next time I will increase the positive ones and avoid the negatives, thus attaining better results"), and passing this knowledge on to future generations, thereby achieving ever-enhanced results ("Not only can you expect water next spring, you can start saving it in reservoirs right away. Then later, when the rains stop, you can have a feast, enjoy abundant food, and dance and sing").

Perhaps motivated by the intense and enduring psychic pain inherent in being self-conscious, a new psychic energy—one could call it the drive to *well-living*—appeared. It aimed beyond mere survival to the goal of seeking to make life as comfortable and pleasant as possible. Over time, and as the influence of this force grew, the notion of "quality of life" was introduced into God's Creation. Though self-conscious beings may fight like other trapped animals to extend their lives, longevity is no longer the overriding goal. While most people will affirm a desire to live as long as possible, their commitment to doing it is often highly conditional. Yes, they want to live long lives, provided they can do so with dignity, exempt from events that violate their sense of what is meaningful or acceptable to them. These may include uncontrollable pain, severe functional decline, increasing dependency on others for the satisfaction of basic needs, seeing their children become seriously ill, and so forth. Such people will willingly sacrifice length of life for the benefits of avoiding psychological and/or physical misery. Recently, a group in Holland, spearheaded by scientists, artists, and intellectuals, requested legislation to make legal euthanasia available to anyone over the age of seventy, no questions asked. The driving force underlying their advocacy was neither incurable physical illness nor overwhelming emotional despair but rather a desire by certain people to avoid enduring the decline that inevitably accompanies elderhood.[4]

From the perspective of an instinctually driven physical body, the actions taken by an individual's desire for well-living are often experienced as undermining the commitment to survive as long as possible. Contrariwise, seen from the perspective of a self-reflective, self-conscious mind, a physical body's yearning to survive at all costs can often be experienced as cruel and oppressive. In contemporary culture this split in goals and values is reflected in such conflicts as those that pit the people who define themselves as pro-life versus those who are pro-choice, those who support some form of euthanasia versus those vehemently opposed to it, and those who approve the use of embryos created through in vitro fertilization for stem cell research and those who perceive this as a crime against the innocent and defenseless. In each of these areas of cultural dispute, the collision of these two fundamental drives is defining.

Recently, I had occasion to witness this psychic tension play itself out in the case of a 92-year-old woman diagnosed with advanced lung cancer. To her closest son, the one she regularly leaned on for help, the afflicted woman expressed a desire to approach her condition "conservatively." She declared, "I'm willing to receive some form of anticancer treatment as long as it doesn't diminish the quality of my remaining life. I understand my life is now in its final stages and that I don't have many more months, never mind years, left free from serious physical and mental decline. I am willing to sacrifice some time for quality and dignity." Though some siblings strongly supported her wishes, others did not. They felt their mother was shortchanging herself and deserved every available medical intervention capable of prolonging her life for as long as possible. For them, quality of life was not the defining consideration, and they sharply resented their brother for supporting their mother's wishes. For them, the drive to live was paramount.

The human yearning for a life free of suffering has often been confused with a death wish. But there is no death wish in all of nature. Contemporary discoveries in cell biology have revealed that cells, the units of life, are genetically programmed to die at a certain time in their life cycle, but this fact doesn't at all imply an urge to die. Instead, it reflects the importance that timely death has for the general well-being of all living organisms. Without such deaths there would be no growth, no renewal; without such preprogrammed deaths at the cellular level, unregulated reproduction takes place creating the condition we call cancer. Rather than wanting death, people who are driven by well-living want to live free from persistent pain and anguish. Oncology patients often say, "I want to die;" but what they really mean is, "If I have to continue to endure the symptoms and the distress I am suffering daily, then I want to die. But if you can help me overcome these terrible problems, I want to live!"

Given our human condition, liberation from suffering only occurs either when we are completely detached from our feelings (extreme stoicism) or when we return to a state of unconsciousness. In many grave instances, the siren song of unconsciousness lures us toward what appears to be ideal pleasure but in actuality delivers us to lethargy, boredom, drug addiction, alcoholism, and other conditions that prevent us from facing challenges that threaten our well-living. Our deep and general yearning to return to the unconsciousness we had in the womb—mythically portrayed as returning to the prelapsarian Garden of Eden—is no "death instinct" but merely a by-product of our difficulty in accepting aspects of life as it necessarily is—complete with its incurable imperfections and dissatisfactions, irremediable pains, and inevitable finitude.

By recognizing the psychic split between instinctual forces driving us to survive regardless of the quality of that life and those that drive us toward well-living, we can more fully understand why the most enduring of our origin myths presents God's actions in a similarly bifurcated fashion. On the one hand, He prohibits the first human couple from becoming self-conscious creatures—and why, after all, would a loving and caring God not want us to live eternally and free of suffering? On the other hand, the myth presents God as omniscient, which clearly implies He knew exactly what the primordial couple was going to do, and thus, their becoming conscious may have been precisely what He intended for them in the first place.

Indeed, the Eden myth repeatedly puts forth ambivalent messages, viewing self-reflective consciousness as both desirable and undesirable. For example, the narrative exalts the merits of prelapsarian unconscious living: "The two of them were naked, the man and his wife, yet they felt no shame" (Gen. 2:25). But almost at once, the narrative goes on to illustrate the benefit of conscious living: man can now cover his nakedness by fabricating loincloths. It is not too much to say that this detail alone foretells the promise of all sorts of future manufacture of clothing and other inventions useful for promoting both survival and well-living.

According to biblical lore the vision of the world that man's Eden myth embodied ruled his understanding for generations. During that lengthy period, man invested himself in fulfilling its divine directives—"to fill the earth and master it"—hoping thereby to reduce the discomfort provoked by his awareness of the threats that the physical world posed to his overall happiness. We can also imagine him inventing more satisfactory technologies for husbandry, and food procurement, building more hospitable environments, and similar efforts. The invention of God and the origin myth, however, while effective in relieving some of his insecurities and anxieties, saddled man with the terrible illness already described: a sense of original fault, of inherent human corruption, and the fiction that someday, somehow, somewhere, through his acts of contrition and obedience, and through God's just nature, he would be able to reclaim his bliss and innocence. Once he conceives himself to be responsible for his misery, he then embarks on a never-ending effort to expiate his fault and return to some version of Eden—in heaven, paradise, the afterlife, somewhere. And, as we shall see, many of the following books of the Hebrew Bible can be read as a record of this evolving effort.

PART II

Covenant, Commandments, and Law

CHAPTER 4

The Basic Jewish Biblical Narratives

Overcoming the Primordial Illness and Returning to Paradisiacal Existence

BIBLICAL SCHOLARS HAVE LONG seen an evolution in the picture of God given in the Old Testament, even attributing different dates of composition and different human authors to whole sections of the Hebrew Bible.

What will be emphasized here is that the unrolling of the biblical narratives as we experience them now, when reading the books of the Bible consecutively, as the compilers of the Hebrew Bible arranged them, corresponds to a multiplex evolution: the image of God changes, the relationship between God and man changes, and the understanding and portrayal of the human being advances as well. This evolution in the biblical narrative can be seen as the progressive development of adaptive responses—in the form of better mythical formulas—by our forebears to the problems of unremitting guilt, shame, and fear humans felt as a result of the terrible thing the original couple committed.

The Story of Cain and Abel: How to Please an Unknowable God

The story of Cain and Abel, which directly follows man's expulsion from the Garden of Eden, gives expression to that which differentiates man from all other living creatures: his capacity to distinguish right from wrong. This wondrous gift, acquired as a result of falling from grace, is precisely what will help him stir his life toward happiness and goodness and away from despair and evilness. But while man may often know what is right he is not always able to act righteously and whether he does or not will also depend on how those with whom he interacts respond to him.

Cain and Abel's drama illustrates this difficulty well when it confronts head-on the problem of sibling rivalry, parental preference, and man's proclivity to give offerings to those on whom he depends for care and protection. This inclination to please seems innate, hard-wired into our DNA. Recently, a friend told me how his grandchildren engaged in this practice regularly. Nobody taught them or encouraged them to do this, but they must have realized, intuitively perhaps, that when they made offerings to family members, nannies, others—like gifting a leaf, a flower, a drawing, a small pebble—they got favorable responses, motivating them to do this even more. The experience was clearly reassuring and evocative of good feelings for them. It is not surprising, therefore, that the first action by the first set of children described in the Hebrew Bible is to try to ensure the graces of their heavenly Father by making offerings to Him.

As the story goes, Cain, the firstborn of Adam and Eve, and his brother Abel bring offerings to God. Abel's offering is gladly accepted while Cain's is not. Noticing his distress, man's imagined God addresses Cain saying, "Why are you distressed, and why is your face so fallen? Surely, if you do right, there will be uplift but if you do not do right sin couches at the door; its urge is toward you" (Gen. 4:6, 7). While the Bible does not explicitly convey why Cain's offering was unwelcomed by God, the implication is that he didn't bring the best of his produce, as Abel did. In other words, he had made a conscious choice to act in ways "not right." In this direct, straightforward way, the principle of reward and punishment became firmly established: Do good and you will be rewarded. Do bad, and you will be rebuked and punished.

Being reproved by God evokes intense pain in Cain, as it does in every child when reprimanded by his father. On the one hand, Cain feels spurned by the heavenly Father; on the other, he is envious of the positive attention his brother received. Unable to confront the source of his pain and anger, given his utter dependence on God, he unleashes these feelings on his younger brother, killing him.

The story of the first human murder, a fratricide, illuminates important aspects of man's character and how these impact the quality and length of his life. It acknowledges his capacity to act morally and experience blessings and praise from within and without as well as his capacity to act immorally and experience reproach and chastisement from within and without. Man is indeed the first animal that kills because he is consciously aware of being emotionally hurt, humiliated, or rejected. His inclination to violence for psycho-emotional reasons is a distinctive feature of the newest member of the animal kingdom, another of the unintended consequences of the emergence of our kind. It is also a powerful reminder of his presumed innate badness, which cost him the loss of paradise.

This tragic act also establishes the premise that man's survival and well-being on Earth is intimately linked to how he behaves in the world, rather than simply to repetitive events outside of his control. When fulfilling the expectations he imagines God holds for him, he can expect to be appreciated, protected, and loved. But when he fails to do so, evil will surely fill his life. There is a foreshadowing here of a much more elaborated ethical contract that comes in later biblical books and that can be seen as a further evolution in man's struggle to subdue in his nature those aspects of self that bring him suffering.

Cain and Abel's powerful tale also anticipates man's great difficulty in living a moral, principled life, given the profound insecurities afflicting him and, not surprisingly, the imagined God he worships. These insecurities cause his God to react with disdain when feeling slighted by man (as when Cain offers Him what He perceives as not being up to the expected standard) and cause man to experience deep hurt and fury when admonished by the highest authority, which in Cain's case leads him to act out his rage on his unsuspecting brother. These emotional vulnerabilities in the deity are a displacement of man's own vulnerabilities and his propensity to react violently and viciously to perceived slights when in a primitive stage of development, as Cain was then, and as many of us, unfortunately, still are now. This archaic state of functioning creates an explosive mixture that augurs poorly for the future of man, who surely will not always divine accurately what it is his God wants or needs from him. Yet his well-being depends on the actions of this omnipotent divinity whose bad moods—revealed in those acts of nature causing man great suffering—ironically hinge on a creature whose behavior He cannot control.

It is hard to imagine Cain intentionally spurning his Maker knowing, as he indubitably must have, what this same Divine Being had done to his parents when they disobeyed His command in Eden. And even if he did not know (supposing this was concealed from him by his parents), he knew he was dealing with an omniscient, omnipotent, and omnipresent deity who would not take being displeased lightly. A more reasonable explanation is to adduce that he was unaware of what God expected from him, as often happens between children and parents, and if he did know, then this was a covert action of hostility triggered perhaps by a perceived favoritism from God toward Abel.

In either case, had Cain been dealing with a more mature, self-assured, balanced, truly compassionate and loving Father/God, one imagined by an equally mature and more resourceful human being, he would have responded in a very different way. We can imagine, for example, such a God engaging Cain in a dialogue aimed at understanding the meaning of his actions and thus helping him articulate his feelings and thoughts. A more developed deity would have educated him about what good comportment toward his Creator would look like. Such actions by a more evolved deity would have prevented Cain's hurt and rage from escalating and degenerating into murder. But man could not imagine such a God at this point in his psychological unfolding. Instead, he envisaged a super-sensitive, insecure, thin-skinned God inclined to fits of rage and to punishing man severely, often beyond what his deeds called for, and at times seemingly for no apparent reason.

At this early stage of his mythmaking project, however, there is a glimmer of hope for man, for God, despite His admonishing tone, finishes His communication by telling Cain he can overcome his inclination to do wrong: "If you do not do right sin couches at the door; its urge is toward you, *yet you can be its master*" (Gen. 4:7). This verse suggests a developing awareness within man that his inclination to

act immorally, dishonestly, and unfairly, as defined by the culture in which he lived, can, with effort, be conquered. But how to conquer his evil disposition is not revealed; centuries will pass before man is ready to attempt to get a handle on this. But at least for now, he is told by his higher conscience—God—that it is doable, something within the scope of his human capabilities.

Cain's Punishment: Man's Enduring Insecurity and Sufferings

Following Abel's murder, the Bible has God forcing Cain to acknowledge his crime. Surprisingly, He does not claim Cain's life: His ruling is not based on the law of an eye for an eye but rather on inflicting suffering on the transgressor, suffering that would last for the rest of his existence. So he condemns Cain by telling him he will struggle mightily to provide food for his sustenance, as the earth will not "yield its strength to him" (Gen. 4:12) and that he will be a "ceaseless wanderer on earth" (Gen. 4:12), that is, feel threatened and unsafe no matter where he goes. And yet to ensure nobody lays a hand on him and kills him, and in this way frees him from his torment, God places a sign on Cain's forehead so that wherever he goes he will be easily recognized as being off-limits. Cain's punishment is emblematic of how primitive man must have often felt about his world and his God: alone, forsaken, unwelcomed, and continuously unsure of his ability to provide for his sustenance and for that of his family.

It is notable that while God's first order of business was to introduce order into the primeval amorphousness—"God said, 'Let there be light;' and there was light. God called the light Day, and the Darkness He called Night. And there was evening and there was morning, a first day" (Gen. 1:3–5)—the first thing man does is to reintroduce disorder: first by transgressing the divine injunction and then by killing for the redemption of his hurt. Such breakdown of order was inevitable given the limited intellectual and emotional resources available to him then, a condition that resulted in him acting impulsively, aggressively, and irascibly when confronted with life's challenges. Man has been struggling to overcome this enduring disorderliness in both his personal and communal life ever since.

After the Flood: Limited Psychosocial Evolution and the Covenant

The first stories in Genesis reveal man as a corrupt, devious creature inclined toward wrongdoing, all of which must have been deeply offensive to that part of his humanity capable of imagining himself as a just, caring, loving being. At some point in time, though, his corruption and evilness reached a critical point, demanding something drastic be done. So out of the depths of the noble side of man's soul, a new image of God developed. Whereas He was originally pictured as a deity somewhat aloof from His Creation, God is next visualized as actively functioning in the world. Having come to the realization that man's deviousness had no bounds and that his disregard for God's commands was blatant, the myth creators have God start humanity's tenure on earth again. This time, however, they begin with a good and noble man, Noah. After instructing him to build an Ark and bring his family and a pair of each of the species of animals inhabiting the land into it, God unleashes a devastating flood that kills every living being on earth except those Noah invited into the Ark.

While new beginnings usually raise hopes and expectations for a better tomorrow, the fact that this one came on the heels of a cataclysmic event that killed nearly all living creatures and destroyed everything man had built thus far allows us to assume it provoked on those lucky survivors a profound loss of faith and painful thoughts that the outer world was chaos and that the God they worshipped and depended upon wasn't, after all, just, predictable, or omnipotent but rather an irritable, destructive, out of control God capable of inflicting unbearable pain on His children.

A new understanding of his living reality became urgently needed, one that would make sense of what had occurred and thus would restore trust in God's fairness and the future. Being expulsed from Eden for transgressing God's command was at least understandable to ancestral man, but that God would destroy all living beings including animals with no culpability for any of man's transgressions was shocking and frightening and difficult to countenance. Thus a further development of the mythical relationship between God and man surfaced. This time he imagined the voice of God rising to proclaim: "Never again will I doom the earth because of man since the devisings of man's mind are evil from his youth; nor will I ever again destroy every living being, as I have done. So long as the earth endures seedtime and harvest, cold and heat, summer and winter, day and night shall not cease" (Gen. 8:21, 22).

By acknowledging God had gone too far in His punishments and making Himself promise He will never do so again, man was acknowledging his need to know that nature, of which he was an integral part, and the world in which he lived were controllable and under some kind of supervision and restraint.

Looking back in time, our forebears also doubtless saw the aggressive lawlessness that partly characterized antediluvian human behavior (from Cain and Abel to the continuing evil concoctions of man's mind) as destructive and wrong and thereby responsible for a good part of their distress and concomitant suffering. Intuitively, they understood that humanity had a tendency to manifest a kind of aggression unique among the other species sharing their living space. It needed to be controlled. After the Flood, therefore, our predecessors would have naturally yearned for a society containing a rudimentary system of laws that would hopefully ensure a degree of civility, stability, and equity in human affairs.

Unable to comprehend what causes man's malignant aggression (as difficult today as it was then: witness the massacres in schools, workplaces, and other settings in our country that burst out with alarming regularity), the ancients acted pragmatically, devising rules of comportment and penalties they hoped would ensure a more harmonious coexistence. Among other new injunctions now ascribed to God came this crucial one: "But for your own life-blood I will require a reckoning of every man for that of his fellow man! Whoever sheds the blood of man by man shall his blood be shed; for in His image did God make man." This powerful directive seems to contradict the previous one embodied in God forgiving Cain's life, although it imposed on him what is perhaps an even harsher penalty: that of being outcast from the human community forever. This apparent contradiction reinforces the belief of many biblical students that the Bible gives voice to differing points of view. But it may also illustrate a tension brewing within the collective human soul regarding how best to reduce the frequency with which murder happened in their midst: capital punishment and the belief in terrible suffering in the world to come, or unremitting suffering for murderers in the world of the here and now. In either case, the sanctity of human life was unequivocally affirmed.

An important new chapter in human history now opened, one that we are still exploring today as developments in biotechnology and medicine force us to continuously reassess the meaning of our ethical duty to respect human life and to protect it. Given the remarkable and often unimaginable developments in these fields, we are periodically impelled to redefine what we mean by human life and a human person.

By committing themselves to living by the rudiments of a "rule of law," our ancestors intended to promote a system of social governance that fostered trust between people as well as respect for human rights— like the right to life. At the same time, the system had to retain flexibility to correct its errors either by creating new laws or getting rid of old ones when they stopped working or were ineffective.

The significance of the rule of law for the well-being of the community cannot be overstated. It represents an antidote for human oppression and authoritarianism. To be effective, though, it has to avoid all forms of arbitrariness or preferential treatment of certain groups of people or specific interests. In other words, it must set up laws that can be known in advance and that apply to everyone equally with no exceptions. Amendments to laws and rules will be needed over time, but their introduction must not violate the principle of universal applicability. In this way, authorities cannot become tyrannical despots who impose rules and laws on the citizenry that benefit only them and their allies to the detriment of everyone else.

I had occasion recently to speak to a woman educated in England but now living in the capital of a Third World country: Caracas, Venezuela.

"I don't dare even to walk my dogs," she said dejectedly. "Where I live, there is no personal security, no protection for business interests, no protection of private property, no functioning judiciary, and a police force in cahoots with criminal elements. It is an awful and alarming situation."

Operating by rules and laws does not mean, however, that society renounces being caring, compassionate, and humane with its members and with the members of other species. It is reassuring that even in those primitive times, a semblance of this important sentiment insinuated itself in the biblical account. While man's dominion over all other creatures remained affirmed, in the same breath God is described as directing man to avoid eating flesh with the lifeblood still in it. Clearly, as man's understanding grew, he began to demand of himself certain empathy toward other aspects of Creation, an empathy that he is still working on developing and asserting today, particularly when considering the welfare of members of his own species.

During this period of psychological rebirth that was brought forth by the story of the Flood, man was inwardly driven to ensure that these novel directives were implemented. He must have been aware that his relationship with the Creator/supervising Father God had gone awry from the very beginning. First Adam and Eve disobeyed God's injunction, which led to their subsequent expulsion from Eden. Then Cain, their firstborn son, killed his brother, Abel, drawing God's severe punishment. Finally, given the crass behavior of the human race as a whole, God destroyed most of it with a devastating flood. Yearning to experience more control over existence, and aware of his inherent weaknesses and failings, man's creative imagination gave birth to yet another new mythical concept: *a covenant*, in this instance the cosmic agreement between two highly unequal parties.

Delivering man from fear of another cataclysmic flood or some other terrible disaster, God is imagined as entering into a covenantal relationship with man in the person of Noah and his sons: "I now establish My covenant with you and your offspring to come, and with every living thing that is with you . . . all that have come out of the ark, every living thing on earth . . . never again shall all flesh be cut off by the waters of a flood, and never again shall there be a flood to destroy the earth" (Gen. 9:9–11).

This new mythic emanation, which became the foundational basis upon which our Jewish forebears built their hopes for redeeming suffering, assured man that he need never again fear the worst. Indeed, it envisions Noah and his descendants receiving a perpetual sign, reminding them of the Supreme Being's faithfulness: "I have set my bow in the clouds, and it shall serve as a sign of the covenant between Me and the Earth. When I bring clouds over the earth, and the bow appears in the clouds, I will remember My covenant between Me and you and every living creature among all flesh, so that the waters shall never again become a flood to destroy all flesh" (Gen. 9:13 -15).

No sign is more reassuring after a horrible flood than a rainbow, the harbinger of calm and peacefulness. Storms are powerful, frightening, and seemingly unavoidable, but God promised He would always be there, protecting man and making sure he would not again suffer utter devastation and loss.

The introduction of a sign into the mythical structure—so that "I (God) will remember My covenant with you"—acknowledged the insecurity in man's soul in regard to the controllability of nature and the reliability of the agent responsible for exercising such restraint. In the absence of a specific sign from God, He might easily forget His promises and allow a repeat of the devastating experience man had just endured. This would be intolerable; hence, by providing a sign of His commitment, the myth further reassured man it would not be so.

By making the covenantal idea a critical part of man's relationship with the Divine, God's accountability to man was asserted, for He was now bound to him by a sacred agreement that could not be rescinded. Never again would this God do anything in violation of His promises to Noah and through him to humankind and all living creatures. God's willingness to enter into a binding agreement with man also rehabilitated man's status, the one he lost as a result of his ancestral transgression. From here on, man will hopefully shed the terrible mantle of being a fallen creature inclined to badness and become an equal partner in the redemption of his life with the Creator of the All instead.

This newly minted image of God gave man the opportunity to redeem himself; hence, there was renewed hope that he would eventually find resolution from the suffering that being human, ergo self-conscious, imposed upon him.

A covenantal agreement between God and man was a clever and effective way to restore, at least temporarily, the people's confidence in the world and their created God image, just as other types of agreements between parents and children, for example, build trust and feelings of safety between them. Implicit in a covenant, however, is an understanding that each side has responsibilities and is answerable to the other. Each side knows what it needs to do to fulfill its part. Children, for example, expect to be cared for, supported, protected, and loved by their parents who in turn expect their children to follow their dictates and embrace their beliefs and values. A three-year-old child, when hearing that his mommy and daddy were going out to dinner, said with some anguish in his voice: "And who is going to take care of me?"

Surprisingly, though, in the first articulation of an agreement between God and man, there was no indication that man was to play any active role in it. The myth's silence on this point suggests that man's ego-self may not have been psychologically ready to know what his part in the agreement was going to be and, therefore, also not ready to assume responsibility for it. Developmentally speaking, man was still in an early stage, dependent on a parental authority to guide his life and look out for his well-being. Hence, his primordial inner artist, while able to conceive of a covenant with God, only articulated the divinity's promise to temper His reactions to man's inevitable foibles and remember His commitment to man but was mum as to what man's side of the bargain was.

Babel: Progress and the Limits of Early Science and Technology

Man's evolving postdiluvian mythological emanations must have assuaged some of his fears and misgivings and the suffering these caused. But in the end his belief in the promises his imagined God

69

made to him were insufficient to fully contain his distress. Lesser floods, earthquakes, volcanic eruptions, tornados, wars, famines, lawlessness, social injustice, violence, and similar catastrophes continued to occur, gradually eroding the restored confidence of the community and over time causing great damage to organized human life. Finally, man understood that to attain his desired happiness and security he needed to reign over the threatening forces of nature (including those of his human nature). Expecting that the God he worshiped would perform this essential task had simply not worked.

There followed a remarkable spurt in man's intellectual development, evidenced in the biblical account by his mastery of mathematical, architectural, and engineering principles. Formerly living a semi-nomadic life, the biblical account tells us now that he has become a city dweller, thereby improving his accessibility to critical resources such as food, water, sanitation, and healthcare. The quality and possibly the length of his life have been enhanced. Here we are given a glimpse as to how man's rational, scientifically based approach to resolving existential challenges contributed massively to bringing comfort and safety to his life. But psychologically speaking man needs far more than technical achievements if he is to make himself secure and enduringly happy.

At this juncture in his psychological development, a new myth burst forth: man believes that by building on his technical achievements he can grasp a life free from the fear of pain and suffering. "Come," he said, "let us build a city, and a tower with its top in the sky, to make a name for ourselves: else we shall be scattered all over the world" (Gen. 11:4). But why was building a city—a remarkable feat itself—not accomplishment enough to secure him a name and a better future? Why did the mythical account have to conceive the city as having a tower reaching the sky? And what is man's primordial wisdom saying to himself when his myth describes both his failure to realize the project and his punishment for having tried? For the Hebrew Bible has God descending upon him saying, "If as one people with one language for all, this is how they have begun to act, then nothing that they may propose to do will be out of their reach. Let us then go down and confound their speech there so that they shall not understand one another's speech" (Gen. 11:7).

Here, man's myth creator highlighted a profound contradiction between his conscious efforts to gain mastery of his world and thus attain the feeling of security he yearned for, and his unconscious understanding that this was not feasible, at least not yet; hence, it was not the right path to solve his problem. On the one hand, man's evolving myth recognized his longing to overcome his creatureliness, his vulnerabilities, and his debasing mortality. On the other hand, it recognized the folly in such escapist fantasies. His urge to build skyscrapers, an attempt to become godlike—a logical absurdity—exposed, therefore, an underlying feeling of powerlessness. In describing the failure of his compensatory drive to overcome his fears, he acknowledges the delusory character of his wish. "If I could only reach the sky," he seems to be telling himself, "I will be like God. Then my fears and all my other sufferings will disappear. I will be all powerful, all knowing, able to ward off all the things that threaten my survival, and thus, become blissful again, as I was during my time in Eden." But deep inside he knows that he cannot make it, that he is mortal, and while made in God's image, he is not born endowed with the resources that can ensure his safety and his happiness. Thus, despite his technical prowess and progress and skill, in the story of the Tower of Babel man mythically affirmed the futility of this approach, already signalized at the beginning of Genesis in such language as God's question: "Now that the man has become like one of us, knowing good and bad, what if he should stretch out his hand and take also from the tree of life and eat, and live forever?" (Gen. 3:22).

In his wisdom, man's mythmaker once more rejected the unrealistic and biologically injurious dream of immortality. It is fascinating to think that our forebears' psyche, a cauldron of ideas, images, and wisdom from which these myths emanated, was already aware of the damaging effects that the search for immortality could and would have on the human species. Many centuries later, through the development of the sciences and the deepening of our understanding of the human body and human life, we discovered how counterproductive immortalization at the cellular level could be. Even though our ancestors could not have known this, from the depth of their imagination, something in them did understand that immortality could not be the path leading to the goodness and happiness they so desperately wanted.

Conscious man, however, is a stubborn creature, and so, despite his recurrent failures, he has continued to search for ways to conquer nature and make his life ultimately predictable and safe.

The Polish director Krzysztof Kieślowski's film series *The Decalogue* illustrates our current folly.[1] The series consists of ten episodes, each raising poignant questions about the meaning of each of the biblical commandments. The first film focuses on the terrible dangers associated with our efforts to attain security and tranquility by worshipping either our intellectual prowess or an omnipotent, omniscient God actively involved in coordinating human affairs. The story involves a young widower trying to raise his ten-year-old son on wholesome, enduring, and scientifically sound values. A university math professor who depends on his older sister to attend to the boy while he is at work professes an eminently secular worldview and an understanding of life that is based on knowledge empirically derived. For him, religion is a form of indoctrination based on false premises that poison the minds of believers. In a way, science and technology are his gods, and he worships them with fervor. His sister, a devout Catholic, is concerned about the way her brother has been raising her nephew and uses every opportunity to instill religious faith in the boy. The boy is highly inquisitive and prone to asking difficult questions—"Why did my friend's dog die?" "Where does one go after death?"—which his father enjoys answering. The story unfolds during winter, and the grounds outside the family's apartment building are covered with snow. The boy had asked Santa Claus for a pair of ice skates and the father, knowing how much he wants them, surprises his son by giving them to him a few days before Christmas. A man-made lake in the vicinity had recently frozen, and the boy urges the father to let him go skating after school the next day. Uncertain as to whether the thickness of the ice can withstand the boy's weight, the father consults a weather bureau and, using precise mathematical formulas on his computer, concludes that the conditions on the frozen lake are unequivocally favorable; and so he accedes to his son's request. Next day, upon his return home, he finds out that the ice had broken while his beloved son was skating and he drowned. The occurrence is incomprehensible to him, unacceptable. The formulas he used were infallible, the computations exact, and there was no way the ice could have broken given the child's weight, the outside temperature, and the conditions prevailing at the time. Everything checked out—and yet the ice had broken. Having placed all his faith in the god of science, he feels terribly betrayed and forsaken. Overcome with anguish and guilt, he goes on a destructive rampage.

Experiences such as these remind us that life and the physical world we live in are filled with mysteries we cannot fully vanquish, not even with precise mathematical formulas or computations, and whenever we place our safety in the hands of a god in whose graces we depend on for our well-being and security, the results can be catastrophic.

Abraham: The Emergence of an Autonomous Self

As the biblical myths continue to unroll, they show man stuck in a time when his most profound searches have given him a strong sense of his creaturely limitations. Despite his technical progress, he feels himself to be a youngster whose divine Father is seen either protecting him by trying to keep him out of harm's way or judging and punishing him severely when he misbehaves. His myths primarily show him relying for security and happiness entirely on his heavenly Father's moods and goodwill. At this stage of his development, his intellectual achievements surpass by a large margin his psycho-spiritual resourcefulness. He is able to build cities and to improve his life, but he still has great difficulty reigning over his fears, his guilt, his impulsiveness, and his instinctive drives and overcoming his inability to live in a cooperative, productive way with others.

When Abraham appears in the biblical narrative (a century or so after the beginning of the second millennium BCE) man's evolving consciousness depicts additional possibilities for reducing humanity's juvenile dependency and unthinking submission to an external authority and for making his struggle for happiness more successful. In the past, despite stern warnings and harsh punishments, man was characterized as a childlike creature: bright but crass, too often disappointing his imagined God and, through Him, the higher vision he harbored of himself. But Abraham seems more of a grownup, a person capable, through his actions, of giving expression to those commands and wishes man's myth creators attributed to God. This helped create the social and psychological conditions required for improving safety and welfare and hopefully, once and for all, overcoming the sense of being a flawed, sinful creature. Tuning into the tone and content used by the biblical narrators when describing God's first communication to Abraham, we can see how it already embodied new potentialities: "Go forth from your native land and from your father's house" (Gen. 12:1). This is a call to forsake almost everything that protected and sustained other men, including Abraham himself.

That Abraham obeyed and made the enormous changes in his life demanded by the voice he heard within altered the picture man had heretofore created and accepted of himself. Abraham's heart received his call from an inner dynamism that suggests man had evolved psychologically to the point where an individual could cease mechanically following the mores of his ancestors and willingly give up the collectivity on which he had hitherto based his existence: country, community, and kindred, in particular, his father. Far from the demigod heroes of early mythologies, we have moved to where an Everyman is imagined capable of becoming heroic. Human self-knowledge had experienced a quantum leap in evolution: a single man could engage directly with great powers and take the road less traveled.

But there is more to God's summons. For beyond showing that a man could leave the old, the narrative also demonstrated he could choose a specific new destination, even one far away. In mythic language, man had now imagined his God wanting him to be both free and self-realizing, a critical step in the journey to emotional and spiritual health.

Despite the terrible hardships implied in what are depicted as God's demands, Abraham/Everyman is shown as having the fortitude to respond to his own internal stirrings. The myth further affirmed his steps toward autonomy by showing God as having made many promises and assurances that He would always protect him: "Fear not, Abraham, I am a shield to you; your reward shall be very great" (Gen. 15:1). In following his calling, Abraham allowed himself to venture into an unfamiliar, somewhat mysterious destination. Until then, he had lived in what was intellectually the epicenter of civilized life, but socially and psychologically he was part of a rather primitive tribal-based society in which individual needs and yearnings were subjugated to those of the clan, the tribe, and the community. What he was willing to leave behind was the known, the certain, the tested; what he was willing to do was expose himself and his family to a new world shrouded in mystery. Would he have the resources and the resilience to overcome the many challenges he would surely face? He didn't know. Nonetheless, something deep within him was convinced it was the right thing for him to do; in fact, it was the only thing he could do. It was the thing that would, in the end, hopefully, make his life meaningful and give him the emotional uplift he sought.

As great as Abraham's first steps were, the mythmaking powers inherent in the human psyche saw him as symbolizing more than human individuation. He also symbolized righteousness, the human search for and adherence to ethical norms. When God first summoned Abraham to "go to the land I will show you," the promised new place was understood to symbolize a new human project to create a better way of being. It was the first adumbration in literature of a Utopian vision. The Bible has God further saying, "I will make you a great nation, and I will bless you; I will make your name great, and you shall be a blessing . . . and all the families of the earth shall bless themselves by you" (Gen. 12:1–3). Here was a statement of nothing less than an ethical mission, a vision of reorganizing society, first in Abraham's descendants and later, through their example, the whole world—that would be God's "blessing." Above all its other important implications for human progress, the Abraham story was man's mythic way of explaining society's evolution in ethical directions, where autonomy and personal rights and duties are of great import.

The myth underscores this ethical import in many places. For example, when a famine forces Abraham to sojourn to Egypt, he is immediately tempted to surrender his wife Sara to the powerful Pharaoh, who desires her for she is a woman of beautiful appearance (Gen. 12:10–16). But once God (understood as man's conscience or his Higher Self) intervenes to tell the Pharaoh that Sara is indeed Abraham's wife and not his sister (as he had insinuated) she is returned seemingly untouched, unsoiled. Here the myth associates Abraham with an implied norm of family sacredness, especially conjugal inviolability. This event can also be taken as the beginning of humanity's education in higher social norms, the first step toward later biblical codifications of the sanctity of marriage.

When his and Lot's herdsmen quarrel, Abraham lets Lot choose which part of the land he wants to keep for himself. Lot, of course, chooses the better part. By accepting the decision, Abraham shows a judicious willingness to make personal sacrifices for the sake of keeping social peace. The myth shows humanity beginning to move toward personal responsibility for enhancing harmonious human solidarity.

A number of similar Abrahamic stories attest to his dedication to a more principled way of life. For example, he would not take anything belonging to the king of Sodom as recompense for successfully fighting and defeating the king's enemies (Gen. 14:22, 23). Here the virtue of generosity is affirmed. Moreover, to take extra payment from the king would have compromised Abraham's valued independence. Legend also tells us that disgusted by his family's worship of idols, he smashed them, thereby affirming God's righteousness. At another point in the biblical account, he realized that much of his misery stemmed from the way he approached his interpersonal relations. His inability to confront issues and assert himself emotionally, for example, led him and others to despair: "Sarah saw the son whom Hagar the Egyptian had borne to Abraham playing. She said to Abraham, 'Cast out that slave woman and her son, for the son of that slave shall not share in the inheritance with my son Isaac.' The matter distressed Abraham greatly, for it concerned a son of his" (Gen. 21:9–11). And yet Abraham said nothing; submissively he did what his wife told him to do, perhaps to keep peace at home. Similarly, legend tells us that after his wife Sarah found out that he was prepared to sacrifice their son Isaac she never spoke to him again and died shortly thereafter.

What might have prompted Abraham to consider sacrificing his son is unfathomable, to say the least. Some authors have interpreted this as reflecting the kind of sacrifice the sacred covenant with God demanded. Others, like Kierkegaard in his book *Fear and Trembling*,[2] portray Abraham as the "knight of faith" who is asked to renounce, for the sake of his faith and love in God, his beloved son, as well as his humanly engendered ethical ideals. What seems clear to me, though, is that the portrait the Hebrew Bible gives of Abraham is that of a man living on the interface of two seemingly incompatible worlds: the world of ordinary human reality—marriage, children, family, mundane day-to-day activities—in other words, the world of the here and now, and the world of what contemporary psychologists may call the transpersonal realm of existence, a realm concerned with issues of collective, environmental, and planetary import and under the command of what is perceived as belonging to the divine, the eternal, the sublime. These two worlds pull human beings in opposite directions, each one demanding total allegiance. The world of ordinary reality makes sure we provide for our physical and material needs, pay our bills, pick up the children on time, and take a vacation once in a while; the transpersonal world alerts us to the conflicts in the world, the decay of the environment, the lack of justice, and our duty to fight for these causes with complete abandon.

It is conceivable that Abraham's love for Isaac (it is in God's summons to sacrifice him that the word "love" appears for the first time in biblical lore), his care for him, may have threatened that other part of him that was supposed to be fully devoted to the directives coming from the Divine Voice that had been guiding his life. An unbearable inner tension may have developed between these seemingly incompatible loyalties causing him to perceive, albeit erroneously, that by loving Isaac so much he was betraying the Divine Voice that had assisted him with such devotional care. The same God that had reassured him that he and Sarah would have a son of their own despite their advanced age had surely the right to demand he sacrifice that son as unequivocal proof of his unfettered loyalty to Him. Fortunately, moments before committing what would have been an irremediable outrage, his more rational side realized the absurdity of what he was about to do, stayed his hand, and thus prevented him from committing a terribly immoral and destructive act.

Nikos Kazantzakis, in the prologue to his book *The Last Temptation of Christ*, describes this tension with great clarity and passion: "My principal anguish and the source of all my joys and sorrows from my youth onward has been the incessant, merciless battle between the spirit and the flesh.

"Within me are the dark immemorial forces of the Evil One, human and pre-human; within me too are the luminous forces, human and pre-human, of God—and my soul is the arena where these armies have clashed and met."[3]

Abraham's allegory teaches us that what felt to him—and still does to many others—like an unsolvable incompatibility between the world of the mundane and the world of the transordinary is just illusory. Allegiance and dedication to one do not have to diminish dedication to the other necessarily. Ordinary and transordinary realities are in fact complementary, and we must learn to balance and integrate them if we hope to attain psycho-spiritual wholeness. Concern for our personal and familial needs—children, marriage, work, health—does not require betraying our more transcendent calling: participation in remedying the ills of our community, the health of our society, our environment, or the conflicts that poison the relationships between ethnic groups, races, and nations. But accomplishing this balancing act is very hard for most of us.

The biblical narrative does not tell us whether Abraham's experiences heightened his awareness, leading him to a new level of psycho-spiritual functioning, one that enhanced his ability to live morally and attain inner peace. But at least it represents the beginning of man's evolving understanding that beyond the effects of nature's uncontrollable powers on his life, man's success in overcoming suffering and attaining the happiness he seeks ultimately rests in his own hands.

Regardless of how knowledgeable he is, man cannot control nature—not even his own nature—a good part of the time. But what he can do is affect the way he responds to the events of his life and, depending on the quality of that response, foster health and wellness and peacefulness for himself and others—or the opposite.

In the mythic world of Abraham's story, the pathway toward the redemption of human suffering has moved beyond the vision of living according to the Rule of Law, adumbrated earlier in the narratives, to the subjective *internalization* of right doing. The importance of the ethical sense and its sway over people's inner lives cannot be exaggerated for it is essential to the attainment of communal harmony. This ethical sense is indeed the condition that ensures that regardless of how its members understand their relationship with the Divine and the beyond, whatever their metaphysical differences may be, they can still live according to ethical principles they can all agree to, and thus co-exist in peace. For this to work, though, the operative term is wholehearted *acceptance* of ethical principles by all involved. Whether it is the sanctity of life, of marriage, of the physical world, the duty to care for the poor and the ignored, respect for autonomy, or respect for the rule of law, all such principles need to be embraced with sincerity; otherwise the social system will descend into turmoil and conflict and ultimately collapse.

The biblical description of God's ways as "righteous" allowed ancestral man also to view Him as accountable for His actions for He created, after all, the potential for a moral world to which He, too, was bound. Thus, in a totally unprecedented act, fully exercising his newfound sense of right and wrong, the narrative shows Abraham questioning God's justice. Hearing of God's intention to destroy Sodom and Gomorrah, he asked: "Will You sweep away the innocent along with the guilty? What if there should be fifty innocent people within the city; will You then wipe out the place and not forgive it for the sake of the innocent fifty that are in it? Far be it from You to do such a thing, to bring death upon the innocent as well as the guilty." The Lord answered, "If I find within the city of Sodom fifty innocent ones, I will forgive the whole place for their sake" (Gen. 18:23–26). Once again, man's myth creator introduced order, safety, and reliability into the ruthless world that he was learning to manage, and with that the potential for less despair. The God that rules man's life is portrayed here, the Bible tells us, as responsible and accountable. He responds to man's questions and challenges, revealing man has agency with God. He knows that man is now beginning to watch Him as much as He is watching man. And while the Divine is perceived as all-powerful, He cannot do whatever He wants for He is bound by principles of justice and fairness, just as is man.

A New Covenant: The Ethical Life for Individuals and Community

Man's understanding of his relationship to the great power in the universe—God—had evolved from one in which communication was largely unidirectional (God asking difficult questions and demanding specific actions from man) to one that was dialogical, mutual. This evolved man was imbued with mythic autonomy. Like God, he was free to question even the highest authority. Thus when God tells Abraham, "Your reward shall be very great," he responds, "O Lord God, what can you give me seeing that I shall die childless." Later in the same conversation God tells Abraham, "I am the Lord who brought you out from Ur of the Chaldeans to assign this land to you as possession," to which Abraham replies, "O Lord God, how shall I know that I am to possess it?" (Gen. 15:1, 2, 7, 8). This short exchange illustrates Jewish inquisitiveness and the beginning of Jewish *chutzpah*: the demand for proof and pragmatic answers from our enigmatic, otherworldly divinity who too often speaks in riddles. God makes promises to Abraham and instead of responding with gratitude, total confidence, and trust, he responds by asking for specifications. He seems to be saying something like, "All these promises made to me are nice and dandy, but where is the deed of trust with my name on it? Having that on hand would make me feel much better than all these promises. After all, only You and I know You gave it to me, no one else. Why should they believe my word?" Moreover, he also expects God's answers to be congruent with

His stated promises: "I am a shield to you; your rewards shall be great" (Gen. 15:2, 3); "As for your wife . . . Sarah. I will bless her; indeed I will give you a son by her" (Gen. 17:17).

The more equal the relationship between man and his created God, the less humans are depicted as mere victims of events that cycle and recycle interminably. Instead, they are seen as partners with the Divine in a relationship of reciprocal responsibility and thoughtful consideration. Specifically, dedication to an ethical life entitles man to demand the same level of moral commitment from God. Additionally, the mutuality inherent in the relationship between man and the Divine speaks to the antidogmatic, antiauthoritarian trend in the biblical tradition, revealing some emphasis placed on freedom of thought, freedom of expression, and freedom of inquiry, that is, the freedom to question the veracity of what we are told and taught. All these are qualities of free people living according to a body of knowledge rooted in their actual experiences rather than in some strict dogmatic set of constructs.

Abraham is shown driven by an inner spirit, that is holy, affirmative, and forward-looking. He understands that if his descendants and the generations following them pursue his ethical vision and remain loyal to his chosen path, they will become a blessed community, and through them "all the families of the earth will bless themselves." It is essential, though, that his followers become familiar with his ways and embrace them. But how could he motivate others, more particularly his family members, to follow his example? Uncertain they would receive the same guidance and support from the Divine Inner Voice he had experienced, how could he get them to understand and follow his vision, whatever difficulties might arise?

Man answers this question by introducing a new covenantal formula that goes beyond the unidirectional one he put forth in the Noah story. Now God is depicted as saying, "You shall circumcise the flesh of your foreskin, and that shall be the sign of the covenant between Me and you. And throughout the generations, every male among you shall be circumcised at the age of eight days . . . Thus shall My covenant be marked in your flesh as an everlasting pact" (Gen. 17:11–13).

That very day, he and all the men in his clan circumcised themselves, marking a fundamental transition in the covenantal relationship between God and man. For when man's myth creator had God establishing a covenant with Noah, it was He who made the promises to man and provided him with a sign to remind man and Himself of His commitment. But in the covenant He established with Abraham, his clan, and their descendants, the reverse takes place: it is man's turn now to provide a sign, a physical one, reflective of his unbending commitment to the sacred covenant with God. The irreversible sign in the flesh would serve as a daily reminder of the person's duties and responsibilities to God and the ethical life expected of him. By imagining the need for a permanent physical sign, man's myth creator may be acknowledging man's propensity to stray from his obligations. By having a mark on his flesh, he cannot avoid seeing daily, he would now be in possession of a physical antidote to his tendency to forget his commitments and duties.

During the time of the first covenant, man's ego-self was not mature enough to affirm his role in it. Hence there was silence regarding this. His primordial artist understood, however, the need for man to know that his God was accountable and committed to him. So the first agreement was established between God and a man who developmentally was still young, his happiness resting fully in God's hands. The second agreement, however, has the makings of a relationship of true mutuality in which each party has a well-defined role to play in the reduction of individual and collective suffering and in the attainment of individual and collective peace and happiness.

Psychologically speaking, the Abraham story suggests a type of individual more fully actualized. Such an individual operates at a higher level of psycho-spiritual proficiency and hence is able to act responsibly and more autonomously, demanding similar qualities from others, including from his Maker. Having followed the path he pioneered, Abraham is at a stage in which his thinking is dominated by grand idealistic visions that he is willing to undertake and better yet fulfill. Whether in antiquity or in modern times, people such as these live out great enthusiasms, adventure, engage in passionate acts, and are ready to tackle the big issues of their time. People who arrive at this stage of psychic functioning exhibit a persistent connection to their interiority and to the awareness that there is more to their being than meets the eye. Such people, while living in the objective reality of the here and now, are at the same time in touch with an inner voice/presence that connects them with broader realms of understanding and perception. And even though they are grounded in the world of ordinary occurrences, they cross with regularity into the transpersonal, archetypal world where their true calling lies. These are people whose role is to promote collective prosperity, communal harmony, and peace among races, ethnic groups, religious traditions, and nations. They are socially minded people who make sure that the resources available to the community are equitably distributed. Their challenge is to give expression to the demands of the upper world, an endeavor that will thrust them into unfamiliar, uncharted territories, and at the same time remain connected to the mundane world they share with others. This evolution of mind and struggle between disparate worlds as part of man's journey to freedom from despair is foreshadowed in the stories surrounding the mythic figure of Abraham.

Interpersonal Human Foibles Amplify Man's Sufferings

With Abraham, we have the first biblical image of a more mature and better-integrated person—autonomous, self-driven, righteous, unafraid to break away from old ideas and customs, responsive to his inner calling, and capable of learning how he can intervene in his life and affect his suffering. With him, we also begin to learn how interpersonal dynamics, which are an accurate reflection of the state of our mental and emotional skillfulness, affect our day-to-day living. This important theme is further developed in the lives of his son Isaac and of Jacob and Esau, Isaac and Rebecca's twins.

The denied reality of parental preference, which most parents vociferously refute, had already raised its ugly head with horrendous consequences in the story of Cain and Abel. Now a similar event takes place in the lives of Isaac and his wife Rebecca, giving expression to the persistent competition for attention and favors between offspring and to how this source of distress and anguish magnifies our suffering when not addressed.

The Bible tells us that even during her pregnancy Rebecca experienced agitation in her belly, prompting her to go to the Lord to inquire about its meaning. "Two nations are in your womb," God tells her. "Two separate peoples shall issue from your body; one people shall be mightier than the other, and the older shall serve the younger" (Gen. 25:23). Notably, this is the first and only time God speaks directly to a Jewish Matriarch. Almost from birth, Isaac favored Esau, the burly, more aggressive, more masculine firstborn son, while Rebecca favored Jacob, the gentle, smooth-skinned man of the tents, the one who emerged holding Esau's ankle. One day, taking advantage of his twin brother's physical exhaustion, Jacob, for a bowl of lentil soup, buys from Esau the privilege of receiving the blessing reserved for the firstborn from the father. Later on, and under the instigation of Rebecca, Jacob deceives his blind and dying father by pretending he is Esau in order to receive the blessing he had manipulated his brother to sell him. When Esau discovers what happened, he reacts with unbridled fury. Jacob flees and must thereafter live away from his parents, most particularly his mother, whom he adored. Esau, the son Isaac loved, and Rebecca feared, as the only child left at home, presumably now receives all the attention he desires from his parents. Nonetheless, once again, he experiences parental rejection, this time from both when they disapprove of the wives he has chosen for himself. Clearly, the home of Isaac and Rebecca was not a paragon of familial harmony. Instead, it exemplified the kind of prototypical conflicts that have repeated themselves throughout the ages in almost every household: children competing for parental attention and favors, parents often treating children preferentially but never acknowledging it, and hurts and wounds lingering for decades, causing familial tensions, troubles, and not infrequently abusiveness, even violence that may mar the lives of its members for generations.

Wrestling Jacob: Autonomous, Inspired, and Subject to the Shadow

From Abraham onward, we see the relational bond to our interiority, our spiritual calling, strengthening and humanity deepening its appreciation of what it means to be human. More concretely, we find in the biblical myths a line of people whose objective reality, the one construed on the basis of sensorial information, is being complemented and supported by a progressively developing subjective reality emanating from their interiority in the form of dream imagery, visions, inner dialogues, feelings, and intuitive insights interpreted by them as communications from God. These are people whose private inner lives are as real and important as the public, sensorial, ego-centered ones they can readily share with others.

Of the psycho-spiritual developments responsible for reducing man's suffering that took place during this four-hundred-year nomadic period, one of the most important was Jacob confronting his repressed self, whence he overcame the profound anxiety caused by his past misdeeds—deceiving his father and stealing his brother's birthright, among others—for which he had not suffered the expected consequences. The night before reencountering his twin brother Esau, Jacob was forced into a bloody battle with a mysterious figure that unexpectedly appeared in his camp. This battle can be seen as symbolizing the inner struggle between Jacob's conscious self, the one rationalizing and explaining away his questionable past misdeeds, and his emerging darker side—repressed guilt for wrongs committed against brother and father and repressed fears of reprisals—that tells him otherwise. Though the arduous fight that ensues hurts Jacob in his thigh, near his sex organs, in the end, he emerges stronger and able to meet his brother with less fear and guilt. Consequently, their reencounter goes well, and they part ways in peace.

This biblical story metaphorically describes what we must endure if we are to integrate aspects of the psyche that every human being carries and demonstrates how, once this happens, better outcomes from our difficult experiences follow. The night Jacob was confronted by the shadowy figure he seemed to have reached a new level of psychological resourcefulness. He was able to recognize the terrible guilt and shame he harbored in his soul for having stolen from his brother, Esau, their father's blessing and for having deceived his blind father. Once he was able to recognize that he was battling his own strong resistance to acknowledging his deceptive nature and his tendency to take advantage of others when he was in need or insecure, he felt more protected, connected, and less fearful. Now he was able to face his brother without emitting those subliminal messages we usually convey when our shadow remains constellated in our interior, away from consciousness. These messages may communicate to others something like, "I did you wrong and deserve your rage. Punish me!" Absent such conscious confrontation with his inner demons, these forces would have continued to live in the recesses of Jacob's being, manifesting in subtle, confusing ways, causing conflicts and suffering.

It is not surprising that on account of Jacob's remarkable confrontation with his inner demons, the biblical narrators change his name to Israel because "he had striven with beings divine and human and had prevailed" (Gen. 32:29). By struggling with his guilt, fear, and shame he faced what Jung would call his "psychological shadow,"[4] thus allowing him to move now to a more integrated psychological stance. He had become a different person: Israel, the father of a great nation to be, and a man now less afraid of his world and life.

Personal growth, however, is a slow, irregular, arduous, nonvolitional process that usually unfolds in stages. We can set the intention to attain it and become involved in experiences that may induce it in us, but ultimately its progress is not completely under our control. But maturation and consciousness expansion are essential if we hope to reach a new understanding, new resourcefulness, and new skills with which to engage our lives in more meaningful ways and with fewer afflictions. So even though Jacob was able to overcome some of his perturbing feelings regarding his ill-treatment of his brother and thus avoid persistent enmity with him, this development was not enough for him to secure an enduringly peaceful, happy life.

Earlier on his deceptiveness and opportunistic character came back to haunt him when he was deceived by his father-in-law, Laban, who replaced Rachel, the woman he loved and desired to marry, with Leah, the oldest sister, the one his father-in-law wanted to be married first. Jacob's household suffered continuously from competition for his love and favors by the two women who knew well whom his heart preferred. As fate had it, the one he did not love was the one who had no trouble bearing children, while Rachel, the one he adored, was barren, which Leah did not fail to exploit to her advantage as often as she could. Then, when Rachel, at last, was able to bear him a child, Joseph became his father's favorite, raising great animosity and jealousy from his eleven brothers who felt dismissed, ignored, and mistreated. These ill feelings led them to conspire against their brother's well-being, culminating in Joseph being sold to a caravan of Bedouins en route to Egypt and them lying to their father about it, telling him that Joseph had been devoured by a ferocious animal that left behind only his blood-soaked tunic.

Losing the child he doted upon and loved dearly evoked despair in Jacob's soul, from which he never fully recovered. His sons paid the price for their deception by witnessing the daily suffering their disconsolate father endured. Unable to relieve his distress by telling him the truth of what had occurred, they were thereby unable to relieve their own.

Joseph and a New Human Gift for Healing

Another transcendent development during the patriarchal period that aided man's efforts to overcome suffering was the discovery, symbolized in the Joseph story, of the influence that dreams have on people's ordinary lives. Interpretation of dreams by a presumed divine oracle may have preceded the Joseph story, but he was the first biblical character endowed with the capacity to understand his and other people's dreams. Joseph could tap effortlessly into the mystery of this nightly occurrence, which connects dreamers with relevant events in their lives and/or in the life of their community and gives them the opportunity to intervene favorably and make individual and communal life better and healthier. How Joseph came to be such a good dream interpreter the Bible does not say. What is clear, however, is that he had lived a troubled life and had been exposed to many hardships: the jealousy of his brothers, the forced separation from father and kin, and the false accusation of sexual harassment by the wife of his employer in Egypt, which would result in his incarceration. All these may have served as inductive experiences that heightened his sensitivity and his ability to connect to his inner mystery.

As he explored dreams, Joseph at times intuited that they were prophetic, that is to say, they made us aware of events likely to occur at a future time. So when the Pharaoh's chief cupbearer, who was serving a prison sentence concurrent with Joseph, tells him about a dream in which he sees one of a three-branched vine budding, its blossoms and clusters ripening into grapes, Joseph interprets it to mean that he will be released from prison in three days and reinstated to his old post, which indeed happens (Gen. 40:9–13). Later on, the Pharaoh tells the now free cupbearer about a dream in which seven fat, sturdy cows are swallowed by seven skinny ones. The dream tormented the Pharaoh and yet none of his magicians or seers could offer a satisfactory interpretation. Remembering Joseph, the cupbearer recommends him to the Pharaoh, who calls upon Joseph to interpret the dream. Joseph presages seven years of great abundance in Egypt to be followed by seven years of famine and desolation, which encouraged the Pharaoh to store grain and nonperishable foods so that he could feed his people during the lean years (Gen. 41:17–36). Through the figure of Joseph, our ancient narrators described man being inducted into a new possibility: that of entering into an even deeper relationship with a source of knowledge and wisdom (i.e., God) that, while occasionally communicating during man's waking hours, did so consistently through nightly visitations.

Joseph's ability to decode the meaning of dreams symbolizes man's advancing relationship with the hidden side of himself, the one he has no willful access to. Given the understanding of human nature our forebears had at that time, it is inconceivable that they could have imagined dreams originating in their unconscious minds. For them, only an extracorporeal source—God and His angels—could be creating their dreams, and thus their content revealed information the Supreme Being had chosen to share with them for their benefit and that of others. An additional channel of communication had opened up for them between the domain of the Divine and the domain of the objectified self, a channel all human beings can regularly access, as we all dream daily and remember at least some of our dreams with enough detail to draw from them at least some of their teachings. Dreams are indeed the royal road into our inner lives, giving an honest insight into the foundation of our being in the world: our psyche. Through our dreams, we can learn about the hidden forces that drive our daily lives and what our total personality needs. And while few people in contemporary times are either born with or develop Joseph's uncanny ability to tap into the meaning of dreams, there is nothing to suggest that this ability cannot be induced or developed to some extent, if not in ourselves, then at least in some other members of our communities to whom we can go for assistance and guidance.

The Ethical Emphasis in Patriarchal Mythmaking

In a general sense, the stories of the patriarchal biblical period emphasize how man's tranquility is directly dependent on his ability to maintain his righteousness. Such practices as concealment (Abraham's readiness to sacrifice Isaac while keeping his intentions from his wife), deception (Jacob deceiving his blind father Isaac or Laban deceiving Jacob), parental preference (Jacob favoring Joseph or Isaac favoring Esau), parental disapproval (Isaac and Rebecca disapproving of Esau's spouses), and spousal submission (Abraham submitting to Sarah's demands and ridding himself of Ishmael and Hagar) are all revealed to cause strife, animosity, and unhappiness. In fact, the Babylonian Talmud definitively states that when an individual is brought before the heavenly court for judgment, the first question he will be asked is whether he conducted his business affairs honestly (Shabbat 31a). In other words, what matters most, in the end, is not whether he followed each of the Torah's precepts while behaving in reprehensible ways but whether the individual behaved decently and ethically during his sojourn on earth. Honesty, transparency, fairness, justice, truthfulness, compassion, acceptance, and love—these are shown to be the attributes of mind that breed harmony, peace, and wellness, and those who practice them will be naturally walking in God's path and be rewarded with happiness regardless of whether they believe in Him or observe all His revealed precepts. It is not our beliefs that matter to heaven but rather the behaviors our beliefs promote in us.

It is notable that during this period spanning the lives of the Patriarchs and Joseph, God's communications with them—as conceived by the creators of these stories—were always affirmative. Never does God show dissatisfaction, frustration, or disillusionment with any of their actions. This does not mean they lived unblemished lives or that they always trusted their God or His promises. For example, after waking up from an awesome dream, Jacob makes a highly conditional vow to God saying, "If God remains with me, if He protects me in the journey I am making, and gives me bread to eat and clothing to wear, and if I return safe to my father's house—the Lord shall be my God" (Gen. 28:20, 21). But what if He does not? Clearly, there is a lack of faith behind Jacob's vow despite the wonders he had already seen and/or heard about. And yet God does not rebuke him for his doubt, his demands, or his conditionality.

Though some of these men's actions were indeed reprehensible, their intentions were good. Despite their obvious failings, they were committed to the ethical life and hence, more often than not, acted constructively. God's persistent validation of their lives indicates a strong endorsement of the ethical pathway for the resolution of man's existential challenges. In essence, God's attitude was one of empathy and support toward those trying to better themselves. Man, we are given to understand, is an imperfect, fallible creature, but as long as he tries to improve himself, he will draw compassion, support, and encouragement from those around and above him.

From a developmental standpoint, the patriarchal period saw the establishment of Abraham's descendants as a group of families endowed with a better understanding of their environment, their needs, and their overall human nature than had been in place before when they lived in Ur. These people lived a seminomadic life: they wandered in the land of Canaan without a country they could call their own or a defined form of governance. Nonetheless, these were people who understood that the way they behaved in the world and the way they treated each other and themselves went a long way in defining how much or how little they suffered.

In the absence of archeological evidence to support their existence, it is impossible to tell whether the Patriarchs and Matriarchs are historical figures or fictional characters created by the authors of these important stories as vehicles to express the evolution in human understanding taking place over the centuries in which these legendary figures purportedly lived. In either case, their stories do confirm that man had a path he could now follow that would hopefully help him redeem, if not all, at least part of his anguish. He had ethical principles to live by; he had agency and could intervene effectively in reducing suffering; he had access to communications from the beyond through his dreams, enabling him to relate to his interiority and live a better integrated and more balanced life. And, finding himself once again in God's good graces, he fashioned an improved self-esteem. He had good reason for expecting that his life would improve now and that he could be happy, enduringly so, his base nature notwithstanding.

CHAPTER 5

One Nation under God

TO ESCAPE THE TERRIBLE famine ravishing the land of Canaan, the biblical narrators tell us that Jacob, his eleven children, and their families and servants journeyed to Egypt. With this move, an unexpected change occurs in the biblical stories: from exploring the efforts of individuals, families, and small clans to live according to the ethical standards of comportment God purportedly expected of them, we are presented with a lengthy narrative—the Books of Exodus, Numbers, Leviticus, Deuteronomy, and the Prophets—detailing the dedicated efforts of a much larger group, an entire people, to become established as a sovereign nation-state that lives according to the same behavioral ideals. These are people who, after centuries of enslavement and terrible oppression, yearn to become a dignified righteous community in which collective suffering will yield to collective peace, prosperity, and well-being.

That such an important transition, as well as others, later on, was bound to happen is implied centuries earlier by God's promise to the Patriarchs that their descendants would be as numerous as the stars and would give rise to a multitude of nations (a forecast, perhaps, of the diverse religious traditions that would emerge from Judaism over the centuries, Gen. 17:4). But we are given no precise motive for this sudden shift in narrative emphasis. We are told only that "the Israelites were fertile and prolific; they multiplied and increased very greatly, and the land [Egypt] was filled with them" (Exod. 1:7).

Living Well in a Good Society

It stands to reason that, having moved to a land blessed with a navigable river and fertile soil, a land capable of sustaining large populations, the Israelites increased considerably in number, thus becoming a real threat to the indigenous population. The Hebrew Bible makes this point perfectly clear when it has the Egyptian king say to his people, "Look, the Israelite people are too numerous for us . . . in the event of a war they may join our enemies in fighting against us" (Exod.#1:8–10). The king's fear led to the dastardly practice of slaughtering all newborn Israelite males as well as committing the people to years of hard labor until, at last, a new phase in the evolution of man's consciousness set in: nationalistic fervor and a desire for self-determination was born into those who had been enslaved and deprived of their basic freedoms, rights, and needs. These were people who understood that to attain inner wellness and happiness they needed to be free to decide the direction in which to steer their lives without fearing subjugation and genetic manipulation by despotic rulers. In other words, they needed to be free to express their political and spiritual will and establish a social and economic order that was fair and equitable.

In the Book of Genesis God's actions were centered on the individual lives of the Jewish Patriarchs and Matriarchs who established some of the moral values and ethical principles that, when followed, reduced suffering arising from human intercourse and general action. God's image initially was that of a Father-God who first raised children, then cared for them during their adolescence, and finally, as they became adults, engaged them in a relationship of mutuality. The challenge now was to find ways to ensure that the same values, virtues, and moral principles—honesty, fairness, personal responsibility and accountability, autonomy, respect, dignity, and self-realization—embraced by these trailblazers would be embraced by a whole society of beings.

That a selected few could follow consistently in God's path and feel the inner harmony inherent in it had been borne out by experience, but this achievement would have had little social significance if it could not be expanded to include a much larger community of beings and, eventually, all of humanity. But for peace and prosperity to reign in a nation-state the majority of its people need to live in freedom, have the chance to prosper, and feel protected from unmitigated physical pain and suffering inflicted on them by others.

According to text, the force motivating the large Israelite community to seek redemption was the terrible suffering they had endured in Egypt. That suffering was necessary to spur further social, political, and psycho-spiritual evolution had been hinted at in an earlier narrative about Abraham. Then, at a time when he came to understand that it would be centuries down the road before vast rewards would be conferred upon his descendants, a dark dread descended upon him. As the sun settled on the horizon, he heard the voice of God say to him, "Know well that your offspring will be strangers in a land not theirs, and they shall be enslaved and oppressed for four hundred years; but I will execute judgment on the nation they shall serve, and in the end they shall go free with great wealth" (Gen. 15:12–14).

What might have constellated in Abraham's interior to produce such bewildering, contradictory statements is impossible to know. We can speculate that our ancestors' inner wisdom, manifested here as the voice of God, knew that for Abraham's descendants to attain the clarity of purpose and the strength of conviction with which he had been graced and to ultimately enjoy a happy life, they would be required to endure the growing pains he had personally experienced collectively. Abraham well knew how much he had struggled before finding the strength to leave his father's home and pursue his calling. And how, once having left, he still had to face many more challenging situations, some critical, when trying to establish himself in his new home and give form to a new way of life. Hence, following his acknowledgment of the freedom and goodness implicit in such a choice, complementary images of enslavement and deep sorrow for those following him made themselves known. By the same token, when considering that what we are reading is not necessarily historical but more likely allegorical material written centuries after the facts described therein, we can understand that the author(s) of these stories, knowing the complexity involved in translating an individual's accomplishments to a large human collective, added to the mythical revelation Abraham received a clairvoyant insight into the future travails of the Israelite nation as a whole.

The oppression under which Abraham's descendants lived in Egypt was a dark yet necessary part of their journey to collective freedom and a happier life. During this stretch of time the original clan of seventy people—Jacob's twelve children and their families and servants—became a community of six hundred thousand souls, all of whom may have known something about a covenant between God and their forebears and may have even lived according to some of its precepts but not many. It is more logical to think they had no reason to trust in any covenant with God or cause to believe it conferred special privileges on them. More likely, they felt forsaken and abandoned, for the Bible tells us that the God who frequently communicated with Abraham and Jacob had not uttered a single word to them for centuries.

This miserable period of Israelite life came to an end sometime during the last quarter of the second millennium BCE with the rise of Moses, a man capable of guiding his people to the Promised Land.

The emergence of Moses signaled a dramatic shift in the people's mental and emotional condition for he was a man embodying the energy of the liberating hero, a man who could and would lead the Israelites' uprising against their tyrannical ruler. But his appearance also signaled a readiness in the Israelite population for reclaiming and hopefully recapturing their freedoms and their rights.

The biblical description of Moses is indeed heroic. He is God's anointed, a man exhibiting extraordinary powers and capable of remarkable deeds. Psychologically speaking, he epitomizes a resourceful, charismatic, outstanding yet still all too human leader. Having been brought up in opulence and having enjoyed great power, he is up to the task. Hence, when he discovered his origin of birth and the condition under which his people lived and labored, he rose against those whom he had previously served. And being who he was, he had the strength and credibility to lead his people out of the quagmire in which they found themselves.

This strength and fortitude, however, were slow in developing. In fact, when he received the call to go back to Egypt and free his people, Moses initially struggled against the idea of being the right man to redeem the people of Israel from slavery. So when the myth creators have God speak to him from a "burning bush" that does not consume itself, he tries to circumvent God's demand that he fulfill his destiny. It had been several years since he had murdered an Egyptian taskmaster who was mercilessly beating a fellow Israelite, compelling him to escape Egypt. He was now a married man, a shepherd, and the father of young children. The sudden confrontation with a voice that had grown progressively stronger and more insistent, a voice telling him he must return to Egypt and persuade the Pharaoh to let his people go, overwhelmed him. Ordinary Moses could not conceive of doing such a thing. Who is he to go to the Pharaoh, the Egyptian king/god, and tell him to free his people? He feels inadequate and small, with no standing and no authority to make such a demand. A stutterer from early childhood, he does not even know how to speak clearly, let alone persuasively (Exod. 4:10).

Another side of Moses, however, the one residing in his unconscious and belonging perhaps to the archetypal self, encourages him to go back. Despite his personal misgivings, he is indeed the liberator, the man who can complete the task. This inner force imbues him with conviction and strength and prepares him to face the brutal oppressor. In the end, this aspect of Self prevailed. Moses returned to Egypt and became engaged in the lengthy process of freeing a people that had been enslaved for centuries.

Becoming a liberator is a complex process. Even after having decided he was up to the mission, Moses had to overcome a final hurdle yet before being fully ready to stand up to a stubborn, powerful king/god and succeed. The Bible tells us that at a night encampment, while on his way back to Egypt, the Lord encountered him and sought to kill him (Exod. 4:24). It is through the decisive intervention of Moses's wife, Zipporah, that the murder is prevented. Aware of the imminent danger facing her husband—women are more able to see what men are often blinded to—she immediately proceeds to circumcise her son and then touch Moses's leg with the foreskin she has removed; in this way, the threat that had constellated for her husband was defused (Exod. 4:25, 26).

This unexpected, unprecedented act is mind-boggling. Why would the creators of this mythology have their imagined God, who had just commanded Moses to return to Egypt, endanger his life and almost cause the collapse of the whole mission? The Bible gives no explanation for this bizarre occurrence. We can speculate, however, based on the way the threat was diffused, that it may have reflected a lingering ambivalence in Moses toward the mission and, more importantly, toward the part of him that commanded him to take it on. After all, he had failed to circumcise his son, even though this was a critical part of the covenant God had established with his ancestors, thus demonstrating perhaps a persistent conflict between his ego-self and the inner voice driving him forward. Having failed to demonstrate his full loyalty to the mission may have evoked a destructive force ready to annihilate him—as liberator—and preempt the task at hand; for without total commitment, he would not be in the right frame of mind to undertake it. It took the intervention of the feminine counterpart in Moses's psyche, embodied in the story by Zipporah, to call off the serious threat Moses's ambivalence had engendered. Once the latter was resolved through the affirmative act of circumcision, Moses was free to proceed unhindered.

The man who returns to Egypt is very different from the one who left. He is now an imposing figure: mature, resourceful, honest, dependable, unrelenting, and unyielding. A visionary leader who will give no ground to the stubborn Pharaoh: precisely the kind of political and spiritual leader the Israelites needed to break once and for all the chains of bondage holding them back. The story of the Exodus from Egypt also gives testimony to the inner strength and confidence that come along when we respond to our calling and allow ourselves to move beyond the boundaries of our ordinary living. In doing so, the fear of what may lie ahead is replaced with the strength of conviction of the rightness of our aims and misgivings with the certainty that it is our duty to fulfill them.

Historically speaking, it remains highly questionable whether the Israelites were ever enslaved in Egypt, for no one has found convincing archeological evidence supporting this claim. Those who believe it do so more by faith than tangible evidence. Nonetheless, a victory stele dated 1220 BCE tells about a battle won by the Pharaoh against Israel in Canaan, thus suggesting that if there was an exodus, it was a few years before this date. Regardless of whether it is a historical fact or not, the account stands as a vibrant part of a narrative that voices the oppression and despair experienced by human beings who, saddled with suffering for centuries, experience the decisive intervention of their God. This God has herein added two new mythical images to his repertoire: that of the performer of acts defying human comprehension—like the plagues that afflicted Egypt before the Exodus; and that of a military commander capable of protecting the people of Israel from the might of an army as sophisticated as that of the Egyptians.

These new images were of monumental import, for they created a convincing argument for why the people should return to the worship of the God of their ancestors who had been, it would seem, absent from their lives for so long. In fact, a few days after the Israelites left Egypt, the narrators of the Bible make the Lord Himself make this point clear to them as He calls on Moses from the mountain, instructing him to say to them: "You have seen what I did to the Egyptians, how I bore you on eagles' wings and brought you to Me. Now then, if you will obey Me faithfully and keep My covenant, you shall be My treasured possession among all the peoples" (Exod. 19:4, 5). In this speech the God of Israel has elevated the status of the previously enslaved, suffering Israelites, thus priming them to welcome and, more importantly, abide by the terms of a new covenant that was immediately forthcoming.

During the celebration of the Passover Seder Jews are encouraged to regard themselves as the people who were enslaved in Egypt and whom God emancipated through His overwhelming power, His magnanimity, and His grace. In this way, people will be helped to remember that regardless of the external conditions under which they currently live, they have all been, and continue to be, enslaved by something or someone and in need of freeing themselves from any and all oppression by appealing to the same divine energy that brought their Jewish ancestors out of Egypt. Enslavement by an inner authority—an inner Pharaoh that batters and demeans us, is something humans have experienced for ages regardless of their religious persuasion; it can be as despairing as being subjugated by an outer one and, at times, even more so.

We should not forget that all of us are oppressed by the reality of unremitting suffering that our human condition inexorably and indistinguishably imposes on us. The primordial wound associated with being a sentient human being and the additional suffering this provokes as a result of our encounter with the ruthless forces of life and nature is neither avoidable nor curable. Consequently, entrapped in misery, humanity is always seeking for ways to rid itself of a level of displeasure, which every generation preceding and every generation to follow us has and will experience. It is little wonder, therefore, that in the story of a people struggling to overcome suffering their experience of enslavement and their subsequent burst into freedom figure prominently.

An Ethical Constitution for Relieving Man's Hurts

In describing the birth of the Israelite nation, a community of people who, after hundreds of years of hard labor, established themselves as a national entity in their own territory with their own culture, beliefs, language, and lifestyle, the Exodus symbolically expresses humanity's perennial struggle to emancipate itself from all kinds of subjugation, restriction, and abuse. Man's drive to freedom is encoded in his soul. He yearns for liberty and for the opportunity to self-actualize and self-rule. He wants to be his own master and have the privilege of choosing how he lives his life. But, as in ancient times, it is often only after suffering great pain and experiencing protracted inner and/or outer cruelty that he builds up enough strength, courage, and determination to allow his own Moses to come forth and release him from his shackles, whether self-imposed or actual. Until then, efforts to promote social and political change and institute a more developed, mature, egalitarian, and equitable system of governance and social intercourse are doomed to fail. They did so then and continue to do so now, for we are not to forget we are still a very young species working at finding harmony and happiness in the context of our reality and our human capabilities.

Moses, as a member of the Egyptian royalty, may have found their religious beliefs and practices disagreeable. Once realizing he was a member of the Israelite community, he might have become aware of the ethical principles and moral traditions underlying the lives of the men and women preceding him. He might have even adopted them. Nonetheless, he was well aware that for such a system to be embodied collectively, in particular by people enslaved for centuries, it would take more than encouragement and inspiration for them to follow on this path. Intuiting that for his people to live righteously and honorably, they needed a well-formulated set of principles—a constitution—Moses, who is soaked in theistic beliefs and imagery, would naturally attribute his inspired visions, his insights, and the powerful creations of his heightened spirit to be emanations from the Divine Itself. He would see himself as a Prophet, an intermediary, a powerful conduit between God and His people of Israel, and feel energized by his understanding—better yet, certainty—that his vision was holy, nothing less than the product of a higher power channeling itself through him.

And so, ascending to the heights to receive divine inspiration, the Bible tells us that Moses intuits the Ten Commandments, which contain the principles that later on served as the foundation for the 613 complementary precepts he presumably wrote to guide the people's lives. Given that God revealed the commandments Moses offered the Israelites, they were irrevocable. They did not require justification or persuasion and were meant to be inviolable and to be accepted unconditionally: do not murder, do not steal, do not covet your neighbor's wife or his possessions, do not pervert justice, do not slander, honor your mother and your father, do not worship other Gods. There is nothing to be added or subtracted from them. They are beyond reproach. When uttered, a core component of our human soul reverberates in response to them for it recognizes their holiness.

They embody universal values, truths known intuitively by man to be essential for personal well-being and harmonious communal living. But they are principles that need further elaboration to function effectively in society. Do not kill; but what if attacked or dishonored? Do not steal but what if one is dying of hunger or one's children are sick and need medicine one cannot afford? Honoring one's mother and father is laudable; but what if they are abusive and injurious?

Moses must have understood these nuances and the need for amendments because, in addition to the foundational principles, he came up with an elaborate set of laws and rules that applied to some of these specific circumstances. Spelling out how human beings were to behave if they aspired to safety, prosperity, peace, and happiness, Moses gave the Israelites important foundations for becoming a thriving nation that could serve as a light to all other nations. Such thoughtfully crafted rules and laws were meant to guide their interactions with each other, their environment, their neighbors, and, of course, God. To reduce their individual and collective suffering and flourish, all they needed to do was to faithfully follow Moses's Instruction as described later on in the Book of Deuteronomy, which seems to have appeared for the first time in written form during the reign of King Josiah in the seventh century BCE. It is impossible to know how many of the 613 precepts were known to the Israelites before Ezra, the scribe, produced the written version of the sacred Torah in the year 445 BCE. Nonetheless, in mythical time, the Hebrew Bible tells us that, sometime in the twelfth century BCE, the Israelites, already in the desert, received this revelation and have been held accountable for its fulfillment ever since.

Providing the people with a set of laws and rules to guide their daily lives did not, however, hinder their freedom to choose and self-determine. In the end, it was up to them to decide whether to abide by this Instruction or not and thus endure the positive or negative consequences of their choices, whatever they may be.

The Inability to Live according to Moses's Ethical Constitution

The major thrust of Moses's constitution taxed people's level of psycho-spiritual proficiency by demanding they: (a) maintain a consistent feeling of gratitude for their blessings and an appreciation of their good fortune; (b) establish socially sensitive societies that provided for the poor, the sick, the orphaned, the widowed, and the powerless; (c) enforce a fair civil and criminal justice system in which murder, theft, fraud, embezzlement, and other offenses were severely punished; (d) master their instinctual drives and sexual appetites so that physical violence, rape, incest, and adultery were maximally reduced; and (e) live in communities where the rights of racial minorities, ethnic groups, foreigners, and women were respected and honored. In principle, these are laudable aspirations and if fulfilled do lead to a life that is meaningful, purposeful, and suffused with a richness that heightens and brings great joy. But to meet such lofty standards requires a population whose basic physiologic needs—food, shelter, healthcare—are well attended, that feels safe, and that is highly mature and resourceful, a goal that we have not yet accomplished even a few thousand years later.

Traditionally, Jews have identified themselves as members of the chosen people. This is based on the belief that God chose the Patriarchs and Moses to deliver His message of how He expected man to live and what norms He expected him to fulfill and follow if he wanted to restore himself to the happy life he once had. This message, which was first expressed for the benefit of the few, was later directed to the six hundred thousand souls that left Egypt as part of the Israelite nation. Based on this narrative, God entered into an inviolable covenant—first with Noah, then with the Jewish Patriarchs and Matriarchs, and now with Moses and the people of Israel—stipulating they would live according to His revealed Instruction in return for His protection, support, compassion, and love. But when this narrative is understood to reveal instead humanity's deepest yearning for justice, fairness, respect, freedom, and safety and for living a moral, principled life, it takes on a very different meaning. Then the Israelites (and contemporary Jews) are not to be seen (or to regard themselves) as the chosen people, but rather as *the people that chose* and continued to choose out of their free will to follow a path dictated to them by leaders responding to an inner voice imagined as coming from God.

Whether there is a God out there with the attributes described for Him in the Hebrew Bible, and whether this God actually spoke to Abraham, Moses, and the others is a matter of faith, but in the end, it does not matter whether this did or did not take place as described. What matters is the kind of lives these people lived or tried to live, the ethical principles guiding their actions, and the goals they managed to attain. Whether commanded by directives coming from the Creator of the All or personal insights emanating from the depth of their mysteries, there is no doubt that Abraham left his homeland for Canaan to establish himself there and give expression to a different way of life; Jacob fought his inner demons and conquered at least some of them, developing psychological and spiritual strength; Moses heard the inner voice asking him to go and free his people from bondage, and he did; and the Israelites embraced Moses's Instruction and made efforts to fulfill its mandates, even though most of the time they failed to live up to its high standards. Whether these figures are historical, allegorical, or both, the ethical principles embedded in their life histories and exemplified by the commandments, precepts, and laws they proposed for the purpose of bringing order, justice, and equanimity to the relationship between men and between men and God, are part of the legacy the writers of these stories and the creators of these myths left for us, a legacy that continues to this day to guide the lives of billions of people struggling, as did their ancestors, to overcome suffering and live a meaningful, joyful life.

Knowing he was now old and drawing near death, Moses invested himself in gaining the Israelites' trust and their allegiance to his Instruction. Already the chances of their commitment enduring were not good. For one, the people were soon going to be deprived of their spiritual and political leader, the man who had brought them out of bondage, guided their journey through the wilderness to the edge of the

Promised Land, protected them from God's fury when they transgressed, and gave them the commandments and the laws that were supposed to direct their lives forever. And while Joshua, son of Nun from the tribe of Ephraim, had been handpicked by Moses to take his place at the helm, there was no evidence he had the competence or the maturity to fulfill the task. Having established his reputation by leading the Israelites to victory against the Amalekites during their desert wanderings, Joshua had been primarily a military commander rather than a bona fide spiritual leader. With Moses's absence, the Israelites would have to depend on their own conviction and commitment and that of the tribal leaders, at least initially, to maintain faith in his directives.

By providing the people with a comprehensive set of laws to guide their lives, laws founded on ethical principles, Moses had hoped they would be compelled to live morally—even if not genuinely convinced of the virtue of some or even most of these laws—and as a result become a prosperous, peaceful, and progressive nation that later on may develop the moral conviction needed to make the joys of such a way of life sustainable. But already in the desert, before the people even had a chance to reenter their ancestral land and fulfill their dream, Moses's deep understanding of the human condition forewarned him of what was likely to happen to his people once they exposed themselves to the pagan cultures prevalent in Canaan, cultures that did not tax their citizens with demanding norms of conduct as a precondition for the attainment of safety and prosperity. In what is one of the most arresting and moving passages of the Torah, the myth creators have God say to Moses: "Know that . . . You are soon to lie with your fathers, this people will thereupon go astray after the alien gods in their midst, in the land that they are about to enter; they will forsake Me, and break My covenant that I made with them. Then My anger will flare up against them, and I will abandon them and hide My countenance from them. They shall be ready prey; and many ills and troubles shall befall them. And they shall say on that day, 'Surely it is because our God is not in our midst that these evils have befallen us.' Yet I will keep My countenance hidden on that day because of all the evil they have done in turning to other gods" (Deut. 31:16–18).

Prodded by this profound insight, Moses writes for the people of Israel a poem—he calls it Haazinu ("Oh listen," or "Please listen" in Hebrew)—for them to read aloud daily as they enter the Promised Land. In this poem Moses reminds the Israelites that God is their Rock, that He is faithful, fair, and just. That He is their Father, the One who created them and allows them to subsist. That He will protect them and shield them from harm. But having given them the gift of free will, He cannot prevent them from hurting themselves, so woe to them if they were to forget His way and all He had done for them and stray from His path (Deut. 32:4, 6, 10, 12). This poem was meant to serve as God's witness against the evil Moses expected the people of Israel to engage in once they entered the Promised Land, for as he so well stated, "Even now, before I bring them into the land that God promised them on oath, their minds are devising ways to violate God's Instruction" (Deut. 31:21).

Moses's insight into the struggles the Israelites were going to endure should not amaze us in the least: becoming self-reliant and self-determined is tough enough for an individual let alone for a whole nation whose people are at different stages of their individual psychological and spiritual maturation. Nation-building is indeed a daunting task. Its success ultimately depends on whether the political leaders can persuade the people that abiding by the "Rule of Law" and respecting their adopted constitution is in their best collective interest. In theory, it seems rather straightforward, but as we saw with the Israelites, to live honestly and have gratitude for what their many gifts brought them, to respect other people's rights and master their animal impulses, and to sustain all these collectively and thus bring joy into people's lives, was a rather lofty goal that they would not be able to reach consistently.

National Security Entails Ethical Compromises and Violations

To this point in time, the biblical narrative emphasized the importance of embracing the ethical way of life for the welfare of a budding nation of six hundred thousand souls released into the reality of self-determination. For this human collective to become a nation-state, however, it needed a land on which to build its dwellings and establish its institutions. According to the Hebrew Bible, 440 years before Moses led the Jews out of Egypt a clan of seventy people inhabiting part of the desired land—the Promised Land—had left to go to Egypt; few of their descendants, presumably, had returned. However, it is argued that not all the Israelites left for Egypt and, in fact, a substantial number of them remained in Canaan, although never functioning as a nation-state.

In the meantime, during those 440 years, tribes of different ethnic origins occupied the land, cultivated it, and built cities on it. These people were obviously not prepared to recognize the returning Israelites' right to the land based on some historical claim to it. The fact that their ancestors had lived on these lands for several generations and owned them was of no importance to the current dwellers. A moral conundrum ensued pitting the Israelites' desire to create a society respectful of the lives, property, laws, and cultural mores and customs of others (as long as these were not imposed on them) and their need for land on which to live as an autonomous, self-determined nation free of foreign occupants, rules, and systems of belief.

To understand how this conundrum was resolved we must remember that myths generated by people sharing religious ideologies, economic interests, and/or the desire for a specific piece of land will tend to be self-affirming. Although these narratives may address universal concerns, that is, self-determination, freedom of expression, threat of annihilation, the challenge of unremitting suffering, and so forth, they will often present a perspective favorable to the originators of the myth and detrimental to the interests of any other group or community. Early on, when the God of the Bible was made to speak to Abraham after he arrived in Canaan, He tells him, "I will assign this land to your offspring" (Gen. 12:7). Later on, after Abraham returned from Egypt, the biblical account has God saying to him, "Raise your eyes and look out from where you are, to the north and south, to the east and west, for I give all the land that you see to you and your offspring forever. I will make your offspring as the dust of the earth, so that if one can count the dust of the earth, then your offspring too can be counted. Get up, walk about the land, through its length and its breadth, for I give it to you" (Gen. 13:14–17). The implication of these affirmations is profound and transcendent. The interlocutor was none other than the Supreme Being, God Almighty. He had created the land: it belonged to Him; hence He could dispose of it as He wished, regardless of who may be living on it at any given point in time.

In fact, when the Israelites finally reached the eastern bank of the River Jordan following the exodus from Egypt, the biblical narrators have God saying to them: "Start out and make your way to the hill country of the Amorites and to all their neighbors in the Arabah, the hill country, the Shephelah, the Negeb, the seacoast, the land of the Canaanites, and the Lebanon, as far as the Great River, the river Euphrates. See, I place this land at your disposal. Go, enter the land that the Lord swore to your fathers, Abraham, Isaac, and Jacob, to assign to them and to their offspring, after them" (Deut. 1:7, 8). Upon hearing this edict, it is relatively easy for the returning Israelites to justify the merciless killing and utter destruction presumably inflicted on the people inhabiting the land and to experience no remorse, panic, or disabling guilt. After all, they may have thought, the land belonged to God. He had explicitly given it to them. He knew there were other people who had lived there for centuries, cultivating the land, building its cities and vineyards, and despite this, He demanded their extermination. He must have had good reasons, morally sound reasons for doing it this way, so why was it their business to question Him? This is how He wanted it, and this is how it was going to be. God's justice was inscrutable, and their task was simply to abide by it. So when Moses tells the Israelites, "The Lord God Himself will cross over [the River Jordan] before you; and he Himself will wipe out those nations [living in the Promised Land] from your path and you shall dispossess them. The Lord will deliver them to you, and you shall deal with them in full accordance with the Instruction that He had enjoined upon you" (Deut. 31:3–6), his declaration seems righteous and moral. Their job was to purge the Promised Land of people worshiping foreign idols and never veer from their sacred mission.

This type of mythic demand—God sanctioning murder and violence against people upholding different religious beliefs and cultural values—has been repeated innumerable times throughout human history. It conferred upon the Israelites the right to annihilate those who inhabited the land they coveted; it gave the right to Christians to persecute Jews and burn other Christians they viewed as heretics; centuries ago it gave license to Muslims to kill Jews, Christians, and all other infidels and still does today.

Such a permissive, immoral pattern of thought and action is common, perhaps even inevitable, during the initial stages of the life of a new nation established on religious grounds, and it was on full display in the narratives contained in the Books of Joshua, Judges, 1 and 2 Samuel, and 1 and 2 Kings. These initial periods before the nation and its religious traditions became fully established and consolidated are fraught with conflicts and religiously inspired violence. Infidels, that is, those who do not live in accordance with the tenets and dogmas of the new religion, are seen as threats to its integrity and that of the nation; they must be addressed harshly and definitively. Over and again in the biblical narrative, we find God sanctioning the annihilation of the people living in the land and severely punishing the Israelites when, out of self-interest or compassion for the conquered, they fail to comply fully with the strict demands of this Divine Order and let some of their enemies live.

As expected, the conquest of the Promised Land was terribly bloody. The God who gave Israel a code of moral living became a fierce warrior God commanding the Israelite army to conduct a campaign intent on cleansing the Promised Land of all those who had occupied it while the Israelites were enslaved in Egypt. Children, women, elders, and men of different tribes and ethnic background were slaughtered mercilessly, their homes burned, their cities destroyed. The directives given to the Israelites by the mythmakers could not have been clearer: all people inhabiting the Promised Land before their arrival had to be killed or dispersed. The land had to be cleansed so that the ethical culture they were commanded to establish could flourish. No persons were to be spared, regardless of how innocent they may seem because, in the end, they would not follow in God's path or recognize God's sovereignty. Strict adherence to God's commands was mandatory, and not only were those punished who transgressed the command, but the whole Israelite nation was punished for even the smallest infraction. Before overtaking the city of Jericho, for example, Joshua tells his people the following: "The Lord has given you the city but everything in it is to be proscribed for the Lord. But you must beware of that which is proscribed because if you take anything from that which is proscribed you will bring calamity upon Israel" (Josh. 6:17, 18).

Unfortunately, one man of the tribe of Judah took of that which was proscribed, incensing the Lord. As a result, in their next battle, the mythical God is made to cause a significant number of Israelite men to be killed, men who had nothing to do with the described offense (Josh. 7:1, 5). Given that according to the creators of this biblical story God was the mastermind behind the Israelites' war effort, the notion of killing the people and destroying their cities was perceived as moral and righteous.

Ownership of land by nation-states has never been built on ethical principles or moral argument but rather on the law of the jungle: those who are the strongest or the more numerous prevail. In this case, at least initially, it was the Israelites. The second truth is that the feelings of guilt and deep remorse associated with the savagery needed to be placed in a redeeming context or else it would have been impossible to execute and even less possible to endure. By having these acts framed as divine mandates the perpetrators are implicitly expiated from responsibility. In essence, all religious wars, whether in antiquity or in contemporary times, are founded on this basic principle: God mandates the annihilation of those who do not share one's beliefs and who dare to question the validity of the assertions one's God makes. Such a mythical structure also contains the kernel for ethnic, religious, and social cleansing by supporting the removal from society of those it perceives as threatening its wellness and long-term success, a brutal process executed numerous times by one group of human beings upon another.

Supported by this kind of narrative logic the blatant inconsistency between the mandate to live ethically and the need for land where this ethical living was to take place was happily resolved. Annihilating the people living on the desired land was morally justified because God, the epitome of justice and righteousness, mandated it; therefore, it was the people's duty to fulfill it, regardless of whether they could justify it convincingly to themselves.

The story of the conquest of Canaan by the returning Israelites seems to have repeated itself in modern times with the establishment of the State of Israel in parts of what thousands of years ago was the land the Israelite God promised them in perpetuity. Other people—Palestinians—once again inhabited some of these lands and while they were not constituted into a nation-state of their own, they had been in Canaan for generations. Some of them ended up losing their homes and their land as a result of the establishment of the State of Israel as an autonomous, self-reliant Jewish state. War inevitably broke out between the newly established state and several Arab states that attacked it in response.

It is true that a thriving, progressive, highly sophisticated Israeli society has flourished in the State of Israel. This society's scientific, technological, and artistic achievements have made and will continue to make important contributions to the well-being of the citizens of the state—Israeli Arabs included—as well as humanity as a whole. Nonetheless, these accomplishments stand on a foundation of loss, pain, and great suffering for another people; in the end, this has not brought tranquility, peace, and enduring happiness to the Israeli community, their great successes notwithstanding.

We are far away from being able to live according to the dictum "one planet for one people." So we live in nation-states with borders and with land that by and large has been conquered by force. I know of no nation in which the land was obtained in any other way, and therefore every nation stands on the skeletons of those who inhabited it before and were overwhelmed by invaders stronger, better equipped, and better armed than the indigenous population. And so, despite the great strides humanity has made in science and technology and the improvement of people's living conditions, we still live in a world in which nation-states fear invasion and occupation, a world in which wars break out as a result of real or perceived threats to security, access to essential natural resources, or as a way to protect themselves from the aggressive designs of other nations. Witness the two world wars of the last century and the death toll they exacted from the human community, not to forget the practically nonstop wars in the Middle East and North Africa since the 1950s.

Following the campaign to conquer the land, Joshua remained faithful to Moses's Instruction and guided the people toward a life of peace and collective wellness. Nonetheless, their faithfulness to the prescribed path was always on fragile ground. As Joshua approached death, he reminded the elders, the commanders, the magistrates, and other important tribal officers that they were the beneficiaries of lands they did not labor for, towns they did not build, and vineyards and olive groves they did not plant. Given these seemingly undeserved privileges he exhorted them to remember who gifted these to them, and hence, to revere the Lord and serve Him with undivided loyalty and devotion (Josh. 24:13, 14). Despite reassuring him they would do so unconditionally, their proclamations were unconvincing. Joshua knew how difficult it had been for him to keep his behavior in check, let alone that of the whole nation, and how much harder it would be after his death. Anticipating what he feared would happen, and using brilliant reverse psychology, he said to them: "You *will not be able* to serve the Lord [after my departure] for he is a Holy God, a jealous God not prone to forgive your transgressions and your sins" (Josh. 24:19, 20).

Joshua's intention here may have been to stimulate the Israelites' competitive spirit and motivate them to remain faithful to the path he had charted for them and thus prove him wrong. Unfortunately, time will show that his concerns were well founded.

Under Joshua's direction the conquered land was divided equitably among the twelve tribes based on their population size (with the exception of the tribe of Levy, whose male members were to serve as priests and religious leaders and hence received no land, their sustenance coming from the contributions made by the members of the other tribes for their service). Evidently, although not surprisingly, the Israelites, upon their return from centuries of slavery in Egypt, maintained their tribal identification and their allegiance to their tribal leaders while living there, even though they were able to recognize Moses and later on Joshua as supreme leaders.

These newly established tribal enclaves operated like autonomous states and were ruled by military leaders (a chieftain or judge) whose main function was to foster prosperity and to provide protection from subjugation by neighboring tribes—Israelite and foreign alike. Based on the strong tradition of equality among the tribes and their yearning for freedom and self-rule, they resisted the idea of creating a centralized government in the Promised Land, one that would surely tax its citizenry heavily in order to pay for its functionaries, the maintenance of a strong army, and whatever adventure the king or ruler would want to undertake. They preferred instead to have God as their commander in chief and expected Him to help them fend for themselves when attacked or threatened. They were willing, though, to enter into temporary alliances with each other, as the situation so dictated. This type of organization, however, created unavoidable vulnerabilities in the tribal states, especially when they were confronted with more sophisticated, experienced, and numerous enemies.

During this historical time, which lasted over two centuries, a number of chieftains, Prophets, and priests rose to prominence to become judges in Israel. Many of these men were of humble, even questionable origin. Ehud, for example, was left-handed, which during those times was perceived as reflecting an inborn defect; Jephthah was the son of a prostitute; and Samson was a wild, violent, half-witted strong man. These heroes were expected to rule the land according to God's laws and commandments (creating what some would call a democratic theocracy), but their accomplishments, by and large, reflected their abilities, determination, and strength, although to enhance their status the biblical narrators presented them as being the frequent recipients of God's favors. Despite having wonderful qualities, none of these strong leaders were able to secure a lengthy peace for their individual tribal state or, for that matter, the Israelite nation as a whole. They did, however, see significant improvement in the quality of the people's lives. Nonetheless, once the euphoria of the conquest passed and their sovereignty became better established, significant threats to the people's well-being arose, threats that brought new sources of suffering into their lives and thus the need for prompt attention and resolution.

Regaining the ancestral land was indeed an achievement of great import, and maintaining tribal autonomy self-reinforcing. But to establish a thriving nation capable of fulfilling its spiritual calling the people needed to feel that their individual and collective safety, prosperity, and happiness were not only secure but also enduring.

CHAPTER 6

Struggles in Resolving Suffering
Adaptation, Development, and Failure

FOLLOWING THE ESTABLISHMENT OF the budding nation, foreign enemies, more particularly the neighboring Philistines, attacked Israelite tribes and occupied different parts of the conquered land. Technologically and militarily superior to the Israelites, they represented a formidable foe for the new nation and were able to suppress any attempt by the Israelite tribes to rebel and regain their land. In one of these battles, the Philistines captured the Ark of the Covenant, symbolizing the subjugation of the whole tribal confederacy of Israel.[1] As a result of these disastrous defeats, the Israelites needed new figures in their mythical landscape that would help them address their military, economic, and spiritual concerns. These figures came in the guise of *the Prophet*, the human conduit for God's message to the people of Israel and their rulers and the community's alter ego, tasked with reminding its members of their duties to God, to themselves, and to others, and *the king*, whose role was to rule and protect the whole nation from foreign invaders and maintain the economic welfare of the people.

Samuel, the first of the Israelite Prophets to appear after their return from Egypt, was no ordinary man but one destined to serve God and His people for the duration of his life (1 Sam. 1:28). A revered leader, Samuel was thought to be in contact with a Divine Voice that offered him insight, vision, and guidance; he was therefore respected and held in high esteem in the community. Whenever he made a pronouncement the people knew to trust it because it would inevitably be fulfilled.

As Samuel's life entered its later stages, the elders of the tribes of Israel approached him, demanding he appoint a king to rule over them. Having been a political and spiritual leader for most of his life and aware of how complementary these functions were to each other, the request to separate them deeply troubled Samuel for he understood that such an action presaged something bad for the nascent nation.

Surprisingly, though, he was encouraged by none other than God Himself to heed their request; the Lord reminded him that their desire for a king was not in opposition to his well-intended actions—designating his sons as his successors—but rather in response to their discomfort in relying exclusively on Him as their king and protector. "Heed their demand," the myth creators have God telling Samuel, "but warn them solemnly about the practices of any king who will rule over them" (1 Sam. 8:9).

Understood as an intrapsychic dilemma, God's command reveals indecision brewing in the Prophet's interior. Part of Samuel's personality, the part he identified with the most, appreciated the perils associated with selecting a king to rule over Israel while another part, the one that revealed itself in his meditations and dreams, understood that despite the risks this posed the people needed something more tangible than relying on an abstract God that communicated with them exclusively through His Prophets. The threats surrounding the Israelites were tangible, and they needed tangible solutions to their collective and individual fears.

So Samuel does as God suggests, forewarning the people of Israel that the king they were clamoring for will take their sons and appoint them as his charioteers and horsemen, and force some of them to run in front of his chariots. Some will be chiefs of thousands; some of scores, while others will have to plow the king's fields, reap his harvest, and make weapons and equipment for use by his army. He also tells them that the king will take their daughters as perfumers, cooks, and bakers; he will seize their choice fields, vineyards, and olive groves, giving them to his courtiers. A tenth of their grain and vintage will be his, and he will give it to his eunuchs and noblemen. He will take their male and female slaves, their choice young men, and their animals and put them to work for him. He will take a tenth of their flock, and they shall become his slaves. Then the day will come when they will cry out because of all the terrible things their chosen king had done, but the Lord will not answer them on that day (1 Sam. 8:11–18).

Despite Samuel's stark forewarning, the people, having still fresh in their memory the suffering endured by their ancestors when enslaved in Egypt, and their own more recent distress caused by the losses incurred at the hands of the Philistines, insist on having a king: "We must have a king over us, that we may be like all other nations," they tell him. "Let our king rule over us and go at our head and fight our battles" (1 Sam. 8:19, 20).

Samuel acquiesces to the people's demands and anoints Saul as king of Israel, entrusting him with the task of delivering Israel from the hands of the aggressive and powerful Philistines threatening their sovereignty and their lives (1 Sam. 9:16).

The remarkable exchange between Samuel, God, and the elders of Israel gives voice to an evolving conflict in the soul of Israel's returning tribes: their need for freedom and autonomy versus their need for safety and security. The realization that to fulfill one set of soul yearnings required the abdication of part or all of the other further heightened this tense situation. Protecting the lives, property, and safety of the Israelite tribesmen required the establishment of a central authority possessed of a powerful military and bureaucracy to administer the kingdom and implement the laws. Such an establishment would, of course, open the door to authoritarianism, corruption, nepotism, and to the trampling of the many freedoms the people had enjoyed since recapturing the land.

In the case of the people inhabiting the Promised Land at the time, however, collective security and safety had primacy over tribal as well as individual autonomy and rights. The possibility of being subjugated by a foreign power and once again exiled to a foreign land, thus losing the privileges they had fought so doggedly to regain, was a major source of angst for the tribal leaders, and something they were not prepared to endure again. Moreover, what value was there for personal freedoms when one's life was constantly threatened?

Tensions and ethical dilemmas such as these afflict our nations today. Threatened with acts of violence and terrorism, political leaders struggle to determine how far to impinge on personal privileges to improve collective safety; the answer to this ethical question remains elusive and under continuous review.

God Assures David That Israel's Sovereignty Will Endure Forever

Saul's rule of Israel was fraught with difficulties. Failing to follow God's command to annihilate the Amalekites, he fell in disfavor with God. Disgraced and defeated by the Philistines, he falls on his sword and dies an undignified death, after which David, son of Jesse, whom God had chosen to be the second king of Israel, replaced him.

During David's reign, the kingdom of Israel expanded considerably in size. Able to finally defeat the oppressing Philistines and recapture the lost land, he expanded the kingdom in all four directions. David was a charismatic and capable military leader, and all his campaigns enjoyed God's blessings. This was a time of glory for Israel and one of internal harmony, prosperity, and happiness. All this notwithstanding, there was still angst in the people's hearts regarding their ability to maintain these gains and the goodness that came along with it. The process that led to their success had been difficult and taxing and associated with great loss of life. Aware of what the people needed, the Prophet Nathan offered David and the house of Israel a new iteration of the sacred covenant that would help them gain the confidence they were seeking.

Speaking with great assuredness and in the name of the Lord, he delivered to King David the following message: "Know that I took you from the pasture, from following the flock, to be ruler of My people of Israel. Know that I will establish a home for My people of Israel and will plant them firm, so that they shall dwell secure and shall tremble no more. Evil men shall not oppress them any more as in the past . . . I will give you safety from all your enemies.

"When your days are done and you lie with your fathers, I will rise up your offspring after you, one of your own issue, and I will establish his kingship. He shall build a house for My name, and I will establish his royal throne forever. I will be a father to him, and he shall be a son to Me. When he does wrong, I will chastise him with the rod of men and the affliction of mortals; *but I will never withdraw My favor from him as I withdrew it from Saul,* whom I removed to make room for you. Your house and your kingship shall ever be secure before you; your throne shall be established forever" (2 Sam. 7:12–16).

Nathan's reassuring words addressed the main source of anxiety of any community: being invaded, subjugated, enslaved, and/or annihilated. The prosecution of many wars and the persistent threats to their national security caused the Israelites apprehension and distress. The knowledge that they could be crushed by their enemies at any moment restricted their ability to pursue the loftier goals to which they aspired. Being able to deploy a large and effective military had gained the respect of their foes, but there was always the chance that a stronger, more competent enemy would arise and erase all their gains. Moreover, for the monarchy to gain ascendancy among the people of Israel, God's imprimatur was needed.

When the elders of Israel first approached Samuel and requested he anoint them a king, God encouraged him to do so, but this did not mean He had wholeheartedly endorsed their demands. But in the narrative Nathan delivers to David we hear the voice of God rise to deliver the strongest, sweetest, and most reassuring message the people could have ever hoped for. And to further assuage the angst associated with the uncertainty of who may follow in King David's footsteps, the Prophet Nathan assures them that David will be succeeded by one of his own offspring whom God will treat like His own son. Finally, He reassures David and the kingdom's citizenry that they can always count on His support, protection, and help.

Feeling protected and safe, the nation's mood lifted. There was confidence and a heightened state of goodness. David captured these sentiments beautifully when, in a burst of poetic inspiration, he sang to God: "O God, the rock wherein I take shelter. My shield. My mighty champion . . . He rescued me from my enemy so strong, from foes too mighty for me . . . He brought me out to freedom. He rescued me because he was pleased with me" (2 Sam. 22:3, 18, 20).

But why was the house of David deserving of such favorable treatment? What had David done to be rewarded so amply? The question is answered with total clarity with this passage: "I, David, have kept the ways of the Lord and have not been guilty before my God. I was mindful of all His rules and have not departed from His laws. I have been blameless before Him, and had guarded myself from sinning" (2 Sam. 22:22–24).

David's moving poem ends with a song declaring his unconditional loyalty to God: "You, O Lord, are my lamp . . . With You I can rush a barrier . . . the way of God is perfect, the word of the Lord is pure. He is a shield to all who take refuge in Him . . . Exalted be God, the rock who gives me victory" (2 Sam. 22:29–31, 47).

David's poem beautifully illustrates the experience of a man for whom everything is working out, a man who has no worries. He was free, safe, joyful, protected, and secure. The world was his oyster and his state of jubilation and euphoria moving and contagious.

We know, however, that David's existential bliss did not last too long. David was not the epitome of perfection he claimed to be, and his life was visited by strife, calamity, and disconsolate suffering not once but multiple times, and not just for him but also for the whole of Israel. For now, however, it all seemed to be working perfectly well, and his words offered reassurance and hope. His life experience was proof that following in God's path was indeed the way, the only way, to enduring happiness.

Before David's ascendancy, the nation's attempt to build a moral and ethical society had been hindered by the state of insecurity and instability under which the tribes of Israel lived. Having recognized the need for a king, an organized army, and a centralized government looking out for the people's interests, the elders of Israel had gotten their wish. Now that God had given His seal of approval to this new form of governance they felt safe and able to proceed forward to the fulfillment of their higher calling.

Responsibilities to God versus
Responsibilities to Kindred

But living an ethically principled life was (and still is) a tall undertaking and some of the challenges it imposes are well illustrated in the story of Eli, the high priest, and his rogue sons. According to the biblical narrative, Eli was aware of his children's shameful and undignified behavior: "He heard all that his sons were doing to all Israel, and how they lay with the women who 'performed tasks' at the entrance of the Tent of Meeting" (1 Sam. 2:22). Knowing this was causing distress and fear in the population, Eli exhorts his sons to desist of their ruinous ways. His words falling on deaf ears, Eli faces a daunting moral dilemma: As high priest and supreme religious leader he is expected to preserve the well-being of the whole community by enforcing God's Law, which in this case called for severe punishment for his sons: if he did not, a higher power would be exacting the punishment. On the other hand, these young men were his flesh and blood. He brought them to life, nourished them, raised them, loved them, and cared for them, and he could not conceive subjecting them to their well-deserved chastisement. Paralyzed by his paternal love, and more significantly by his desire to avoid the shameful and painful feelings he would experience were he to act as the law prescribed, he lets their iniquities go unpunished. We then hear the voice from within—the voice of God—first through the words of an anonymous "man of God," and then through the voice of the Prophet Samuel, telling Eli of his forthcoming rebuke: "I sentence his house to endless punishment for the iniquity he knew about—how his sons committed sacrilege at will—and he did not reprimand them. Assuredly, I swear concerning the house of Eli that the iniquity of the house of Eli will never be expiated by sacrifice or offering" (1 Sam. 3:13, 14).

Most people when reading this story will sympathize with Eli's actions. After all, what was he supposed to do? Kill his sons? When a loving father is confronted with unruly children, he has a very hard time bringing them to account. By and large, he tries to justify and rationalize their behavior, covering up their destructive actions, hoping they will eventually understand the error of their ways and change. The narrative, however, leaves no doubt that such an approach to this challenging dilemma is unproductive and erroneous because it compromises the common good, a most undesirable and unfair outcome. Having been called to ethical living, morality and justice are supposed to have primacy over the love of kindred. In other words, in such a world blood cannot be considered thicker than water because once the ethical foundations sustaining a culture are compromised, whatever the circumstances may be, a slippery slope is entered upon, one leading to the gradual erosion of its moral fiber. This was contrary to what the Israelites intended and wanted to see happening, hence the stark forewarning of the dire consequences their actions may have on future transgressors.

King David faced a difficulty comparable to that of the high priest Eli when he became aware that one of his sons, Amnon, raped his half sister, Tamar. David is terribly afflicted by this occurrence but does nothing to address the offense. When receiving word of the transgression that had taken place, Absalom, Tamar's brother, is incensed both by it and by his father's inaction. He takes it upon himself to redeem his sister's loss and shame by killing Amnon, his offending half brother. This leads to years of alienation between David and his beloved son Absalom, ending with the youth attempting to usurp his father's throne and then being killed in battle by David's men. Once again, filial love, moral confusion, and indecision cause a father to fail to act, leading to conflict, destructiveness, and to individual and collective suffering.

What could a loving, more psychologically resourceful father have done? For one, he could have acknowledged what had occurred and demanded accountability from Amnon, for example, had him admit publicly that what he did was wrong, cowardly, and despicable; he could have then made him ask for forgiveness from Tamar, his brothers, his father, the community at large, and of course, God. He could have also made every effort to clear Tamar's name and honor, ensuring that the community understood she had absolutely no responsibility for what had occurred. David could have also issued a public condemnation of Amnon, letting him and others know how hurtful and shameful his actions had been and the dire consequences that befall such perpetrators. Finally, he could have demanded Amnon serve Tamar and the community for a reasonable period of time with no compensation as a way to expiate his terrible offense. Actions such as these may have prevented the violence that inaction unleashed and perhaps staved off the death of two of David's beloved sons.

The dilemmas confronting Eli and King David, however, continue to be ever present in our modern world, causing additional suffering: parents rationalizing and covering up their children's misdeeds, and children, whether young or adult, often overlooking their parents' abusive, neglectful, and damaging behaviors. To expose intimate ones to the consequences of their wrong actions is exceedingly difficult. However, I read a story about parents who, after seeing footage of their fourteen- and sixteen-year-old sons burglarizing a store, turned their kids into the police; and another about a father who forced his twelve-year-old son to stand on the corner of his home street with a sign hanging over his chest that read: "I stole from a store."

God: Severe Judge or a Compassionate Father?

When examining how the myth creators framed God's responses to the moral lapses of the Israelites we repeatedly encounter a harsh, severe, and unforgiving voice coming forth. This must have felt terribly frightening to a young, budding nation in the process of maturing socially and psychologically. The harsh intransigence of their imagined God exposes the existence in their soul of an aspect of self that was rigid, strict, judgmental, and punitive. Jewish Kabbalists, centuries later, identified this aspect of self as the embodiment of the energy of Gevurah, or strength in God, identified by psychoanalysts in contemporary times as a strong, overbearing *superego*. That our ancestors imagined their God this way must have reflected their experiences growing up under the tutelage of fathers or authority figures that manifested similar character traits as well as their internalization and symbolic expression of the impact on them of the harsh, ruthless, and unforgiving natural world in which they lived.

Held in balance, this energy is naturally compensated by the energy of compassion and loving-kindness (Hesed), which embodies the feminine side of man's soul. But at this point in the evolution of the Israelite nation, this compassionate side of man was less accessible to the Israelites than the judgmental side, thus giving expression to an experience of God that often felt retaliatory, vengeful, and punitive rather than empathic and compassionate toward His suffering children. This latter configuration of the Divine did not seem to comprehend that humanity's failings were not by-products of their baseness, weaknesses, or evil inclinations but rather the result, given the early stage of their psychological unfolding, of having imposed upon themselves standards of comportment not commensurate with their mental and emotional abilities.

From Judgment to Forgiveness and Compassion

The transition of power from David to his son Solomon, the third of Israel's kings, was anything but smooth. Aware of his father's old age and weakening soul, Adonijah, David's son by Haggith, anointed himself as king over Israel. Upon hearing this disturbing news, King David pronounced Solomon king, thus fulfilling his promise to Bathsheba, Solomon's mother, and to the Prophet Nathan. Afraid for his life, Adonijah recognized Solomon as king of Israel, thus avoiding unnecessary bloodshed.

During Solomon's reign, the nation attained an unsurpassed confidence in its political craftiness and ability to use diplomacy rather than military force to ensure its safety and the stability of its territory and its previous gains. Solomon highlighted his many accomplishments and successes by building majestic palaces and later on a permanent home for the God that had protected and guided him and the nation to such prosperity and happiness. At no other time in its long history was Israel stronger, wealthier, or more secure. Through Solomon's leadership, the Israelite nation reached its highest glory, becoming the envy of its neighbors. The Temple he built was imposing; upon entering it, one could immediately sense the presence of the Divine. The priests, when in the sanctuary where the Ark of the Lord that contained the two tablets of stone received by Moses resided, were unable to perform services, for the presence of the Lord had filled the sanctuary with a dense cloud (1 Kings 8:10, 11).

Being a very wise man, Solomon knew that the future of the Israelites depended on the quality of Israel's leadership. He knew his father had been a great leader and that he had inherited similar qualities, but what about his children, and his children's children? Would they have the strength of conviction and the vision to keep the people on the right path? Would they keep the citizenry accountable for their actions and more importantly would they be accountable for their own actions and choices? He also knew how hard it was to follow the moral precepts Moses left for the Israelites and how easy it was to slip into lawlessness. Having reaffirmed the basic principles under which the last version of the covenant had been formulated, he introduced a soothing and most reassuring novelty: the idea of a forgiving God, one who exhibits compassion for the poor mortals He created who, despite their best efforts to live according to His ways, are often unable to restrain themselves from transgressing His Law. They are, however, able to repent and show genuine contrition for their actions, a most laudable trait.

Aware of the fallibility of his contemporaries, and for that matter his own, and deeply concerned with the terrible consequences these failings had brought upon the people of Israel in their recent past—and could bring yet again in the near future—Solomon aimed to soften the blow by creating a system for dealing with man's limitations, a system that was more sensitive, caring, and humane. Appealing to the merciful side of the Lord (and by extension that of man) he tried to make this dimension of the soul more present and accessible in its interactions with the rational, ego-centered side of man's personality. Thus, as he proceeded in his address to God he challenged Him by asking, "Will God really dwell on earth?" He then implored God to listen to His servant, to keep His eyes open day and night toward the House he had built for Him, and when hearing the supplications which His servant and His people of Israel offered toward this place, to give heed, and pardon (1 Kings 8:27–30).

To ensure that God (and more importantly, the people) understood the meaning of his words he proceeded to describe in detail instances in which he hoped the forgiving side of the God of Israel would hold sway and absolve his fallen children. Thus he said: "When Israel is routed by an enemy, when the heavens shut up and there is no rain, when there is a famine in the land or pestilence, blight, mildew, locusts and caterpillars, when an enemy oppresses them in any of the settlements of the land, when they are afflicted by plague or disease, when a foreigner who is not of Your people of Israel comes from a distant land for the sake of Your name, when they sin against You for whatever cause—for there is no man who does not sin—and You are angry with them and deliver them to their enemies who carry them off to an enemy land, near or far, and yet, they turn towards You and acknowledge they have acted wickedly, perversely, and cruelly, they show remorse, they pray in Your direction and turn back to You with all their heart and soul, oh God give heed to their supplications and their prayers and exonerate them. Render to each man according to his ways as You know his heart to be—for You alone know the hearts of all men—so that they may revere You all the days that they live on the land that You gave to our fathers" (1 Kings 8:33–50, 52, 53).

Solomon's amazingly candid plea to God acknowledges indirectly the terrible distress and anguish the covenantal agreement, and more precisely God's harsh, punitive hand, had stirred in the people's heart. Considering how much man desired to follow the lofty ethical principles prescribed for him by his imagined God, and in so doing overcome his suffering, we can readily understand his deep disillusionment when he realized that regardless of how hard he tried he would invariably fail, for there was no man who had not sinned, and surely more than once. Consequently, he will not only fail to overcome his innate suffering but suffer even more as a result of an internal voice speaking harshly and judgmentally against his actions, thus reinforcing his ingrained belief in his inherent wickedness. Given this incontrovertible truth it is not surprising that, as an antidote against man's enduring anguish, man's myth creator was at last compelled to bring forth the complementary energies of compassion and forgiveness into the relationship with God.

Until this particular moment in the evolution of man's relationship with the Divine, and given his inherent limitations and his personal awareness of God's violent temper, the knowledge of the covenant often elicited fear, intimidation, and a sense of foreboding in him. This is not to say that man had not also experienced the gracious, caring aspect of the Divine because he most definitely did, but not consistently, and not without having paid dearly for those elusive moments. Such an experiential background weighed heavily on the people's hearts, breeding an undercurrent of resentment, discontent, and rebelliousness, all of which discouraged allegiance to God. By imploring for compassion and forgiveness, Solomon sought to draw a new type of energy from God toward His fallen children. Aware that his contemporaries transgressed repeatedly and that future generations would inevitably continue to do the same, he asked for something that would reassure man that his failings were not fatal, that God's ire could be mollified, and that banishment from divine love was not an inevitable part of his earthly existence.

By entreating God for compassion and forgiveness, Solomon, and with him the Hebrew nation, acknowledged several truths: firstly, that these attributes of soul had been somewhat dormant in them, hence they were often absent from the actions of the God they had imagined; secondly, that when people are able to express remorse for past misdeeds, it motivates the recipients of their contrition to respond with sympathy and a willingness to pardon. Consciousness of our failings, public acknowledgment of them, and humility, so long as they are genuine and heartfelt, are effective in fostering conflict resolution and social harmony. But if the words we utter are not linked to the right sentiments and actions, the recipient will feel misled and deceived, and instead of responding sympathetically, he will react with anger and repudiation. So drawing this kind of energy into human intercourse can be problematic: expressing genuine remorse when having acted improperly is not just a cognitive act but an overall psychological stance dependent on the level of refinement of the offender. Everyone can learn to say the right words, but very few people can do it with the right senti-ments attached, which can then produce positive outcomes.

Solomon's speech also reaffirms the existence of another reassur-ing avenue for the redemption of man's suffering by demonstrating how, through prayer and supplication, particularly when offered in the Temple he had built for God to dwell in, the people could succeed in changing God's mind and gaining forgiveness for their misdeeds. Whether similar results could be obtained by offering these prayers elsewhere is not intimated, thus raising awareness of the symbolic importance the Temple had and would continue to have in subse-quent centuries for the people of Israel. Here was the place where they expected to find their God and where their offerings and prayers would have had the highest chance of attaining their aim: less judg-ment and less suffering.

Once King Solomon finished building the House of the Lord, the myth creators have God appearing to him one night and saying, "I have heard your prayer and have chosen this site as My House of sacrifice. If I shut up the heavens and there is no rain; if I command the locusts to ravage the land; or if I let loose pestilence against My people, when My people, who bear My name, humble themselves, pray, and seek My favor and turn from their evil ways, I will hear in My heavenly abode and forgive their sins and heal their land. Now My eyes will be open and My ears attentive to the prayers from this place. My eyes and My heart will always be there" (1 Chron. 7:11–16).

It is easy to imagine the profound sigh of relief God's response to Solomon's supplications must have had on the population given its powerful confirmation of God's acceptance of them. Hearing the sooth-ing voice of the benevolent, forgiving, loving side of man's personality articulated as a pronouncement coming from God himself must have evoked wonderfully good feelings in the collective psyche; yet it did not preclude Solomon from later on violating the covenantal agreement with impunity and showing little remorse for having done so.

In 1 Kings, chapter 11, we are told that Solomon loved many foreign women from the nations of which the Lord had said to the Israelites, "None of you shall join them and none of them shall join you, lest they turn your heart away to follow their gods." Despite this warning, Solomon turned away from the commands of the God of Israel and followed other gods, even though the narrators of the Bible had made the Hebrew God appear to him twice and explicitly prohibit him from doing so. On the surface, the changes in Solomon's behavior toward the end of his life are puzzling and difficult to reconcile with those he exhibited in earlier times. Known as the wisest man in Israel, why would he indulge himself in actions he knew were forbidden and would bring forth severe punishment for him and for the people he ruled? Is it possible that Solomon had lost his way and gone rogue? Or is it more likely that, as he grew older, he came to realize that his strict adherence to "God's path" had deprived him of pleasures and satisfactions he no longer wished to give up? A colleague shared with me an experience with a patient who at an office visit declared: "I want to make it to eighty-five." "Why eighty-five?" asked my puzzled colleague. "Because once I get to eighty-five I can start smoking again." Perhaps, like my colleague's patient, Solomon concurred that once you reach a certain age—or level of psychological polish—you can indulge in pleasures and action that would have been detrimental at an earlier time. Clearly, Solomon's actions in later life seemed to have been driven by dimensions of his personality different than those that expressed themselves so eloquently in his earlier years. Perhaps for him, as an individual, doing what he did was neither destructive nor detrimental, but as an example for the whole citizenry of Israel, his behavior could not be sanctioned.

So it is no wonder that his comportment drew God's ire and repudiation; the Bible has God telling Solomon, "Because you are guilty of this—you have not kept My covenant and the laws which I enjoined upon you—I will tear the kingdom away from you and give it to one of your servants. But, for the sake of your father David, I will not do it in your lifetime; I will tear it away from your son" (1 Kings 11:11, 12). And so, as forewarned by God, after Solomon's death the Israelite kingdom splintered into two political entities in 928 BCE: Judea and Israel (Samaria). Instead of cooperating, the two new countries fought each other, each declining in power and prestige and eventually losing their sovereignty, thus bringing misery and despair to the lives of large segments of the Israelite population.

In the story of God's punishment to the people of Israel, we learn an important lesson: the damage done in one generation has repercussions for the generations to come. Even the actions of a single leader can affect how much suffering or happiness and peace future generations experience. Ergo, beware of whom you choose to lead you at home, at work, at the local, state, and national level because it can affect not only you and your children's well-being but also that of many generations to follow.

CHAPTER 7

The Rise of the Prophets' Influence
A Shift in Mythopoeic Strategy

THE ANOINTMENT OF KINGS to rule over Israel brought great personal suffering to its citizens. While Israelite history shows periods in which affluence, security, and overall goodness prevailed, more often than not they were short-lived and did not prevent the nation from descending into lawlessness and disorder. Instead of fostering peace and collective prosperity, the institution of the monarchy benefited only the few. Eventually, it led to a psychological regression for the nation that resulted in the crushing loss of the privileges and rights its people, with great sacrifice and effort, had previously gained as citizens of a sovereign country. During this lengthy period, which extended for more than four hundred years—from King Saul, who reigned between 1030 and 1010 BCE, to the fall of the kingdom of Judea, to the Babylonian king and the exile of many of its citizens to Babylon during the reign of King Zedekiah, between 598 and 587 BCE—the influence of the Prophets as spiritual leaders increased considerably.

Having set themselves up as conduits for God's irrefutable truth, the Prophets felt free to make bold pronouncements, whether directed at kings or commoners. That their insights, guidance, and clarity implicitly came from the Divine Himself had the potential of profoundly impacting the people's mood and actions. Hoping to stimulate a return to a moral and more harmonious way of living, they reminded the people of their transgressions against God's Law and their overall wicked behavior. Their concerns were centered on preserving the moral essence of their religious tradition rather than its ritualistic practices, setting them apart from the religious and political leadership that was concerned instead with issues of political and economic power and other mundane needs. Additionally, the Prophets recognized it was their moral duty to forewarn the Israelites of the dire consequences facing them were they to fail to repent and mend their ways; that in fact to be free of moral responsibility for all that happened around them it was not enough to simply avoid wickedness and evildoing in their lives. Instead, they had an obligation to be proactive and intervene on behalf of those who were evilly inclined and make sure they were properly forewarned of the immediate and future consequences of their misdeeds.

Of Kings and Prophets

To gain ascendancy the Israelite Prophets needed to gain the people's trust. Given the ominous and heart-wrenching quality of some of their pronouncements, they understood that it was counterproductive to place themselves above the fray and assume superiority to the people to whom they ministered. They had to be prepared to acknowledge their failings and fallibilities and act like regular folks; otherwise under what authority could they demand others do what they would not? It is with this in mind that we hear the Prophet Isaiah share with the community he served that once, when God appeared to him, he felt so intimidated by His presence that he responded by saying, "Woe is me; I am lost! For I am a man of unclean lips and I live among a people of unclean lips. Then, one of God's seraphs [His guardian angels] flew over to me with a live coal, which he had taken from the altar with a pair of thongs. He touched it to my lips and declared: 'Now that this has touched your lips, your guilt shall depart and your sin will be purged away'" (Isa. 6:5–7). Isaiah is confessing here to times when he was slanderous, judgmental, and verbally offensive, even verbally abusive with others; in doing so, he acknowledges how words can injure and cause great pain and that he had been cruel and injurious at times. The remedy for such an offense is figuratively a "burn," a temporary injury to help the offender extinguish the undesired behavior.

Having gained the people's trust by acknowledging his limitations, Isaiah, in one of his first speeches, addressed the desolation afflicting the Israelites' outer world, which he attributed unequivocally to the people's coarse, indecent behavior. Admonishing them, he says: "Why do you seek further beatings that you continue to offend? Hear the word of the Lord you chieftains of Sodom; give ear to our God's Instruction you folk of Gomorrah! What need have I [your Lord] of all your sacrifices? Thus says the Lord, 'I am sated with burnt offerings of rams, and I have no delight in lambs and he-goats. Who asked that of you? Trample my court no more; bringing oblations is futile, incense is offensive to Me'" (Isa. 1:1–5, 10–13).

Isaiah's message to the Israelites is precise and sobering: For him, what the Lord God cared about was how people behaved toward themselves and each other and not whether they pretended to be righteous and pious people. Those who honored the Divine with their lips but kept their hearts from Him were distasteful to the Lord. God cared for justice—social, economic, political—and for those who were respectful, empathic, and compassionate to their fellowmen, people who lived a truly righteous life. In short, He cared for people who lived their lives ethically and lovingly. To further emphasize this, the biblical narrators had God say to the Israelites, "Your new moon and fixed seasons fill Me with loathing; they have become a burden to Me, I cannot endure them" (Isa. 1:14), meaning people should be more concerned with what they do than with ritualistic formulas that obfuscate their intentions and deeds. It is the only way toward a life in which suffering will ebb and be replaced with harmony, justice, love, and joy.

The Prophet's pronouncements to the people of Israel serve as powerful rebukes of Temple worship, as well as of the standing and prestige of the priestly aristocracy that developed as a result. He also denigrated the delusion that if the people paid a tax to the Temple and offered animal sacrifices to God, He would look favorably upon them. Isaiah's harsh words apply equally well today for, as we have all seen, it is not uncommon for people who profess to be pious and to follow religious doctrine and law to be leading duplicitous lives filled with deception, abuse, and sinfulness of the body and mind.

Like Isaiah, other Prophets after him continued to forewarn the people of what their God had in store for them were they to fail to amend their sinful ways, but with little success. Speaking through the Prophet Jeremiah, we hear the voice of God reminding the people how their kings, officers, priests, and Prophets made objects of wood to be their father and objects of stone to be their maker while turning their backs to Him, and yet in their hour of need they cried to their forgotten God to arise and save them. So, in an ironic tone, He asks them, "And where are those gods you made for yourselves? Let them arise and save you if they can, in your hour of calamity? Why do you call Me to account? You have all rebelled against Me" (Jer. 2:28, 29).

When reading passages of this kind, we see important aspects of human nature made clear: an intellectually committed people wielding a tradition of accomplished leaders yet lacking the mental and emotional resources to fulfill lofty moral and ethical standards regularly. Regardless of how much they might have desired to do what their imagined God expected of them, they simply could not. Humanity was left with feelings of self-defeat and self-blame. Though there would always be hope for future redemption via adherence to the high ethical standards implied by the covenant, man's tragic outlook became strongly reinforced: ill fortune was his lot, and he himself was to blame.

While these tragic stories repeated themselves many times in the history of the Israelites, there were clear and reassuring exceptions that may have helped sustain the people's hope and confidence in a better tomorrow. King Asa, who reigned from 911 to 870 BCE, for example, abolished the altars and shrines dedicated by his predecessors to foreign gods, ordering the people of Judea to turn to the Lord God of their fathers and observe the Teachings and the commandments He revealed to Moses in Horeb (2 Chron. 14:1–5). As a result, Asa and the people of Israel received respite and special support from God in times of need. When confronted by an enemy far more numerous and strong than his well-equipped army, King Asa directs himself to God and asks Him for help, to which He responds by helping Asa rout his enemies, making them flee in terror (2 Chron. 14:10, 11).

Similarly, the story of Hezekiah's reign in Jerusalem, between 726 and 687 BCE, gives testimony to the care and special favors the people of Israel and their kings received when following God's Instruction and His Law. The Bible tells us that this king gathered the priests and the Levites and told them: "Our fathers died by the sword, and our sons and daughters and wives are in captivity on account of this. Now I wish to make a covenant with the Lord God of Israel, so that His rage may be withdrawn from us" (2 Chron. 29:9, 10). True to his word, Hezekiah kept God's commandments consistently, which motivated the people to do the same. As a result, he was blessed with good fortune, which led him to feel that God was always at his side and led the people of Israel to feel protected, cared for, and valued.

The moral of these stories is that when fairness and justice prevail in the world, when loyalty and unity are ever present when, the path revealed to Moses is followed with conviction, things turn out well for the nation, despite the serious threats and problems it regularly faced.

This overarching principle also applies to the lives of individual citizens as the story of Hezekiah's health challenges attests. At some undefined point in his life, the Bible tells of the king falling dangerously ill and the Prophet Isaiah coming to him to tell him that the Lord commanded him to set his affairs in order, for he was going to die. Upon hearing the divine proclamation, Hezekiah wept profusely, for he did not want to die. Turning his face to the wall, he prayed to the Lord, saying, "Please O Lord, remember how I have walked before You sincerely and wholeheartedly, and have done what is pleasing to You." The king's plea moved God to reconsider His decree: He ordered Isaiah to return to the king's palace and inform Hezekiah that the God of his father David had heard his prayers, seen his tears, and was ready to heal him. "On the third day from now, go up to the House of the Lord and He will add fifteen years to your life," Isaiah told the despairing but now deeply reassured King Hezekiah (2 Kings 20:1–3, 5, 6). This moving narrative must have built confidence and trust in the people for it affirmed the existence of a powerful God who could make decisions over life and death, who could heal the terminally ill, and more importantly, whose decisions were never final. Men could change His mind; through righteous behavior, devotion to Him, and a pious life, man's fate could be altered. There was indeed hope for humanity no matter how bleak life might seem at any given point in time.

Healing Words

Additionally, the Prophets understood the need for redemptive narratives capable of restoring optimism in the population, narratives that would offer relief and inject hope into their battered souls. For example, Isaiah told the people of Israel that, despite the dire circumstances facing them, not everything was lost. A shoot would indeed spring forth from the house of Jesse, David's father, and introduce a new era, new leadership, and a new vision that would reduce suffering and promote well-being. "When this new growth reaches maturity," he said to them, "it will foster harmony and happiness for all the inhabitants of the land. Then, justice will prevail and people will act with wisdom and insight, and with courage and equanimity in their dealings with each other. It will be a time of calm, of cooperation and tolerance, one in which the people of Israel will recapture their standing as exemplars to the world, and suffering will most definitely ebb" (Isa. 11:1–10). By making sure to keep the date obscure, Isaiah allowed the people to decide when this welcome occurrence was to take place.

A similar pronouncement can be found in the writings of Jeremiah, the Prophet who witnessed the destruction of Jerusalem and its majestic Temple and the expulsion of a good part of the Judean population to Babylon. Responding to the enormous distress afflicting the people of Judea at that time, Jeremiah reassured them with beautiful thoughts coming from none other than God Himself that things would most definitely mend: "But you have no fear, My servant Jacob," declared the Lord. "Be not dismayed, O Israel! I will deliver you from far away, your folk from the land of captivity and Jacob shall again have calm and quiet with none to trouble him" (Jer. 30:10).

A few years later, another Judean Prophet, Ezekiel, who had been forced into Babylonian exile, had a powerful vision that provided uplift and hope to those who yearned to return to Judea and to a time of glory. In his vision the hand of the Lord came upon Ezekiel, lifting him up and setting him down in a valley full of bones that were very dry. "O mortal, can these bones live again?" the Lord asked Ezekiel, to which the Prophet replied, "Only You can know that." "Prophesy over these bones and say to them, 'O dry bones, hear the word of the Lord,'" God tells Ezekiel; then, directing Himself to the bones, He says, "I will cause breath to enter you and you shall live again, and you shall know that I am the Lord." A rattling sound is suddenly heard, and the bones come together, bone to matching bone. As Ezekiel looks upon the bones he sees sinews appear on them and flesh and skin forming over them, but there is no breath in them. Then he hears a voice saying, "Come, O breath, from the four winds, and breathe into the slain, that they may live again." Having prophesied as God requested, the breath entered them, and, standing up on their feet, a vast multitude came to life.

Then the biblical narrators have God say to Ezekiel, "These bones represent the whole House of Israel. They say, 'our bones are dried up, our hope is gone; we are doomed.' Prophesy and say to them, 'Thus said the Lord your God, I will open your graves and lift you out of the graves, O My people and bring you to the land of Israel. You shall know, O My people, that I am the Lord, when I have opened your graves and lifted you out of your graves. I will put My breath into you, and you shall live again, and I will set you upon your own soil'" (Ezek. 37:1–14).

A vision such as this must have elevated the mood of the people, giving them genuine hope that their God had not forsaken them. In fact, God had made it clear He was committed to curing their injuries and wounds, which had seemed intractable. There would be a resurrection of Israel and what had seemed irrevocably lost would come back to being. Israel's future, therefore, was bright because compassion and loving-kindness had been aroused in the heart of the Lord, their God.

Despite these many reassuring proclamations of resurrection, redemption from suffering, healing of wounds, and even of the arousal of the God of Israel against her enemies, they did not translate immediately into tangible, palpable, visible changes in the quality of the day-to-day life of the people and the nation. Gradually, therefore, a deep frustration crept into the larger Israelite community as they realized that redemption from suffering was not forthcoming, at least not in the short term. The promises made by the Prophets in God's name may have been truthful, but they were to be realized in a distant future, one that did not help alleviate their misery or that would afflict their children and their children's children.

Skills Needed for Psychological Ripeness

For people to be able to respond equitably to threats and other challenges to their interests and wellness and to do so in a measured, thoughtful, and constructive way, a way that avoids escalation of conflict, requires competency. To reign effectively over sexual appetite and instinctual drive and respond healthfully to distressing and unpleasant feelings does not depend on intellectual savvy but rather on psychological ripeness, a rare finding to be sure. To respect the laws of the land and honor people's rights and to be moral agents operating within the "rule of law" requires the development of certain skills one cannot achieve by simply deciding one will do so. We witness almost daily how individuals who have dedicated decades of their lives to building a position of importance in their communities engage in unexpected behaviors that, in no time, cause them to lose all they have worked for. The trials and tribulations of some of the political, religious, business, and spiritual leaders of our generation are a perfect example; community leaders, the very men and women we are supposed to look up to, often disappoint us with their questionable personal conduct. Given all this, it is not surprising that nations, as well as religious traditions, have failed to sustain an ethical way of life. To avoid this recurring misfortune and the shame and despair people feel as a result, we need to understand that we are still now at a very early stage of our unfolding as a species and therefore should not burden ourselves with lofty goals we cannot yet fulfill. The imaginings of our ego-selves, the more objective part of our personality, give rise to aspirations and expectations that do not take into account those other parts of us that are expected to fulfill them; our actions, more often than not, stem from baser desires not yet under our volitional control. Awareness of this can prevent unnecessary conflicts, disappointments, and misery for we can then understand that when people do something undesirable, a wrong to others, more often than not it is because they are not equipped to do right. In short, they lack the required psychological maturity to enact rightness, rather than such failure resulting from laziness or irresponsibility.

Such an understanding of our human limitations was certainly not prevalent a few thousand years ago, and, as it is still absent from the consciousness of many contemporaries, it is not incongruent to see that our ancestors justified their miseries by some misperceived inborn human flaw. With time, however, this type of explanation lost some of its inherent power. As painful experiences accumulated, man began to feel that something was seriously amiss with his underlying religious beliefs about the cause of his pain and distress.

In fact, toward the end of the Book of Jeremiah, members of the Judean community who had escaped to Egypt convey to the Prophet that something about the covenant had gone awry. Threatened with terrible punishments if they continued to serve foreign gods, the men, who knew their wives had indeed been offering incense to the queen of heaven and, parenthetically, agreed with their actions, and all the women standing before Jeremiah—a great crowd—along with all the Judean citizens who dwelt in Pathros, were unmoved by Jeremiah's words. Defiantly, they answered that they would not listen to the words he spoke to them in the name of YHWH and instead would continue to offer incense to the queen of heaven and pour libations for her as they had done before in Jerusalem because when they did so they had their fill of bread and they lived well and saw no evil. By contrast, when they stopped serving the queen of heaven and served the Israelite God, they lacked everything and met their end through the sword or hunger (Jer. 44:11–19).

The response of the people to Jeremiah's exhortations was novel and provided another explanation for why the covenantal myth was not able to sustain people's trust and faith in it as a pathway to the redemption of their angst. Traditionally, when the people of Israel suffered, whether at the hands of their own or foreign rulers, they attributed it to their utter failure to live according to God's revealed moral path. But the community of people who escaped Judea and settled in Egypt was suggesting that they had abandoned their commitment to the God of the covenant because He had failed to uphold *His side of the bargain*, causing misery and despair for them—and for no good reason. In other words, they claimed to have noticed that in numerous instances they were visited by calamities even though they had behaved well. Perhaps their behavior was not perfect, but it was pretty much in accordance with God's expectations of them. By contrast, when shifting their loyalty to the queen of heaven and other foreign gods they were rewarded with goodness, peace, and prosperity, thus confirming and affirming the power and reliability of the gods they were now worshipping.

Given the randomness associated with natural events, the erratic nature of human behavior, and the uncertainty surrounding human life, it is easy to imagine that by mere chance the people's fortunes and the fulfillment of their wishes and expectations occasionally coincided with the times in which they worshipped foreign gods and failed to materialize during times in which they worshipped the God of Israel. It follows from this that, at least for the Jews living in Egypt at the time, the failure of the covenantal agreement between Israel and God was due not only to their difficulty in living according to the expected standards but to the observed failure of God to protect and reward them as they felt they deserved. This example gives further voice to an evolving crisis that was brewing in the collective Israelite consciousness regarding the faithfulness of the God they had been indoctrinated to revere.

Not unexpectedly, as collective misfortunes kept mounting and catastrophe seemed to follow catastrophe, people gradually came to feel their suffering was indeed unjust. Not only did they seem to be built to fail at attaining the lofty standard of living that God had set up for them, but despite what the Prophets repeatedly affirmed, the punishments meted by this God for their real or assumed misdeeds seemed unfairly severe and the extent of their sufferings unwarranted.

The problem of undeserved suffering, no doubt, must have troubled man from the time he became self-conscious, but he had usually been able to avoid facing it head on. Though following in God's path had been difficult it had often benefited the Israelites, if not collectively at least individually, so they were able to remain engaged and faithful for many centuries. Yet the greatness of their mounting afflictions seemed to show that, even if they could imagine a man endowed with psychological capabilities surpassing those of all other men, and hence able to fulfill all of Moses's precepts with no deviation, he would still be afflicted by great suffering. Such a realization must have enhanced their frustration and disillusionment. To resolve it, the Israelites were compelled to overcome their next major hurdle—perhaps the most critical one: untying the knotty problem of undeserved suffering.

The Problem of Undeserved Suffering

Of the unforeseen consequences brought forth by the dawn of consciousness one of the most significant was the introduction into human life of the capacity for moral perception. Suddenly the universe, which until then had operated solely on the basis of physical and chemical laws, contained a new component, a subjective component—man—that judged matters according to how he experienced them, how he felt and thought about life's diverse manifestations. To a world of natural flows and rhythms man now superimposed a filter of moral judgment that divided the world into good and bad, right and wrong, truthful and false, a world in which rewards and punishments were dispensed according to the behavior of an individual or even a group or, for that matter, that of ancestors who lived generations earlier. In the context of such an organized world, the notion of fairness and justice appeared for the first time and with it the idea of deserved and undeserved consequences for one's actions.

Accepting the notion that an always just Supreme Being had created our world led man to the inevitable conclusion that his suffering was always deserved. As long as this belief dominated his discourse, suffering was acceptable regardless of its intensity or duration. Nonetheless, even at the very beginning of recorded human history, an undercurrent of resentment and frustration regarding his fate might have been simmering in the recesses of man's troubled soul. Having been deprived of the paradisiacal life he was meant to enjoy for eternity for having done something he could not have avoided, he felt undeservedly punished. These feelings and the conclusions they evoked, however, were unacceptable in early times and had to be repressed at all costs. The persistence of suffering over centuries, perhaps millennia, more intense than anything man could have imagined deserving, made it progressively harder to continue to attribute this burdensome situation to his own faults. But if man's flagrant limitations—his inclination to act immorally and unethically—were not the sole causes of all his suffering, then what else could it be? Was it possible that he was being punished for moral reasons beyond his limited comprehension? Or that there was a dark side to life that he refused to see or acknowledge, a side that functioned arbitrarily and hence punished him for no cause? In either case, if such occurrences were under the supervision of his God it would be a violation of the spirit, if not the letter, of His covenant with man and thus He could not be thought of as God, at least not in the way He had been initially conceived.

The deep hurt and anger resulting from occurrences perceived as causing undeserved misery eventually found their way into the biblical writings. It began with the response the Israelites in Egypt gave to the exhortations of Jeremiah, followed by comments from several Prophets, the psalmists, and culminated with those of the authors of two books that became key components of Israelite wisdom literature. The voice of man's increasing disillusionment with God's governance of His world was rising ever more clearly.

Only centuries after Abraham's questioning of God's justice do we find King David making a similar inquiry of the Supreme Being. Informing us that Satan, the challenging angel, had motivated King David to undertake a census of Israel, the Bible tells us that God was terribly displeased by this. Responding to this affront, the Bible has God send a pestilence over Israel that caused the death of seventy thousand people. In addition, He sent an angel to Jerusalem to destroy it.

Seeing the angel of the Lord standing between heaven and earth with a drawn sword directed against Jerusalem, David says to God, "Was it not I alone who ordered the numbering of the people? Therefore, I alone am guilty of having caused severe harm; but these sheep, what have they done? O Lord my God, let Your hand fall upon me and my father's house, and let not Your people be plagued" (1 Chron. 21:1, 14, 16, 17). Later on, in the poetry of the Prophet Habakkuk, we find other biblical rumblings about God's lack of fairness and disregard for cruelty and justice: "How long, O Lord, shall I cry out and you not listen, shall I shout to You 'Violence!' and you not save?" (Hab. 1:2).

Many of the psalms, including Psalms 69, 71, and 74, echo a similar level of bewilderment and discontent; in Psalm 89 they reach a climax. There the unspeakable is finally uttered: God, who is supposed to be the epitome of justice and compassionate love, has inexcusably violated His promise to his own anointed David and his descendants. This demonstrates a profound change that has taken place in the way man, or his myth-creating aspect, interpreted his suffering. This change moved him from attributing his misfortunes to something morally reprehensible in him to attributing them to something wrong with the Divine Being Himself. It was the frequency of calamities afflicting man, their intensity, and quality that suggested something odd and terribly disconcerting was going on with God's behavior. Hence, the psalmist, setting the ground for his approaching indictment, begins by reminding God of His words and deeds: "Remember how You said, 'I have exalted one chosen out of the people, I have found David, My servant. I will establish his line forever, I will not betray My faithfulness, I will not violate My covenant, or change what I have uttered. His line shall continue forever'?"

Following this rhetorical, accusatory question the psalmist proceeds to thank God for all the wondrous favors He tendered upon the anointed one.

Then, unexpectedly and shockingly, he changes direction drastically, unleashing a scathing indictment of God's wrongful acts against David. Gathering all the strength he can muster, he accuses God of having rejected, spurned, and become enraged at David, thus repudiating the letter of the covenant He had established with His servant. He blames the Lord for having dragged David's dignity into the dust and shattered his strongholds. To top it all, he reminds Him how He had cut short the days of David's youth, covering him with shame.

The poem ends with a desperate plea for God to be merciful again and restore His love and favor to the House of David. Overcome with emotion and fighting his tears he asks, "How long, O Lord will You hide Your face, will Your fury blaze like fire? O Lord, where is Your steadfast love of old that You swore to David in Your faithfulness?"

The disarming honesty exhibited here by the psalmist announces a transformation in understanding that took place in the soul of Israel with regard to where its people stood in their comprehension of what was ailing them. This transformation is best appreciated when the text of this psalm is juxtaposed to the words of the Prophet Nathan to King David at a much earlier period. Then, according to the Prophet, God had asserted categorically His commitment to protect the House of David forever and ever. And yet now we are told that this God of unquestionable faithfulness has broken His promise, causing much heartache to man.

In Abraham's time, a direct encounter with the Divine Voice precipitated profound changes in humanity's awareness of how to best proceed in their struggle to overcome their existential angst. Now, as our ancestors discovered the existence of a darker, seemingly immoral side of life they still imagined under the control of God, parallel changes in the belief system of thoughtful men were in the offing. Under these challenging conditions of rising emotional and spiritual distress, a directional shift in the biblical narrative can be detected once again.

Recognizing that the collective effort by the Israelite community to live ethically, as God had demanded of them, had reached the height of its achievable potential, the Bible moved now in a new direction. Implicit in this new vista is the unspoken acknowledgment that the collective failure of man to resolve his suffering is not due primarily to his base and evil nature but rather is a consequence of the misguided interpretation of the origin of this despair as formulated in the myth of the Garden of Eden.

A change in the explanatory narrative of why man suffered so much was needed: more importantly, new skills, resources, and insight to forestall suffering once and for all. For this to happen the narrative moved once again—as it had in Abraham's time—to the experiences of single individuals who served as experiential vessels on which different pathways for the redemption of suffering would be explored and eventually selected before trying them once again on the population at large. Not unexpectedly, the voice of a courageous human being, Job, rose to be heard. His unique journey to healing and psychic wholeness beautifully illustrates what humanity needed to address and do if it aspired to attain freedom from the fear and angst associated with living in a world in which suffering, and more importantly, undeserved suffering, was—and remains— an integral and unavoidable component.

PART III

Wisdom Literature and the Sacred Torah

CHAPTER 8

An Unblemished Man Is Afflicted
by Calamities

THE LOSS OF THE kingdom of Samaria, the fall of the kingdom of Judea, the Babylonian exile, and the apparent injustice associated with the punishments to which the people of Israel had been exposed over time seriously challenged the religious paradigm that had sustained their lives for centuries. The God image they worshiped seemed out of control, dispensing punishments that felt excessive and undeserved. Given these realities, to continue abiding by the prevailing idea of a world ruled by a just and caring God committed to a relationship of mutual accountability with man became a rather unpersuasive proposition for some of the people. A crisis of trust and confidence likely ensued among these members of the Israelite community; this led to the emergence of three divergent responses, each one attempting to resolve this knotty problem.

The first response, embedded in the pages of the Books of Job and Ecclesiastes, details the efforts of two courageous individuals attempting to overcome their despair by formulating a more realistic and sustainable understanding of human experience and man's relationship to nature, more precisely, his own nature. Their inspiring stories signal a transition in man's approach to the relief of suffering from one that was faith-based and centered on a sacred covenant with God to one that is based on man's ability to acquire empirical knowledge through observation, reasoning, deduction, and reflection and use it to better manage the ruthless, amoral world in which he lives.

The second type of response is found in the pages of the Books of Ezra and Nehemiah and is centered on the codification of Moses's

Instruction to the Israelites (with all its commandments, laws, rules, and rituals) into five books detailing the history of God's relationship to man. It begins with Adam and Eve and culminates with the Israelites who, having been emancipated from slavery in Egypt, were getting ready to reconquer the Promised Land. Before these stories were codified into what became the sacred Torah some of them were available to the Israelites, but not all of them, and not with the richness of detail and poetic beauty they took on once committed to the written word. Ever since this happened, though, these books have served as the backbone of the Jewish religious tradition and have sustained Jewish communities, wherever they arose, for the last twenty-five hundred years (this will be dealt with in the following chapter).

The third type of response detailed in the pages of the Book of Daniel offers an apocalyptic vision of the end of time during which God is expected to unleash His wrath on all those who have sinned against Him before shepherding in an era of everlasting happiness and bliss for the people of Israel and humanity at large. And while the idea of such an era was foreshadowed centuries earlier by some of the Prophets, it was not until the Book of Daniel emerged sometime in the last two centuries BCE that an explicit description of the end of time and the process that would eventually lead to it was revealed to our ancestors in more detail (see chapter 11).

Given that historically the Book of Job seems to have preceded the others, its contributions to the collective and individual effort of the people of Israel to overcome the yoke of heaven (the suffering their consciousness imposed upon them) and attain the happy life will be considered first.

Shattering the Religious Paradigm

Prior to Job's emergence as a figure in the biblical tableau, even the suffering of the greatest Prophets and kings of Israel could be attributed to their sinfulness, for they were, after all, imperfect, flawed men who in one way or another had failed to follow God's Instruction faithfully.

But, unlike every other biblical figure, Job was utter perfection according to God's assertion of this truth not once but twice (Job 1:6–9; 2:3). Such a man is supposed to live a happy, wholesome life in which suffering is not expected to be a part. And yet Job is afflicted with chronic anxiety and a persistent sense of foreboding. He attributes his unpleasant feelings to actions he imagines his children may have committed during their regular weekly celebrations, but in reality, they reflect a dread born from Job's utter disconnection from his inner life, which unfortunately had left him ignorant of and vulnerable to much of what was going on in and around him.

Unbeknownst to him, Job was a man foolishly walking into an abyss. Superficially reassured by the idea that following the commandments and precepts prescribed by his religious tradition would redeem him in the eyes of the Lord and thus protect him from calamities, he was terribly vulnerable to the unpredictable ebb and flow of the world he inhabited. Sure enough, unexpected calamities descended upon him, causing him to lose everything he cared for: his possessions, his servants, his cattle, and worst of all, his ten beloved children, all killed simultaneously when a powerful whirlwind demolished the house where they were feasting.

Job's initial response to these earth-shattering events is conventional, measured, and controlled: he tears his gown, shaves his head, and falls to the ground exclaiming his faith: "The Lord gave, and the Lord has taken back. Blessed be the name of the Lord" (Job 1:21). Such a correct and emotionally blunted response may have helped him maintain his external composure and his faith in the conventional idea of how the world of Israel's imagined God worked, but an awakened reader will see it as a feeble, maladaptive reaction. In what amounts to her only intervention in the Job saga, his wife, realizing the true severity of her husband's situation, calls for a novel, even drastically radical response: she demands from her sick, stupefied spouse that he curse God and die (Job 2:9).

To most people, especially those following the tenets of the old faith and those who have embraced the belief in man's innate badness wholeheartedly, her remarks will be surprising. They seem callous, hurtful, and terribly damaging. But they can also and more accurately be seen as nothing less than a wife's attempt at psychological shock therapy. Understanding there is no time to waste and that her husband's life is on the line, she delivers a potentially awakening blow. We might view her as having arrived at her declaration through something like the following thought process: "If Job were to curse God he would, so to speak, die to his old self, and thereby cease to submit to God's whims or to accept his fate. He would also reject the belief in his innate deviousness and realize that his efforts to immunize himself against calamities by following religious doctrine were an illusory pipe dream. Then he could open his mind to as yet unknown realities and possibilities, ones that might move him toward recovery." Job, however, clings tenaciously to his old beliefs and learned behavioral patterns, stubbornly imagining they will secure his salvation.

Neither his wife nor readers of the Book of Job should be amazed at such alarming rigidity for the simple reason that most of us, when faced with overwhelming circumstances, enter into a state of shock and denial and will tend to retreat and find comfort in sticking with the familiar, the known, and the tested, regardless of how ineffective or distorted it may be.

Job's Affective Explosion Announces a Return to Fuller Living

Denial of facts and of the feelings they evoke can only last for so long. Sooner or later repressed feelings break through, and when they do, their intensity can be so great as to distress our bodies even more than the calamities themselves. Hence, as the story advances we hear Job cursing his very birth, giving voice to the depth of his previously repressed agony: "Whatever I fear comes true, whatever I dread befalls me. For me, there is no calm, no peace; my torment banishes rest" (Job 3:25, 26).

From a psychological point of view, like many of us, Job was a man who was haunted by habitual albeit repressed dread, the ongoing price for his being so controlled and limited in what facts and truths he would allow into his consciousness. Instead of dealing with the anxiety persistently stirring within, he felt compelled to abate it by maintaining his assumed perfection at all times and by defending against possible punishment against his children by performing exculpatory sacrifices on their behalf, a taxing undertaking to be sure. Then, when all his efforts to suppress his awareness of life's ruthlessness failed, and when all the sacrifices he had made to ward off dangers seemed useless, he felt doubly betrayed.

Job's cathartic explosion and the many insights it brought to consciousness constitute a pivotal moment in his journey to eventual healing and overall well-being. Initially, when the calamities struck, he was able to deny the hurt and deep anger they had kindled in him. And while fear was part of his daily existence, he had managed to hide it not only from others but also, and more importantly, from himself. Strong, emerging feelings, however, forced him to face aspects of life he had deliberately avoided and to ultimately question everything that until then had been sacrosanct. They brought up for review much of the teachings he had unthinkingly accepted from parents, teachers, and other authorities. They even led him to question what he had been taught about God Himself. Hence, in the midst of his inconsolable suffering, Job hurled a most confrontational question at the Supreme Being: "What is man that you should make so much of him . . . that morning after morning you should examine him and at every instant test him?" (Job 7:17, 18). Evidently, Job had concluded that the God he worshiped, the presumed champion of justice and fairness, was responsible for actions utterly inconsistent with His supposed essence. Emboldened by his immeasurable pain, he questioned God's behavior: "And if I make a stand, like a lion You hunt me down" (Job 10:16). Job's defiant indictment of God's actions sets forth a completely new stage in the evolution of Israelite thinking, perhaps the thinking of all humankind. His statements were nothing less than the beginnings of man's authentic search for deeper understanding and greater resourcefulness in himself rather than in his imagined God, an attempt to ultimately find a resolution for the existential despair his primordial wound and illness had inflicted on him.

Developmentally speaking, Job is now at a crossroads. He has seen the truth but has not yet succumbed to it. On the one hand, he has discovered that good and evil, and right and wrong, are just different facets of a larger whole—what we may term "the world according to God." On the other hand, at this juncture, such knowledge only delivers him into more pain, leaving him excruciatingly at odds with his conventional beliefs and those of his society (Job 12:6–10, 13–15). Life, the greater life within and without, seems to be proceeding in accordance with no rational or comprehensible plan, and this knowledge dismays him.

Transformation: A New Voice Emerges from Within

Following an extended period of deep turmoil and suffering, magnified by the insensitivity and obtuseness of family and friends, Job approaches a first peak in his inner transformation as a new voice emerges from the depths of his soul shouting, "Silence! Now I will do the talking whatever may befall me; I put my flesh between my teeth, I take my life in my hands" (Job 13:13, 14). The Job who speaks now is resolute. He is ready to confront whatever life may bring, exhibiting a confidence lacking up until then.

Prior to this critical moment, Job had been trying to overcome the challenges raised by his emotional and spiritual crisis using traditional cognitive skills and willful maneuvers. Gradually, he realizes the futility of this approach: it leads nowhere. Now he knows that the resolution of his existential challenge rests on his ability to surrender to life's rhythms by allowing the feelings and insights mandated by his situation to come forward and guide him. Unfortunately, as modern psychology has taught us, when psychic material long repressed finds its way into our consciousness the results can be devastating. Dejection and hopelessness may descend on the sufferer, and he may feel so stricken as to wish for relief at any price, even death. Such was already Job's condition when exclaiming, "Let Him kill me if He will; I have no other hope than to justify my conduct in His eyes" (Job 13:15).

Intuitively, Job understands that an irreversible ending, a death, has been mandated but its precise meaning still eludes him. He has not yet comprehended that the moment he dies to his old self, his old ideologies, his old encrusted beliefs, not only will his disturbed state end, but life itself—the greater life—will be able to flow freely, unimpeded in its relentless search for the best means of achieving its ends. But the intensity of his feelings and the uncertainty still surrounding his life make him regress emotionally. He turns back again to contemplate his unhappy fate and God's part in it: "I lived in peace until He shattered me, taking me back by the neck to dash me to pieces," Job laments. "My face is red with tears, and a veil of shadow hangs on my eyelids" (Job 16:12, 16).

Job's words touch our hearts. When tragedy first struck, he bemoaned his fate but continued to bless the Almighty. His powerful denial of facts and his rigid, dogmatic convictions allowed him to keep his inner home from crumbling. Now, as he allows himself to vent his resentment toward God and humans, his decisive tone implicitly acknowledges that his disasters are part of his lived experience. Job seems to be saying to us, "I have eaten from the tree of knowledge of good and bad and my consciousness has broadened. No longer can I feign ignorance. All that has befallen me has undoubtedly happened and I am appalled by it."

Convinced that God was responsible for shattering his life and that his wife and friends have been blindly insensitive to his despair, Job beseeches them to stop acting as if they were divinities themselves and start recognizing the Almighty for what He is: both the source of all light as well as all darkness, a God that rewards and punishes, that protects and simultaneously doesn't care at all about man's fate (Job 29:18–20, 30:20, 21).

As he continues rubbing his face against the hard truth of the facts of his life, the naked here and now, he acknowledges a world apparently unjust to the core, amoral, a world in which "one man dies in the fullness of his strength, in all possible happiness and ease . . . another dies with bitterness in his heart, never having tasted happiness. Together now they lie in the dust with worms for covering" (Job 21:23, 25, 26).

Job's acknowledgment of the amorality of existence combined with the emotional momentum that has brought him to such truth pushes him forward. Unable to revert to his former contrived conventional innocence, he has to figure out how to live with what he now knows as the world's darkness, exemplified by the myriad calamities that had befallen him.

In the meantime, as his journey progresses, his misery expands exponentially and so does his understanding that answers to his existential plight will have to come from within, from spirit, from his own Inner Higher Wisdom. Now that Job's inner eyes have been partially opened, he can glimpse the dual manifestations in nature as arising neither from caprice nor chance but rather from an abiding pursuit of universal balance: destruction following creation, creation following destruction.

We can already see how Job's emotional catharsis has opened gateways. His strong, authentic feelings together with the relentless questioning they evoke have led to discovering some of the mysteries of the world within. In time he will gain access to a large part of it, thereby opening resources and possibilities unimaginable until then. He will grasp a new understanding and begin to transform himself into an aware and intuitive human being, a man capable of connecting to his innate strength. Within this newly revealed inner world, he will begin to mine the depths of the collective unconscious, a cauldron of accumulated knowledge and wisdom, which he and the rest of us share with each other. Awesome truths will become available to him. He will understand, for example, that "to fear God" is to respect the natural order of things, relinquishing any arrogant pretense at knowing what is "right" in nature. Much of Job's and our painful sufferings, perhaps most, come from not accepting the ways of the cosmos, the ways of the world. This intolerance of the way things are, of the contingencies and frailties of human life, of the unintended consequences associated with the evolutionary process that made us, is what formerly drove Job to experience as evil the destruction of health, wealth, and family. But in time he will be able to see these occurrences differently, especially once he ceases denying important realities of life. He will be able to accept, for example, that suffering is an inevitable part of human existence, and instead of complaining and groaning about it, he will become calmer, eventually even able to feel glad that he can enjoy the freedom from unnecessary pain, which his clearer understanding of things now brings. Then, in a general way, he will be able to conform himself to the larger reality in which he partakes and avoid thinking of any of it as wrong or evil.

But that time has not yet arrived. Though Job keeps appealing for an audience with God, he is still primarily seeking relief from the restlessness and oppression caused by his distorted beliefs and vivid imagination. "Who can get me a hearing from God?" he clamors, "I have had my say . . . now let Shaddai answer me" (Job 31:35).

Elihu Prepares Job to Meet His Maker

It is at this point in the evolution of Job's transformative journey that Elihu appears. He is another of Job's friends, a younger one, representing the wise, enlightened teacher who has come to help Job connect to his mystery. Elihu is the composite of two Hebrew words: Eli (my God) and Hu (he is). Thus when Elihu speaks, we must think of it as if an enlightened part of his soul were speaking to Job. Elihu's words must, therefore, be taken in their highest symbolic meaning.

Challenging the truthfulness of Job's persistent claims, Elihu asks him, "How could you say in my hearing, for the sounds of your words did not escape me, 'I am clean, and sinless. I am pure, free of fault. Yet, He is inventing grievances against me, and imagining me His enemy'" (Job 33:8–10).

Interpreting Job's silence as a sign of acquiescence, he proceeds: "Have you not understood that the world God created does not fit man's measure?" (Job 33:12). And so, with these words Elihu opens up Job to the reality of a world that does not function the way our objectified world does. There is a presence there, he alerts him, that knows about those wonderful things Job did for others but also knows what drove him to do them. It knows that goodness and wisdom were indeed part of his motivation but that fear and ignorance were just as important. More often than not, Elihu asserts, "What stirred you to doing 'good deeds' was your fear of God's wrath rather than a desire to truly help others. Ironically you lived your life in fear of precisely what has befallen you. Your exemplary behavior did not derive from attuning yourself to life's grand complexities—primarily because you were ignorant of them—but rather from anxiety and futile attempts to magically manipulate the primitive, inaccurate version of reality you subscribed to. Don't think for a moment that the inner presence was impressed by the sacrifices you kept offering for your children."

In this critical sequence, Elihu has advanced our understanding of human reality and human nature by acknowledging the existence of an interiority that contains our deepest and truest motivations, our unacknowledged struggles, and a wisdom unavailable to our conscious minds and thus not under our volitional control. Others before Elihu had acknowledged the inscrutability of some of the actions of inanimate and animate nature in the outer world, the world accessible to our senses, but Elihu is also acknowledging a presence within that knows everything that goes on in our private realm and reacts to it accordingly; therefore, nothing about us, whether we are conscious of it or not, goes unnoticed.

In the world according to God, Elihu seems to be intimating, sickness and suffering are not tragic occurrences but rather inevitable events balanced by our capacity to heal our lives and by our innate inclination to succor our fellowmen when in distress (Job 33:19–30). Moreover, as Eliphaz said before with such eloquence, "Happy indeed the man whom God corrects! . . . For He who wounds is He who soothes the sore, and the hand that hurts is the hand that heals" (Job 5:17, 18). Job is learning firsthand about the duality that exists in nature and in his own human nature, which, as he will discover later on, manifests often in the world in which we all partake. The latter is not the moral world he had hoped for but a world of rhythms and flows in which exists a self-reflective creature made in the image of an imagined God. That being is endowed with the potential for doing good and bad, thus making his personal life and that of his community moral or immoral. Job does not understand yet the full meaning of Eliphaz's assertion, but in time he will realize that in the sanctum of his own interiority there is indeed a hand that injures and a hand that heals. By accepting these truths, Job will be able to find resolution for his despair eventually. "Listen to all this," counsels Elihu. "No backsliding now! Become God-like, and seek to embrace your consciousness and the totality of what this wonderful privilege brings forth" (Job 37:14).

For a good part of his journey toward healing Job clamored for an explanation as to why he had been struck with so many calamities and why God had not responded to his implorations for an answer. But Elihu reminds him that despite Job's insistence that God has been mum to his supplications, it has been exactly the opposite: the inner voice has been speaking to Job in many ways, but Job ignored them all. "Why do you rail at Him for not replying to you word for word?" asks Elihu in a condemnatory tone. "Don't you know that God speaks first in one way, and then in another, but no one notices? He speaks through dreams, and visions that come in the night, when slumber comes on humankind, and men are all asleep in bed. Then it is He who whispers in the ear of man, or may frighten him with fearful sights, to turn him away from evil-doing, and make an end of his pride; to save his soul from the pit and his life from the pathway to Sheol"[1] (Job 33:13–18). As expected, Elihu's question elicits no response from Job, for what can he say? Elihu finishes his teaching by telling Job not to waste any time but to set forth and find the God he has been looking for inside, and that he must refuse to let fear or any other unpleasant emotion deter him. And the sooner he does so, the sooner he will discover that there is indeed a powerful presence within waiting for him to come out of his stupor and embrace it in a magical, mystical dance.

Calling attention to the fundamental principle of God's Providence—His continued whispering in man's ear to turn him away from evil-doing and save himself from the pit—Elihu is saying that what Job imagined God to be is not the way He really is, but rather He is precisely the way He told Moses He would be, a deity encompassing all that our rational minds could conceive, and more, much more. It follows from all this that when Job lived as if objective reality was all

159

there was he perforce missed knowing it was merely a small part of the grand world in which his life had been unfolding.

Trying to figure out what sustains our human world requires looking deep into the recesses of our soul. There dreams and intuitions and every other aspect of our inner life help us perceive our living reality in a broader, more comprehensive way. Through such a process we discover how ignorant and misguided we have been about what matters most for inner peace and comfort; there we learn that those who seem to be thriving are, when disconnected from their inner truth, living an objectified life, unconscious of much of what is going on (as Job once did) and therefore tainted with cruelty and repression toward self and others. By virtue of their unconsciousness, they are unaware of how insensitive and hurtful they have been—still are—to many of those with whom they come in contact, particularly those closest to them.

It was this unconsciousness that earlier on allowed Job, when celebrating the many gifts with which he had been blessed, to believe in his general goodness (Job 31:19, 21, 24, 25, 29, 30). On the surface, Job may have seemed good, but he was not as good as he imagined himself to be. During the years when he perceived himself wholly good, he had no connection to life's awesome totality. Instead, ridden with worry and anxiety, he rejected or ignored a good part of the world in which he continually acted. Only now, by virtue of all the painful things that have happened to him, is he beginning to blend with a much larger vision of reality, becoming a more complete and resourceful human being.

By confronting Job with previously unknown aspects of his soul's essence, such as its healing power and its willingness to bend over backward to save others from trouble (Job 33:23–28, 34:30–33), as well as the extraordinary power of his darker side (Job 37:2–4), Elihu is forcing the long overdue collapse of Job's naiveté to take place, thus helping him enter into what ancient alchemists called the "vessel," an inner crucible in which the lead of ignorance can be transformed into the bright gold of knowledge, self-awareness, and self-reliance (Job 35:14–16). Job is in the process of completing his rebirth, and this time he is preparing to receive the raw, unadulterated, primordial force of the inner Divine without the benefit of intermediaries, interpreters, or any external filtering. Now Job is going to hear from the inner presence firsthand. And as he unites more fully with it, he is awestruck when the power of this force fills the vastness of what hitherto had felt like a lonely inner universe.

The presence that offers him wise guidance had never absented itself from Job's inner world—or from that of any other human. But, as with most of us, Job's conscious self was largely detached from that richness and hence often felt alone and empty. As he transforms, however, the illusion of loneliness and disconnection will shatter, and deep feelings of communion and soulfulness will arise.

The Birth of a New Man

And so, no sooner than Elihu finishes speaking, a voice erupts within Job's inner turmoil, flinging challenging questions at him, thus lifting his perspective to the vast richness and sublimity of the created world and by a cunning extension that of the creature possessing a private life—man. The voice Job hears from his inner tempest asks him provocative questions: "Tell me Job, which is the way to the home of the light, and where does darkness live? Can you guide the morning star season by season? Have you grasped the celestial laws?" (Job 38:19, 32, 33).

Silence follows and after a rather long pause the pounding questions resume: "Are you the one to find a prey for the lioness and satisfy the hunger of her whelps . . . are you the one who makes provisions for the raven when his squabs cry out to God and crane their necks in hunger?" (Job 38:39, 41). These interrogations are emblematic of Job coming to understand the hollowness of his previous self-righteousness and rigidity. Yet this confrontation with the larger reality that is God's will in the end imbue him with great joy, serenity, and a feeling of deep connection to nature, in particular to his own nature.

His imagination soaring, Job now envisions truths and possibilities completely hidden from him before. The questioning he is being subjected to by this internal voice and its demand for answers alerts him to the great mystery of which he is a part. Job has seemingly penetrated the transpersonal dimension of the psyche and now stands awestruck before the palace of the All. Venturing into this unfamiliar territory he begins to understand reality through his feelings, intuitions, and dreams—those inner voices Elihu had recalled to Job—rather than through cognition alone. As poets and philosophers (one thinks of T. S. Eliot and William James) have said, those having such experiences suddenly feel privy to truths they recognize they have known all along, though parts of themselves and, indeed, of all humankind, have typically been blind to them. I am referring, of course, to the knowledge that we are part of a much larger existence affecting our safety and well-being: a planet, a solar system, and physical and animate nature, all of it. Job's struggles and persistent efforts to repair his shattered life have allowed him to begin to consciously tap into an arena that at first manifested itself to him in the form of terrible nightmares, making him tremble with fear (Job 7:13–15).

Job's initial encounter with this domain of life felt terribly alien to him, but only there, in the transpersonal (and not within the confines of objective existence) will he, and the rest of us, find the answers to our existential concerns: How to understand the irrevocable decline we all experience and our eventual extinction? How to understand human violence and cruelty? How to understand undeserved suffering? How to develop the resources to engage in one's life crises rather than hide from them? How to be truthful rather than deceptive and cunning? Prodded by these challenging questions Job is forced to expand his horizons and begin to appreciate the interdependence of man and the cosmos. He is also beginning to connect with layers of reality that are neither quantifiable nor subject to personal wishes or societal dictates. These are realities overshadowing and overriding all he has heretofore tried to manage volitionally. That is why, at the end of the inner voice's first speech, he humbly says: "My words have been frivolous: what can I reply? I have spoken once . . . I will not speak again; more than once . . . I will add nothing" (Job 40:4, 5). Job's arrogant defiance of his fate and his demands for divine accountability are gone. His voice is now soft, quiet, and unassuming. He has realized the depth of his ignorance and the foolishness of his previous sanctimonious posturing. The softening of his tone can be interpreted as communicating something like: "I am terribly ashamed of having been unconscious of so much that is important to me and deeply regret the terrible damage this has inflicted on me and on the people I love."

While in the throes of his mystical experience, Job is reminded that despite the immense resourcefulness of his human mind he and all other human beings are still members of the vast animal kingdom, a community of beings in continuous interconnection and interdependence with each other, whose lives are under the influence, even the rule, of laws affecting their day-to-day existence. Within this vast kingdom, what is food for an eagle's young may be pain and agony for the children of the fallen person (Job 39:30). In the same light, what we usually call disease often represents the efforts of other organisms to find sustenance for their growth and survival. To avoid unnecessary torments, neither Job nor anyone else should abstract himself from seeing the larger picture of life.

From here on the Book of Job flows forward with some of its most arresting poetry—images of monster-sized created beings, symbols of nature's strength, and, more pointedly, of its potential for the destructive: "Now think of Behemoth . . . what power in his stomach muscles! . . . Should the river overflow on him, why should he worry? . . . Leviathan too! . . . You have only to lay a finger on him never to forget the struggle or risk it again!" (Job 40:15, 16, 23, 25, 32).

Job's foray into transpersonal reality first confronted him with a creative energy responsible for all that exists. Now, however, he is being inducted into the mystery of the Destroyer/Liberator energy, a striking force that makes ordinary people feel as if evil had crushed them head on. But Job is not portrayed as being crushed. It is as if he is now able to understand this force for what it is: powerful and essential. While many readers see Leviathan and Behemoth as representing abominable energies to be avoided and destroyed if possible, others comprehend that they benefit the Creation. Think of what we and the rest of the world would be if we lived endlessly—a moving morgue of aging zombies, never giving new life its chance.

As Job integrates these magnificent images into his reality, he learns that the world in which he lives is one sustained by the balance between the creative and destructive aspects of nature, his own included. Nothing is static here but rather a dynamic plenitude, a mighty cosmic symphony. It is evident that Job has come to understand that in the world he now inhabits his earlier conventional morality, religious beliefs, and psychological conditionings—only constructive forces are desirable and good; goodness is rewarded and sin punished; and submission to authority ensures all would be well—had kept him weak and vulnerable despite the fact that outwardly he appeared strong, successful, and safe.

Having witnessed a deeper, more reliable truth, Job is forever changed. Knowing truth, we may speculate, allowed him to tap the deeper meaning of all that had happened to him. He understands that nothing needs to be added or subtracted from life.

Job is beginning to perceive the interdependence of Man and World, World and nature, and he cannot stop marveling at the complex grandeur of this coherence. With the humility of someone blessed with insight, Job answers the inner voice he believes to be God's by saying, "I know that You are all-powerful; what You conceive, You can perform. I am the man who obscured Your designs with my empty-headed words. I have been holding forth on matters I cannot understand, on marvels beyond me and my knowledge" (Job 42:2, 3).

The deepening of Job's understanding, evidenced by the tone of these last verses, evokes good feelings in him. Realizing that what has happened to him was neither the result of some innate badness for which he deserved punishment nor the product of a wrathful God acting with wanton abandon opens him up to all that life may bring forth. And as his tone further softens we hear, in the next few verses, an emergent calm wisdom: "I knew you then only by hearsay, but now, having seen you with my own eyes, I retract all I have said, and in dust and ashes I repent" (Job 42:5, 6). The old Job, the one we find at the beginning of the story, the man who worships God unconditionally, who believes all he has been told about this God but who has never experienced Him in his own flesh, is dying and being reborn into one who is finally able to accept life and the world in which he lives as it is, as it was meant to be. This is a world in which consciousness is not perceived as wounding, and therefore there is no need to explain human suffering as resulting from an ancestral misdeed. From this new place of understanding and integration he can go forth to tomorrows filled with love, compassion, and true holiness.

Job's inner transformation and the completeness of his personal integration are first revealed by the way he treats his friends. Following his connection to his guiding inner wisdom, the imagined God addresses Eliphaz of Teman, rebuking him and Job's other friends for not having spoken truthfully about Him as Job had done (Job 42:7, 8). By offering prayers for his friends, however, Job not only forgives them for their callous and cruel behavior toward him during his time of need but also demonstrates an ability to transcend his hurt and understand they could not have done any better. By praying for them, his inner being ceases to be divided. Job has evoked a superior function capable of synthesizing opposites that can now coexist under a single roof: Logos, the seat of rationality and mental prowess, and Eros, the seat of desire, creativity, and feeling embraced in an eternal dance. Here is the meaning of God having given him, by way of earthly restoration, "double what he had before" (Job 42:11). To use the language of esoteric disciplines, the two have become one within him. From that unity arise symbols of the blessings appropriate to Job's inner richness: "all his brothers . . . sisters . . . friends of former time sitting down at table with him," and the astonishing increase of living beings around him, "fourteen thousand sheep, six thousand camels . . . seven sons and three daughters . . . no women as beautiful as the daughters of Job" (Job 42:10–15).

Awareness of the persistent presence in his inner mystery of a guiding voice in communication with him through nocturnal dreams and visions heralds the dawn of a new era in human comprehension and functioning. Clearly, Job's crass ignorance at the beginning of his journey caused him great suffering. Now that his consciousness has expanded to integrate a good part of his inner life, natural calamities are perceived as part of the risk associated with the privilege of living. Learning about them, understanding the physical, animate, human world and the workings of the human mind are essential if we hope to live long and well. In an indirect way, all of us today, through Job, are encouraged to let our curiosity, our rationality, our creativity, and our need to know and understand and to find meaning in our lives burst forth freely. By becoming more attuned to what happens around us and less dependent on some external force for the resolution of our angst, we learn to care better for ourselves. The world in which Job and all of us are embedded must be engaged and honored, and we must learn to avoid unconsciousness, for it increases our vulnerability and the potential for unnecessary misery.

Wisdom Experienced, Wholeness Attained

Having realized that to overcome his suffering he had to integrate the light and the dark sides of his human nature as well as that of animate and inanimate nature (symbolized by the towering images of God in chapters 40 and 41 in the Book of Job) and honor his rational side and the human faculties capable of tapping into the nonrational dimensions of his life—like our feelings and intuitions—he symbolically gave birth to a new type of human being. In that sense, the Book of Job can be seen as an emanation from the depths of the Israelite soul of a novel, even revolutionary understanding of human life and the world. The new man heralded in this book is one that has moved away from fear and groveling, from false praise and blame, from accepting he is cursed and thus deserves to suffer endlessly, in short from ignorance, naiveté, and unconsciousness to an unconditional acceptance of all Creation and to an appreciation of the inner life and of the awesome resources available to him there. He is a man who understands that rather than feeling he has a *right* to life he is endowed with the *privilege* of being alive and therefore is invested in savoring every moment of it and never again taking anything for granted.

Those able to embrace Job's evolving worldview will understand that there is no God—or for that matter any other cosmic force—that could have created a world in which death, disease, and physical decline were absent. Even stars blow up. Nor could there exist a world in which creatures enjoy the gift of free will, the beauty of knowing themselves as well as the great reality in which they exist, and still live exempt from the suffering that comes from self-consciousness and fore-knowledge. By breaking the spell hovering over humanity for thousands of years, a spell that institutionalized humanity's evilness, Job's story has the potential of releasing us all to a life of freedom from delusion and distortion, a life of healing and the potential for attaining psycho-spiritual wholeness.

Job's insight into the realities of human existence is still the clearest, most resolving pathway for overcoming the suffering caused by our primordial wound and illness and for the attainment of peace, harmony, enduring happiness, and meaningfulness. To embrace the wisdom embedded in Job is to become liberated, free to move toward ways of living marked by self-reliance, self-confidence, understanding, compassion, tolerance, and the enjoyment of each other and the complex world in which we live. This brings rejoicing and a genuine appreciation of the privilege we have been granted not in some fanta-sized other world but here on this earth, now, in whatever additional time graciously given to us by that which determines how long and how well we live.

Epilogue

Job's journey to health and healing helps us understand that the suffering we experience from knowing our unpleasant feelings is an unavoidable component of our human condition—the way evolution caused it to be. But it also shows us that we are resourceful individuals endowed with mental and physical capacities capable of overcoming most of our acquired suffering and finding peace, harmony, and happiness in the amoral, ruthless world in which we exist. To accomplish this aim, however, we must invest ourselves in discovering the laws and principles by which our physical and human world work because, contrary to conventional wisdom, ignorance is not bliss. Remaining disconnected from the realities of this world may feel blissful at first, but it is a mental stance fraught with grave danger. It is imperative therefore that we search for truth, our truth, and avoid youthful innocence and naiveté. Denial is a useful coping mechanism under certain circumstances, especially when short-lived, but if it persists for a long time it will stifle and delay understanding and growth and make us vulnerable to the destructive forces of nature.

The world revealed to us by Job is a stage for nature's *constructive and destructive* forces in continuous interplay and interconnection. That is why order and disorder, health and disease, injury and repair, life and death, must and will always coexist. One reality begets the other, and thus it is impossible to be alive and not experience the full range of what this awesome privilege implies. Once we accept these difficult realities, understand their significance in the large scheme of things, and learn to integrate them into our systems of belief and our religious and cultural traditions everything begins to fall into place.

Job's saga also teaches us that no one is or can be immune to the vicissitudes inexorably woven into the fabric of our lives. These are inevitable parts of how our world is put together. Not all people, however, will be visited by the same number of calamities, experience comparable degrees of misfortune, or reach the same depth of enjoyment and bliss. These are more a function of the randomness of things than reflections of our moral comportment or God's response to it.

The purpose of life, according to the wisdom in the Book of Job, is to develop, mature, and become a complete human being. This is not possible, however, as long as we perceive ourselves as flawed, weak, and cursed creatures. But once we succeed in freeing ourselves from the yoke supposedly imposed on us by heaven, we can attain the joyfulness and harmony our human condition affords us. To accomplish this, we must learn to know ourselves. This requires help. Hence, we must be open to those capable of enlightening our quest. But most importantly, we must listen to that which communicates with us from the sanctum of our inner ear, our inner eye, and our inner heart. Once we learn to be receptive to our inner guides, we will feel more secure, trusting, and deeply blessed.

Taken as a whole, the story of Job alerts us to the vulnerabilities associated with living disconnected from our feelings, intuitions, and the inner voice that guides us through dreams and visions in the night. Such a disconnect may be adaptive at first, during our formative years, but if it persists it will prevent us from attaining enduring happiness.

The key message Job delivers to all of us can be summed up as follows: If we aspire to a life of less suffering, we must know ourselves and others. If we are interested in knowing how the world works, we must uncover the secrets of the physical, chemical, and biological world in which we live. It also encourages us to become outstanding scientists, artists, mystics, and wise sages. In this way, we will surely draw nearer to the truth of our condition and to our enfolded potential to live a happy, even blissful life.

Unfortunately, these teachings and what they demand from us were too onerous to be collectively accepted and integrated into Israelite society so very long ago. Unable to capture the wisdom revealed in Job, the people were left feeling unstable and exposed. On the one hand, Job's saga had served to collapse their belief in the existence of a reliable, faithful, just God, and on the other hand, it offered a pathway to the resolution of their suffering that was more taxing and overwhelming than the one imposed on them by covenantal doctrine, which parenthetically they had been unable to fulfill with any rigor. Something else needed to come forth, something that would offer them immediate relief and hope and could readily be embraced by all.

This something appeared in the middle of the fifth century BCE in the form of the written holy Torah, a compilation of five books detailing the history of the relationship between God and the people of Israel and that also contained a detailed description of how God expected them to live, as revealed by Him to Moses in Sinai. For centuries some of these Instructions had been passed on to them by word of mouth with, as we have discovered, limited success.

Subjecting these Instructions to the written word raised the hope that the divine revelation would now, in this way, have a chance of reaching its highest potential for doing good.

CHAPTER 9

Ezra and Nehemiah

A Sustainable Pathway to Communal Wellness

WHILE THE BOOK OF Job offered an effective new mythical pathway for the resolution of Israelite suffering, its message was incomprehensible for the majority of the population and may have engendered even more angst and dejection given the image it painted of a seemingly irrational God wreaking havoc on an exemplary man for no good reason.

On the other hand, the Israelite community was in dire need of guidance and support to handle its many sources of affliction. For one, the ten tribes originally inhabiting the kingdom of Israel had been lost for centuries, absorbed into the cultures into which they were dispersed; something similar happening to the Judean exiles in Babylon was not an unfounded threat, to say the least. Additionally, while in exile, the people of Israel often heard scathing and frightening pronouncements by Prophets like Ezekiel, who made sure to remind them how wicked they had been and how much God despised their ways: "Assuredly, as I live (God purportedly said to Ezekiel) because you defiled My sanctuary with all your detestable things and all your abominations, I shall in turn shear (you Israel) away and show no pity. I in turn will show no compassion. And when I execute judgment upon you in anger and rage and furious chastisement you shall be a mockery and a derision, a warning and a horror, to the nations roundabout you" (Ezek. 5:13, 15). Proclamations such as these abound in Ezekiel's writings as well as in those of other Prophets of the same era, all revealing deep concern for the behavior of the Israelite community and what it might portend for the future. In all likelihood, these prophetic pronouncements were intended to intimidate the people into behaving in ways compatible with those prescribed by their tradition and in this manner reduce their strained relationship with God and, more importantly, reduce their suffering and ensure they live a better life. The Prophets' hope was to persuade the people of Israel that without repentance and a return to a moral way of living their future was bleak, regardless of whether they lived in exile, under occupation, or as sovereign people.

It was under these tense social and mental conditions that the written Torah made its historic entrance into the life of Israel. Preceding this transcendental development, the Instruction God had delivered to the people of Israel had been transmitted orally by religious leaders charged with the responsibility of guiding the citizenry's behavior. This had to have limited the citizenry's exposure to the fundamental tenets of the tradition. Additionally, it centered its effectiveness on the persuasive power of the Prophets and priests entrusted with the task of passing along the oral tradition to the masses.

Isolated fragments describing some of the main stories and prescriptions in the Torah existed in written form before the five books of Moses came to light. In fact, in 2 Kings we are told that the high priest Hilkiah, during the reign of King Josiah (beginning in the year 640 BCE), found a scroll of the Teachings of Moses in the House of the Lord; this scroll contained a good part of what is currently contained in the Book of Deuteronomy. When the scroll was read to the king, suspecting God's wrath against Israel was great, he was so overwhelmed by what he heard that he rent his clothes in a show of contrition and deep concern. The king's reaction to the reading of the scroll suggests that he was unaware of at least some important commandments and precepts God expected him and the people of Israel to fulfill. Consulted about the scroll, the Prophetess Huldah, speaking in the name of the Lord, said: "I am going to bring disaster upon this place and its inhabitants, in accordance with all the words of the scroll which the king of Judah read. Because they have forsaken Me and have made offering to other gods and vexed Me with all their deeds, My wrath is kindled against this place, and it shall not be quenched" (2 Kings 22:16, 17). Despite this severe admonition by the Prophetess, Israel did not experience ruin during King Josiah's time. Being a good and righteous leader who followed the ways of his ancestor King David, Josiah succeeded in bringing forth economic prosperity and good fortune for the people.

During that same period, a school of scribes was busy writing manuscripts and commentaries based on the contents of the discovered scroll, thus contributing to the education and instruction of the population. Given all this, it is reasonable to assume that the bulk of laws and duties stipulated in the Torah were known to a good part of the Israelite citizenry at least more than two centuries before the Torah appeared in written form. But even if that were to be the case, the extent and depth of the stories included in the five books of Moses would not have been known in enough detail to overcome the Israelites' resistance to embracing wholeheartedly what amounted to a highly burdensome system of laws and precepts meant to inform and guide their daily lives.

Ezra's Gift to Israel

Under the generous auspices of the Persian king Cyrus, a good number of the Israelites in exile returned to their homeland in Judea and undertook the rebuilding of Jerusalem, the destroyed holy city. Their ultimate purpose was to establish once again a blessed community on the land promised to their ancestors by the Lord. Among those returning were two exceptional men, Ezra and Nehemiah. The first was an outstanding religious and spiritual leader who possessed vast knowledge of Mosaic Law, while the second was an astute politician with impeccable credentials: courageous, honest, and highly principled, he served as an outstanding exemplar for the rest of the population.

All this notwithstanding, these men were able neither to stir the exiles nor those who had remained in Judea toward the kind of ethically based, moral way of life they knew was essential to overcome the people's angst and bring happiness and well-being into their midst. In fact, one of Ezra's first acts upon returning to Jerusalem was to remind the returnees of the prohibition against mixing in marriage with people of different faiths. Ezra's forewarning, however, was disregarded and many of the exiles, including many of their leaders, engaged in this practice with abandon, causing the holy seed of Israel to become intermingled with the seed of people whose practices and behaviors their God presumably abhorred (Ezra 9:1, 2). This prohibition to intermarry, the first one in recorded Israelite history, did not imply some racial superiority but rather an understanding that if it was almost impossible for the Israelites to live according to the moral demands of their revealed Law, how much harder would it be for people not belonging to their tradition? Ergo, it followed that intermarriage posed a serious danger to their moral enterprise.

Understanding that the effort to establish an enduring, ethically principled way of life that was based on the oral transmission of the commandments and precepts revealed to Moses had failed, Ezra surmised the people would need the full set of commandments, laws, rules, and practices bound into a single document that would be accessible to them all. Motivated by these important realizations, Ezra dedicates himself to the daunting task of bringing together the stories of the Creation of the universe: the evolution of man's relationship with God beginning with Adam and Eve and their fall from grace, and following with Noah, the Patriarchs and Matriarchs, the story of the enslavement of the Israelites in Egypt, the rise of Moses as the liberator and redeemer of the Israelite people, the exodus from Egypt and the lengthy journey of the people through the Sinai desert where they received the commandments that were supposed to guide their lives and a detailed account of the rules and precepts they were expected to fulfill as part of their day-to-day living. It is in this manner that the first written edition of the holiest book in the Jewish tradition came to light; it became canonized around the year 445 BCE.

That Ezra compiled and unified the content of the Torah does not mean he authored any of the books. Many of the stories contained therein were known much earlier as revelations to the Israelite Patriarchs and Matriarchs, and their subsequent spiritual leaders passed them along from generation to generation. Ezra wrote down those stories as well as collecting whatever written material was in existence at the time; he organized all of it in more or less chronological order, perhaps refining and editing, and finally binding them into five remarkable books.

The sacred Torah gave expression to a moral code of behavior that made abundantly clear how the Supreme Being expected His people to act. Additionally, the Torah offered a detailed catalogue of laws and rules meant to guide the Israelites' behavior in matters of civil, criminal, social, and military jurisprudence, ensuring the nation would be established on a foundation of justice, respect for the individual, and equality—all essential for attaining the coveted collective contentment. By creating such a document, Ezra established a Code of Law that the people of Israel were asked to follow wherever they found themselves. Given that these laws were of divine origin they were supposed to be unchangeable although always open to interpretation. And so a new type of religious leader appeared—the rabbi, or teacher—whose authority was based not on his position in the religious hierarchy involved in Temple worship but rather on his knowledge of Torah Law and rituals, enabling him to officiate wherever he was and, most importantly, wherever Israelites were.

In addition to writing the Torah, Ezra started what became a millenary tradition of reading the Torah scroll to the community as a way of keeping alive and ever-present the ethical standards favored by their imagined God, the virtues of moral living, and the deep wisdom and teachings about human life and relations embedded in its legends, its parables, and its historical accounts. Last but not least, the Torah provided a roadmap that, if followed religiously, offered people the reward of a happy, healthy, and productive life.

The birth of Torah reading, a significant event in Israelite history, is described in the Hebrew Bible as follows: "After Jerusalem was rebuilt the Israelites assembled in the sacred city asking Ezra to bring the scroll of the Teachings of Moses and read from it to them. Surrounded by priests, Levites, and leaders of the different clans Ezra stood on a wooden tower made especially for the occasion and read from the scroll. On the next day, only the leaders of the clans, and the priests and Levites gathered around Ezra to study in detail now the words of the Teachings, and thus, be better prepared to implement its commandments and the precepts therein prescribed" (Ezra 8:2–13).

This practice promoted literacy in the Israelite community—for it was the duty of every citizen to study Torah and for that to happen the people needed to be able to read—which helped its members prosper when faced with difficult social and economic circumstances. Reading the Torah regularly also gave the sages an opportunity to offer expositions (Midrashim) and interpretations of its verses and stories, in particular as they pertained to the problems and needs of the time. Many of these expositions came to light during a two-hundred-year period between the fourth and the second century BCE and later became codified in what came to be known as the Mishna.

The Living Torah

The writing of the Torah and its eventual availability to the people of Israel marked the official inauguration of the Jewish religious tradition. Blessed now with a collection of books that was authoritative, inclusive, comprehensive, and unchanging, they did not have to depend any longer on revelations of the Divine's wishes through Prophets or sages but could depend on the Instructions He had given Moses centuries before.

Despite the transcendent import that the writing of the Torah had for the Israelite people, the house of Israel did not fare too well during Ezra and Nehemiah's tenure. For one, the promise of a triumphal return of the Israelite exiles from Babylon to Jerusalem offered by the Prophet Isaiah and others had not materialized. What is more, the Temple rebuilt by those who did return lacked the majesty and grandeur of the first one. In fact, the Book of Ezra states that many of the priests and Levites and the old men who had enjoyed the first house of God wept loudly at the sight of the new one (Ezra 3:13).

Profound socioeconomic differences between its citizens had given rise to animosity and instability in the kingdom. The wealthy, highly placed local officials and the priestly elite, now ensured of their well-being by the people's promise to pay their taxes, neglected their responsibility to care for the small landowners, the day workers, and the people at the lower rungs of the socioeconomic strata. Some of these poor, disenfranchised people were even compelled to sell their children into slavery in order to survive. In addition to all the taxes and interest rates for borrowed goods and the service of the House of God, they had to pay the extra taxation imposed by the Persian rulers, which added significantly to their destitution.

Trying to remedy these ills, Nehemiah succeeded to a small degree. But when he left Jerusalem to return to Babylon, everything went awry; the people's dependence on his leadership to maintain civility and stay the course led to a collective collapse. Even when he and Ezra were fully engaged, guiding the people with their example and wisdom and making sure the laws were respected, the Israelites continued to have great difficulty abiding by the precepts and commandments stipulated in the newly written books. As the community's transgressions accumulated, their behavior became increasingly deplorable. In Nehemiah's last speech to the people, he asked God to remember how they polluted the priesthood despite his effort to purge them from every foreign element, as well as their many other transgressions of divine law (Neh. 13:10–13, 15–17, 19, 23–25, 29–31).

The failure to turn Israel into a law-abiding nation dedicated to the attainment of its lofty spiritual goals highlights the difficulty Ezra and Nehemiah and subsequent religious and political leaders encountered when imposing Torah Law and precepts on people who either did not believe in them wholeheartedly or simply were not equipped to fulfill their strenuous demands. Nonetheless, Ezra and Nehemiah did succeed in establishing a religious tradition based on the sacred Torah that was reliable and accessible to the people. They also established a tradition of reading and interpreting passages from the Torah, which evolved from the interpretation of obscure words or sentences to finding answers to the vexing questions and challenges of the time embedded in the stories of the holy books.

There was also the problem posed by precepts and injunctions in the Torah that did not seem to comport to the realities faced by the people with the passage of time; these often needed modification and some were even removed from the canon. By glorifying the five books of Moses, Ezra and Nehemiah created the impression that the Torah was an all-inclusive tractate; whatever God had intended to say to His people of Israel He had already said, and therefore there was no need to add or to subtract anything from it. No further revelations or sacred laws would be needed; everything required to live a hallowed life was there.

Life, however, particularly human life cannot be harnessed within the covers of books, and so it continued to unfold, raising new challenges and needs that demanded new revelations, new laws, and new rules. In the years following Ezra and Nehemiah the Instructions contained in the Torah were amended, complemented, and expanded by later sages and scribes to accommodate the needs of their communities. The stories of the conquest of the Promised Land, the establishment of a sovereign nation with its rulers and kings, the emergence of Prophets who helped shape the behavior and moral compass of the nation, as well as other stories, legends, and traditions, were compiled into a new set of books, some of which were canonized and included in what is known today as the Hebrew Bible. Before the fifth century BCE, there was no Torah and no Jewish canon. By the beginning of the second century, though, a great deal was already there. New legislation and practices were also introduced to the five books of Moses as the changing times and the heterogeneity of the population so demanded.

Now that the Instructions revealed by God to Moses in Sinai were transcribed into books, the community could follow its commands and laws and remain faithful to them as it attempted to find enduring happiness. And while having this set of Instructions available in written form made them more accessible, it did not, as we have seen, make them easier to fulfill on a consistent basis. Nonetheless, for the bulk of the Israelite population living in Judea, the Torah would remain the main pillar supporting their efforts to attain the good life.

CHAPTER 10

The Book of Ecclesiastes
Overcoming the Primordial Illness

BY MOST ACCOUNTS, THE Book of Ecclesiastes appeared sometime during the final quarter of the third century BCE during the reign of the Greek-Egyptian Ptolemies. Centered in Jerusalem, the kingdom of Judea had a precarious autonomy; its citizens were free to practice their religion and customs as long as calm reigned in the land and they paid their taxes. But the influence of Greek culture could be seen everywhere. A priestly aristocracy subservient politically and economically to the foreign occupiers had arisen, which created tensions with Orthodox, pious Jews.

It is in such an environment that the Book of Ecclesiastes emerged to describe the efforts of the preacher Koheleth to quell the suffering permeating his inner world and by extrapolation the inner world of many of his contemporaries. This was a suffering his social status, his many accomplishments, and his vast material successes were unable to dispel.

Koheleth's Pursuit of Enduring Happiness

On first impression, the Book of Ecclesiastes seems to recount the story of a king who sets out to study and to probe all that happens under the sun. By emphasizing wisdom in his efforts, the author of this bewildering book underscores the importance of approaching life's mysteries with intellectual insight and emotional resourcefulness.

The book does not tell us, however, why a man of such privilege and status felt compelled to undertake such an arduous task. Why was it necessary, even imperative, for him to do so? Answering this question becomes particularly relevant when considering the sobering statement with which the author begins his startling tale: "Utter futility," said Koheleth, "Utter futility! All is futile! What real value is there for man in all the gains he makes beneath the sun?" (Eccles. 1:2, 3).

An expression of such abject disillusionment is a most perplexing way to begin a book whose stated purpose is to figure out the meaning of all that happens in the world we are privileged to live in. People who engage in such exploratory quests are wont to conclude that human life is complex, unpredictable, and fraught with cruelty and injustice as well as with immense beauty and awe-inspiring moments, and they may even offer advice as to how to live a more equitable, moral, and healthy life—as Koheleth so eloquently did—but they are not expected to end their journeys by asserting that their inquiries and investigations amounted to nothing more than a pursuit of the wind (Eccles. 2:17).

While many aspects of human life may often seem wrong—the finitude of our mental and physical capacities as well as our lives, the inevitability of errors that can bring great despair into our lives and the lives of our loved ones, the unconscionable cruelty of humans toward each other and their environment—they do not necessarily translate into feelings of futility and a sense that one's efforts to find understanding and meaning are worthless. The fact that it did for Koheleth, and that he ends his quest showing profound disillusionment, attests to the reality that something other than just intellectual curiosity, inquisitiveness, or an abstract desire for understanding was driving his effort. Koheleth's expression of futility (or vanity) suggests he entered his journey harboring concrete expectations as to what he hoped to attain at the end of it. There was something tangible he was after, something he wanted, something that would significantly change the quality of his life and hence carried great importance for him. What that something was is never revealed to us, as he never attained it.

Koheleth's frequent expressions of frustration and disappointment with the way life had unfolded for him allows us to conclude that despite his many accomplishments and successes, and despite his position of power and prestige, he was a man experiencing inner turmoil. His disquieting feelings would reach such heights that on one occasion he even expressed a loathing of life.

But why, one may ask, would a man enjoying so many gifts and privileges experience so much angst? Why would someone who has power, riches, fame, prestige, recognition, and so much more feel a need to engage in a quest for understanding the created world? That destitute, dispossessed, oppressed, needy, enslaved men would harbor such feelings is understandable, but the son of David, king in Jerusalem? And why would such a man invest so much energy in pursuing abstractions when having so many critical responsibilities to fulfill as king, husband, and father?

One possible explanation is that Koheleth suffered from what in contemporary times we would call clinical depression, a condition causing him to feel unhappy and despondent even though his life was filled with good fortune and wonderful accomplishments. Depression is a condition affecting hundreds of millions of people today, and it was surely misunderstood and unrecognized in Koheleth's time. People affected by it may experience life as a continuous torment, especially when they fail to overcome their condition by whichever means they try. These people may likely go on quests for answers, but regardless of what they learn they never feel their inner emptiness has been conquered. These are people who feel alone in a crowd. The text, however, decisively refutes such a presumption by sharing with us the immense satisfaction and joyfulness Koheleth felt when attaining many of the things he set out to examine. For example, when exploring the materialistic and hedonistic way of life, he expresses great satisfaction in both the wealth and power he amassed and in the many pleasures he allowed himself to experience. In fact, he categorically affirms having withheld nothing he desired; rather, he got enjoyment out of all his undertakings (Eccles. 2:10). Depressed people are not able to enjoy many of the pleasures of life. In fact, the hallmark of depression is a blunted affect in response to events others find exciting and joyful, a condition from which he most definitely did not seem to suffer.

Over the years, religious authorities and biblical scholars have tried to counteract the bewildering assertions Koheleth makes throughout the book by offering a more positive interpretation of their meaning and in this way deflect the overwhelming sense of hopelessness that Koheleth displays when he realizes the worthlessness of all that he could attain during his short excursion in the world into which he had been born.

The celebrated biblical commentator Metzudad David suggests, for example, that the futility Koheleth describes throughout the book refers to a feeling common in those "who try to find enduring fulfillment (happiness) in the rewards offered by the world that came into existence during the seven days of creation."[1] Others have tried to twist the meaning of Koheleth's words by suggesting that the Hebrew word "havel" should be translated to mean "emptiness"—as in empty of *meaning*—rather than the more traditional "futility or vanity." Then Koheleth's assertions could easily be seen as a thoughtful warning against the uselessness of seeking meaning in all that is impermanent—material possessions, power, physical youthfulness, the pleasures of the hedonistic life, and so forth.[2] Gordis, on the other hand, while acknowledging Koheleth's loss of faith in both the triumph of justice in this world and in man's ability to fathom the meaning of it all, also asserts that man's fundamental purpose in life is to further his pleasure, his happiness. So to rescue Koheleth from his despair, and for that matter, all the rest of us, he states that while man has an innate desire for happiness, and this impulse was implanted in man by none other than God Himself, its satisfaction does not depend on man's abilities, suggesting we must simply accept our lot even if it may cause us to feel defeated and deflated.[3]

Finding such convenient interpretations for Koheleth's blunt and courageous statements may be comforting to some, but they ignore facts: Koheleth was not a man given to mincing words, and he never asserted any of these purported meanings in the course of his repetitious narrative, even though he had many opportunities to do so. He could have easily stated, for instance, that after decades of pursuing pleasure, power, wealth, and spiritual meaning in the material world he discovered that only by dedicating himself to obeying God's commandments and precepts and to loving Him unconditionally could he experience the enduring happiness he sought. In fact, one of the most revealing features of Koheleth's narrative is his omission of many established tenets of Jewish faith and tradition, presumably because they were ineffective in helping him attain what he searched for with so much vehemence.

Koheleth could have also said that after pursuing transient goods his yearnings for happiness always ended in frustration, but once he understood that only the present mattered, he was able to focus on the moment and become a free, relaxed, and a persistently happy man. But none of this is conveyed by his text. To the contrary, Koheleth insistently reaffirmed his displeasure with his life and with the events he witnessed during his sojourn under the sun.

The Seeker of Wisdom

A more realistic and accurate perspective on Koheleth is to see him as a man driven by feelings of frustration, sorrow, and even despondency that had been lurking in the recesses of his being, possibly from early on. And it was precisely the *persistent nature* of these unpleasant feelings that compelled him, and continues to compel many of us now, to seek resolution for this unremitting state of existential discomfort.

Unfortunately, states of persistent despair can often be hidden from conscious awareness for a long time, either by repression and/or displacement onto others, so that those harboring such feelings can continue to function in the world and pretend all is well. As Koheleth so eloquently stated in his book, "A man's wisdom lights up his face, so that his deep discontent is dissembled" (Eccles. 8:1). This disconnection from our deep discontent and our psycho-spiritual resources is why we often find ourselves searching for some "holy grail" (an external supernatural power) to enlighten and give us the understanding and happiness we so ardently seek, when in fact that which can offer us these most valued treasures lies deep within us, in our inner sanctum. Once those who seek happiness by searching for meaning in the outer world come to understand this truth they are able to see that their lives have been conditioned by an array of beliefs and dogmas impressed upon them by the cultural climate in which they live as well as by personal experiences that have caused them to lose self-esteem and self-worth. It is these entrenched dogmatic systems of belief that are responsible for evoking the inner distress they feel and which they have been trying to overcome by ineffectively looking outside of their selves and into the world out there.

One can feel some measure of confidence when making assertions such as these about someone like Koheleth because people who feel safe, secure, and comfortable in their skin do not spend their fleeting time on earth chasing after purpose, presence of mind, or any other type of admirable goal, for these are already firmly in their possession. Their inner world is fairly calm, comfortable, and integrated and they are satisfied with the array of complex experiences life offers them. This, however, was not Koheleth's reality; his writings reveal a stark dissonance between the bountiful goodness surrounding his outer life and the distress perturbing his inner one.

Based on these realizations we can reasonably conclude that Koheleth was seeking what every human being desires: feeling comfortable, safe, loved, and at ease in his physical body and his social milieu. Saddled with a suffering he could not shake, he yearned to achieve a state of mind imbued with those positive feelings we all aspire to. From such a perspective the Book of Ecclesiastes gives voice for the first and only time in biblical discourse to the remarkable efforts by a prominent Israelite to attain the most coveted of human goals—enduring happiness.

Koheleth's notorious inability to overcome his existential angst can be explained in part by the way his remarkable quest unfolded. Motivated by a persistent inner distress, he embarked on a journey of discovery, self-motivated and self-directed. Accordingly, it was he who decided to seek erudition as well as to explore the hedonistic life; it was he who avoided Temple worship, instead visiting houses of mourning; it was he who looked into the lives of others at his discretion; it was he who decided what to reflect upon and where and when to do it. At no time during this lengthy excursion do we hear of events intruding unexpectedly into his life and shattering the foundations of belief and trust on which he rested. In other words, his quest for understanding was willfully driven, thus lacking the uncontrolled and unexpected experiences that so often provoke the kind of deep psycho-spiritual jolt that leads to a more wholesome, encompassing, and harmonious vision of reality.

Having concluded after many self-imposed trials and tribulations that what he had yearned for he would not attain, Koheleth encourages us to focus our energies instead on what we can achieve and sustain, if not indefinitely at least for extended periods of time, and in this way squeeze out of life as much as possible, wasting no opportunity to rejoice and cherish the privileges we have been afforded.

Koheleth's story of enduring distress seems emblematic of the kind of suffering humanity's *primordial illness* may impose on its unsuspecting victims. This kind of suffering is rooted in the idea that our unpleasant feelings are caused by our inborn inclination to wrongdoing. So whenever feeling distressed, instead of thinking our feelings appropriate—the fear of injury and death, the stress of knowing vulnerability, the sadness of loss, the guilt of having injured others unintentionally, and so forth—we usually automatically attribute them to having done something reprehensible or devious, whether or not that something is apparent to us. Because the unpleasant feelings associated with man's primordial illness are not caused by unique childhood traumas or psychopathologies residing in parents, family members, and/or friends but rather by a system of beliefs endemic in the population and shared by those administering our mental health care, illnesses such as these are, by definition, incurable, hence impervious to traditional psychotherapeutic maneuvers. Moreover, the suffering provoked by our primordial illness is also resistant to the diverse measures our culture has sanctioned for making us happy and fulfilled, as Koheleth so very aptly demonstrated. Unfortunately, our ancestors bought into the belief—and many of us still do—that we are *inherently bad* and deserving of suffering; this belief has been successfully passed on to our children and grandchildren for centuries. This misguided interpretation of something that is innate, unavoidable, and in fact desirable—by this

I mean the existence of conscious, self-reflective beings aware of their unpleasant feelings—represents an implicit refutation of that which is quintessentially human. Rejecting what our biological nature offers us is no way to breed harmony, peace, self-esteem, and cooperation between us.

Can Man Overcome the Primordial Illness?

To overcome a condition such as the one afflicting Koheleth requires sophisticated skills and resources as well as novel ways of perceiving our human reality. Attributes such as these are likely to emerge as part of an evolutionary process of mental and spiritual differentiation. An excellent example of such a process is detailed in the Book of Job and I have seen it also happen in patients with life-threatening illnesses or people facing serious life crises such as those provoked by the loss of a significant other, the serious illness of a child, a marriage breakdown, or the loss of one's home. This does not mean it will happen invariably but rather that the potential for it to happen is embedded in our human matrix and will become actualized under certain circumstances.

It would be ironic indeed if in the end the reason for Koheleth's failure to attain his ultimate goal was his apparent good fortune. Spared by life's inscrutable and incurable randomness, the challenging unforeseen experiences that thrust some fortunate people into the heights of psychological functioning required for this type of undertaking—few perceive it as such, at least initially—he comes up short. His failure does not imply, however, that his journey was fruitless. To the contrary, his explorations taught him—and indirectly us—a great deal about human life and the human condition and how best to live one's life.

By acknowledging that everything has its proper time, Koheleth underscores the reality that it is not our ego-driven selves that decide when and where such moments occur, but rather something else, a divine presence that perhaps "brings everything to pass precisely at its time" (Eccles. 3:11). Aware that all experiences are part of the grand scheme of things, he admonishes us not to attempt to either add or subtract from any of them. Every experience has a place and a time in our life, regardless of how well or poorly we may understand this truth, for who can know which experience can be safely removed from our lives without significantly affecting the final outcome?

With wrenching honesty, Koheleth alerts us to the fact that the fate of the righteous and the wicked is the same, for we are all mortal. This knowledge turned him into a bit of a cynic, leading him to assert that the fate of beasts and humans are one and the same (Eccles. 3:17, 19, 20). Koheleth's statement can also be interpreted as refuting the idea of the immortality of the soul, implying that all we have is but one pass through this earthly life and once it is over there is no more other than becoming food for worms and maggots, just like all other living creatures. What he fails to acknowledge here, though, is that while humans and beasts die and are buried in the same ground, what distinguishes human life from those of beasts is how the life that we were given was lived: how have we responded to life's vicissitudes? Have we used the awesome mental resources we have been endowed with to foster harmony, peace, and wellness in our personal and collective lives? Did we rise to the lofty spiritual pinnacles that consciousness of self and others allowed us?

Later on, Koheleth reminds us that while humanity yearns for justice and righteousness and is committed to it, injustice and wickedness are commonplace in our daily lives (Eccles. 3:16). In such a world, good people may perish despite their indisputable goodness and wicked people may live long lives despite their overt wickedness. He also came across occurrences that seemed innately twisted, dishonest, and afflicting, for example, the good and the pious, "and for what purpose," he asks (Eccles. 7:15). In a humbling tone, he admits that appeasing the wicked, the troublemakers, and the mentally crazed, or trying to put a more humanistic veneer over their behavior and thus not call them to account for what they do, is a sure recipe for self-destruction and unhappiness. And while aware that those who revered lawfulness were sometimes rewarded, he felt frustrated that upright men were sometimes repaid as if they were scoundrels—and the other way around—which is, of course, utterly unfair (Eccles. 8:11–14). "Use your own judgment," he admonishes us, "and learn to discern the moral value of things. Do not be afraid of doing a little bit of every-thing, always avoiding foolishness because that may indeed mar and at times even shorten your life. Balance is indeed the basis for health-ful living and whatever we do, we must do in moderation and with prudence" (Eccles. 7:16). Noticing the oppression under which many live—tyrannical rulers intimidating people, minorities being ignored and neglected, discriminatory policies being applied against people on the basis of gender, race, religious beliefs, or socioeconomic status—he regrets the absence of support and true interest in helping these people recover their rights and their tranquility (Eccles. 4:1).

Koheleth is also amazingly clear about the fact that man's labor and skillful enterprise, his own included, are often driven by jealousy and envy of others rather than by the desire to do something beautiful and good. People might not perceive or portray their actions in this way, but remaining oblivious to this important human truth, he warned, is a recipe for disaster (Eccles. 4:4).

Of all the things he sees happening beneath the sun, the most damaging is the disregard with which human beings act toward each other and toward the bountiful earth God has entrusted into their care (Eccles. 8:9). And while it is true that some people are indeed fair and just, more are cruel and corrupt. People's unconsciousness fosters in them emotional disconnects that turn them into unrepentant offend-ers. Unable to sense what they have done to others, they may commit great harms while remaining convinced that all they are doing is virtu-ous and good.

Our protagonist's sobering realizations did not prevent him from appreciating how wisdom improved not only the quality but also at times even the length of one's life (Eccles. 2:13; 7:11, 12). "Being in the shelter of wisdom is to be in the shelter of a richness far better than whatever money, power, or social status can offer, because it is a rich-ness that preserves and improves the life of those possessing it," he tells us. "Wise people know, for example, that regardless of how hard they may try they will inevitably err, sometimes with dire consequences for themselves and others" (Eccles. 7:20). That is why the wise reflect on their actions and ask others for assistance. Rather than thinking they are good, righteous, charitable people who will always receive in kind, they ask the beneficiaries of their charitable deeds how they feel about their acts of beneficence. Do these acts make them feel nurtured, loved, cared for? And if not, why not? By doing so, one can avoid the folly of acting as both executor and judge of one's behavior. Self-reflection is essential for healthy living—but when dealing with others, it is equally important to know how they feel and think.

Koheleth's Recommendations for Healthy Living

As Koheleth's understanding of human existence evolved he began to glimpse a broader reality, the complexities and beauty of which further revealed themselves as his enlightening experiences unfolded. As he so well put it, "Just as you do not know how the life breath passes into the womb of the pregnant woman, so you cannot foresee the actions of the forces causing all things to happen" (Eccles. 11:5). Life is a mystery, he seemed to be saying, and trying to fit its myriad manifestations into a narrow frame is simply foolish. Nonetheless, being the acute observer of human life that he was, and a dedicated thinker, he managed to discover human virtues and principles of interpersonal relationship that would lead those following them to a healthier and more comforting way of life.

The virtues and principles he reveals in his book are new to the biblical narrative and expand upon those embodied in the Ten Commandments Moses presented to the Israelite community in Horeb. Koheleth's prescriptions for well-living are devoid of laws, commands, or rules. They are simply principles of comportment that stand out on their own merit. They are presented to the human community by a human voice speaking on its behalf, a voice that does not promise rewards to those who follow the principles or severe punishments to those who fail to live by them. For Koheleth, those abiding by his norms of behavior do so because they are motivated by the feelings of gratification and overall goodness that doing so brings to their yearning hearts. We can imagine Koheleth, a preacher, investing himself in teaching these virtues and principles of behavior to all those who were willing to listen to him, at the same time doing his best teaching by practicing them himself, and thus serving as a model for others to emulate.

By exhorting us to respect our promises to others and to never forget that when we vow to do something it creates an expectation that if not satisfied will surely disappoint and sadden, Koheleth reminds us that it is better to abstain from making vows than to dishearten others—and us in return—by failing to follow through (Eccles. 5:3, 4). By the same token, he urges us to avoid rashness of speech because it is seldom beneficial. Before responding verbally or in writing to something we hear or read, or to words that may have formulated themselves quickly in our minds, we must take time to digest what we are about to say because once words leave our mouth, they cannot be retrieved. Saying little in a measured and thoughtful way is always preferable to unleashing a stream of disjointed speech that may cause us disfavor with others. But if we do misspeak, let us not pretend we didn't say it or mean it but instead acknowledge it, apologize, and avoid repeating it in the future (Eccles. 10:12, 13).

Another of his teachings reminds us that some people will be blessed with material riches while others, no matter what they do, will remain poor. But if blessed with material abundance we must avoid hoarding and misusing our possessions (Eccles. 5:1, 2, 5, 12, 13). Regarding greed, however, he was emphatic: "It is an undesirable trait and should be avoided. Don't be surprised, though," he would add, "if those who love money never have their fill of it, and those who love spending it will have never spent enough . . . Working, earning our keep, and satisfying our bodily needs makes sleep come easy to us, even when what we have is little, but when having too much of anything sleep will come hard. For once a large stash of money has been amassed, who wants to lose it? So if we find ourselves in this situation, we must get out of it. Otherwise, we may end up spending a great deal of our precious and irreplaceable time worrying about how to preserve our fortune rather than enjoying our well-earned blessings" (Eccles. 5:9, 11).

In no uncertain terms, Koheleth reminds us that whether or not material possessions are part of our endowment, we must cultivate a good name for it is worth more than any material possession we may ever attain. Being thought of as an honest, fair, caring, generous, compassionate, and loving person is the greatest asset we can attain under the sun (Eccles. 7:1).

Finally, Koheleth admonishes us never to forget, when attending a house of mourning, that death is our irrevocable destiny; thus we should use the opportunity to appreciate the life we have been given (Eccles. 7:2–4).

Bearing in mind the richness of his discoveries we can envision Koheleth retiring at some point in his life to a quiet place and turning his many observations and realizations into maxims left for posterity. Had he done something like that he would have left a carefully crafted guide for how future generations could live a more wholesome life based on what they could learn if they were willing to follow his path and explore, ask difficult questions, challenge the status quo, and overcome the prejudices and narrowness of vision instilled in them during childhood.

Such a guide would enjoin us to live each moment as if it were our last because it could be; to eat our meals and drink our wine with joy and gladness in our heart; to revere the company of the women or men we love and express our love for them in every way we can; to avoid bothering with things we can't control; and when the opportunity arises to act, to do so. Similarly, he would exhort us never to forget that words are powerful weapons and their effects can often last forever. To challenge God's world—the world of nature—is a draining, futile experience that leads nowhere. It is better to conserve our energy and keep vital and strong within the bounds of the knowable and the possible.

In closing, he would invite us to follow his recommendations for healthy living and avoid falling into the trap of expecting fairness, justice, or equanimity to prevail in this world, because it doesn't and it probably never will. That is why races will not necessarily be won by the swift, battles by the valiant, or bread received by the wise (Eccles. 9:11). And if unspeakable atrocities have happened to exemplary people then we can rest assured they can happen to us too.

Lastly, Koheleth reminds us not to forget but to observe the commandments and precepts we have been told God revealed to Moses. While they won't protect us from misfortune or help us attain enduring happiness—at least they didn't help Koheleth—they may make our journey less weary and painful.

Epilogue

Despite Koheleth's profound wisdom and his insightful observations about human life and nature, enduring happiness was not something he was able to achieve. His lasting legacy, in fact, is to alert us to the reality that attaining it is not something that can be willed.

Accepting his legacy may save us years if not decades of striving for things that in the end will disappoint. It is not that attaining material wealth, indulging in pleasurable things, becoming well educated, and being reflective and curious about life and the world are useless pursuits because they surely are not—and were not for him. Each and every one of these pursuits gave him satisfaction and joyfulness; nonetheless, they did not give him what he really wanted—happiness.

Koheleth's stark (and irrefutable) views on life did not preclude him from entering into a state of enlightened resignation toward the end of his journey. Having experienced a considerable expansion of his knowledge and understanding of life, his existence seems to have become easier and more pleasant. Nonetheless, the stark realities of his inner life kept creeping up to the surface once his daily responsibilities quieted down, reminding him that the world was not, as he had wished it to be, his oyster.

From a paradigmatic standpoint, the traditional, covenantal agreement that had guided Israelite life for centuries paradoxically had started to break down almost from the moment it was emanated and did break almost entirely for Koheleth. Saddled with persistent mental distress, he was unable to find solace in the ideas and beliefs supported by the traditional religious worldview in vogue at the time he set out to find a new understanding of man's relationship to himself, to others, and to their imagined God, an understanding that would relieve his angst and his pain. But his journey did not yield a final resolution; it did not hit the desired mark. Nonetheless, Koheleth left a legacy of understanding of the human condition that is deeply moving and realistic, one that offered his contemporaries and the generations that followed a clearer picture of what they could expect during their life on earth and how much they could contribute to better their lot.

It is unknown whether the author of the Book of Ecclesiastes was familiar with the Book of Job, written a few centuries earlier. If he was, he clearly missed identifying—as have most others ever since—the pathway to healing that book offered. It is possible, though, that rather than having missed the teachings in Job, what Koheleth offers is an alternative, a less ambitious, more doable pathway, one that can add a great deal to man's efforts to reduce his suffering and one everyone can undertake without having to go through any major physical or psychological crisis.

Unfortunately, the human collective living during the time this book appeared was not prepared to embrace its excellent contributions to the betterment of human life. Individual members may have been able to appreciate its wisdom and use it to their benefit, but not the community at large. In the meantime, in the years following the appearance of the wisdom books, the sociopolitical conditions under which the people lived became so oppressive they led to a profound dislocation in the socioeconomic status of the population. A powerful and wealthy aristocracy for whom adherence to the covenantal tradition had worked just fine emerged together with an increasing proportion of the population that felt disenfranchised, oppressed, and poor, a population that needed something else to lift their mood. Having worsened over time, their living conditions propitiated the emergence of an apocalyptic literature over the last two centuries before the beginning of the Common Era—the Book of Daniel and noncanonical books like the Book of Enoch—and later on the emergence of men like Hillel the Elder and Yeshua of Nazareth, who embodied the energy of Sophia, the feminine consort of God, His helper from time immemorial and the purveyor of love, passion, and compassion. After having erupted in full strength in the life of exemplary Job, this powerful energy vanished from public prominence for centuries to reappear once again in the lives and ministry of these powerful agents of social and spiritual transformation.

PART IV

Redemption at Last:
The Rightness of Being Human

CHAPTER 11

The Book of Daniel

The Redemption of Man's Suffering

THE SECOND CENTURY BCE was marred by tension and strife for the Judean population. It was a time in which the religious freedom they had enjoyed under previous rulers was threatened by the actions of Antiochus IV, who built altars to pagan gods on sacred grounds and forbade the reading of the Torah and the practice of circumcision. Not surprisingly, a book aimed at rekindling the image of an all-powerful yet merciful God capable of redeeming the Israelites' suffering came to light. The book I am referring to is the Book of Daniel, which not only affirmed the hegemony of the Israelite God—YHWH—over all other deities worshipped in the Levant (a large area in Southwest Asia bounded by Turkey in the north, the Mediterranean Sea in the west, and Mesopotamia and the north of the Arabian peninsula in the east) but, more importantly, prophesied the coming of a glorious era for the Israelite nation at the end of time.

In Daniel, centuries of war, affliction, and utter devastation are foretold for the human community. During this lengthy period cruelty, violence, and misery would attain unprecedented heights, and yet this terrible period was to be followed by an extraordinary one—the end of time, in which peace and goodness would reign in all quarters of the earth.

Daniel's Unusual Powers Help Restore God's Authority among the People

Considering the level of distress afflicting the Judean population they surely had no good reason to continue believing either in the just nature of their mythical God or His ability to change their terrible fate. Under such stressful conditions, getting the people to trust in pronouncements coming from the Divine was rather difficult.

Overcoming this justifiable resistance in the Judean population would require a profound rehabilitation of the tarnished image of their God, who for centuries had been unable to help them restore their lost freedoms. The Book of Daniel accomplishes this skillfully by providing irrefutable proof that the Israelite God was indeed sovereign over life and death and thus able to defy all odds. It does so by showing that when three Israelites who refused to bow to the Babylonian king's statue and worship him as a god are dropped into a fiery furnace they emerge totally unharmed, not even the odor of fire clinging to their bodies (Dan. 3:3–6, 12–27).

A second such proof becomes manifest when Daniel, one of the Judean citizens living in exile, is forced to spend the night in the lion's den for having transgressed some ill-conceived royal decree. The king, overcome with deep anguish, for Daniel was very important to him, rushes to the lion's den the next morning and finds, to his great relief, that Daniel is unscathed. By way of contrast, his accusers, when placed under identical conditions in the den, are immediately slaughtered by the beast. Evidently, it was Daniel's God, and not the lion's ferocity or the furnace's high temperature, that determined who lived and who died.

A further rehabilitation of the Israelite's image of God occurs when profound prophetic visions disturb the sleep of the Babylonian kings. These visions prophesy not only the fate of the kings and their kingdoms but also what humanity in general and the Israelite people, in particular, are going to endure; and only Daniel, through revelation from God, was able to decipher the meaning of the mysterious and terrifying visions afflicting the magistrates. In one of the visions, for example, Nebuchadnezzar is told how his haughtiness and presumptuousness will cause him to lose his serenity and sanity, a process that was to last for years before his general wellness and mental health would be restored to him by the grace of God Almighty. A few years later, the king's son, his successor to the throne, received a vision foretelling him of the fall of his kingdom as a result of his disrespect for the God of Israel, which lo and behold occurs precisely on the day Daniel discloses to him the meaning of his precognitive experience (Dan. 5:25–30).

Awe-inspiring occurrences such as these later on prompt King Darius, the Persian monarch then ruling the Babylonian empire, to order the inhabitants of his royal domain to tremble in fear before the God of Daniel, for He is the living God who endures forever, whose kingdom is indestructible, and His dominion is to the end of time (Dan. 6:27). Darius's assertions helped restore the image of the Hebrew God to a position of power and distinction among the exiles, assisting the Judean people in reestablishing their confidence in a better future for they could now see their God as one whose supremacy and grandeur were worth their renewed reverence and trust.

But what exerted the greatest influence on the Judean community in reinstating confidence in the Israelite God was the revelation, through visions and dreams received by Daniel himself, of what was in store for man at the end of time. Despite centuries of affliction, knowing they would be the beneficiaries of His magnanimity at a future time heightened the Israelite faith in the prophecy their God had presumably revealed through these nightly occurrences.

Possessed now of a myth that explained how the happiness that had eluded them for so long was to be eventually restored, they must have felt reassured and hopeful.

The utopian vision described in the Book of Daniel gave testimony to the profound yearning for a sustainable collective peace and happiness in ancestral Israel. Its content reassured man that the loss of integrity and self-worth he experienced at the beginning of time—immortalized by the curse God levied on Adam and Eve and all their descendants—was to be redeemed, if not immediately at least at the end of time. Man's task was to remain optimistic and maintain his faith regardless of how difficult life became for he knew now that a reckoning of apocalyptic proportions was in the offing and, with it, the final resolution of the pain and despair he had experienced since emerging into the light of consciousness thousands of years before.

Toward the end of the popular musical *Fiddler on the Roof*, the people of Anatevka, a small village in Eastern Europe where Jewish families had lived for generations, are forced to leave their homes for the simple reason that they are Jews and are not wanted there any longer. As they proceed to collect the few belongings they can manage to take with them, one of the villagers turns toward the local rabbi, asking him with great anticipation, "Rabbi, we've been waiting for the Messiah all our lives. Wouldn't *this* be a good time for him to come?" To which the rabbi responds, "We'll have to wait for him . . . someplace else."[1] Clearly, despite the great injustice that was being levied against them and the outrage, anger, and frustration they surely felt, the rabbi's faith in a better tomorrow in some unknown place did not seem to wane. We can imagine him saying something like, "Only God knows when that time will come, but it will arrive one day soon, for sure."

For more than two thousand years of living in the Diaspora, the Jewish people were sustained by their strong and enduring faith. Neither the absence of a home they could call their own nor the centuries of the anti-Semitic violence and destruction to which their communities had been subjected broke their faith in a glorious tomorrow. The resistance some ultra-Orthodox Jews exhibit today against recognizing the legitimacy of the State of Israel is rooted in their deeply held belief that the prophesy of a Messiah coming and redeeming the people of Israel at the end of time is literal. Anything less, like attaining statehood as a result of human enterprise and determination, represents an outrage against God's will and, hence, is unacceptable to them.

Daniel Transforms from Prophet to Healer of Souls

Daniel's awareness of what was in store for his people and humanity at large had a profound effect on his persona. From being a seer and interpreter of visions and dreams who proclaimed God's word to magistrates and commoners alike, he now became a redeemer/healer/sage seeking relief for his suffering people, whatever the cost. The catalyst for this profound transformation seems to have been the eruption of perturbing prophetic visions, this time disturbing *his* nighttime rest. Before, when acting as God's Prophet, his job was to decipher the bewildering dreams perturbing the calm of the Babylonian kings. As such, he assumed the mantle of a wise, emotionally detached interpreter capable of explaining the meaning of these visions. But now, as the recipient of these perturbing manifestations, it is he who is deeply unsettled by the visions, he who is having powerful emotional responses to them, and he who is tasked with deciphering their significance.

Knowing that Jerusalem was to remain desolate for seventy years caused him to become terribly dispirited and depressed. Daniel's suffering is akin to that of someone, an elder perhaps, who, having seen with clarity what is in store not only for himself but for all those he loves and deeply cares for, wants to prevent their suffering as well as his own, to stop the destructiveness that has taken hold of them, to do something immediately and thus alter the undesirable outcome he envisions forthcoming. Yet it is not within his capacity to affect the future. So turning himself toward heaven—both the one without and the one within—he solicits forgiveness in prayer, fasting, sackcloth, and ashes.

While imploring mercy from God, Daniel assumes responsibility for everything happening in his world, confessing with devastating honesty the transgressions his people have committed against Him. "All Israel has violated Your teachings, and gone astray disobeying You," he clamors. "So the curse and the oath written into the Teachings of Moses, your loyal servant, have been poured down upon us, for we have sinned against You . . . O our God, hear now the prayer of Your humble servant and his plea, and show Your favor to Your desolate sanctuary, if nothing more than for Your own sake" (Dan. 9:11, 17). Daniel's plea rents the heart. His contrite tone evokes feelings of love and compassion for him and for the suffering people he is asking God to pardon. One can easily imagine similar feelings being evoked in the Divine Being, to whom Daniel's prayers are directed. By confessing the people's sins with genuine repentance, Daniel is trying to rouse God's bountiful mercy and His natural inclination to forgive, and thus bring solace to their ailing souls. But Daniel was not the kind of healer that could embody the healing energy, at least not yet. Instead, he depended upon an external source to touch the bodies of members of his community, so, in lieu of respite for himself and others, his plea is followed by a visitation from a figure that identifies himself as the angel Gabriel.

This humanlike angelic presence tells Daniel that the painful process the people were enduring could not be altered or for that matter shortened. He reassures Daniel, though, that his prayers are being heard and, in time, will be properly rewarded. In the end, eternal righteousness will indeed be ushered in, and the Holy of Holies anointed.

Daniel is profoundly afflicted when hearing the angel Gabriel affirm that desolation had been decreed for humanity until men end all wars. "When might that be?" he seems to be asking. Daniel's supplication for mercy and forgiveness has not measurably improved the Israelites' burden. But his initial failure to amend what he perceived as God's terrible decree does not stop him from continuing to try. "Perhaps, if I show God how remorseful I am, how willing to deprive myself of all joy," we can imagine Daniel thinking, "His heart will soften and I and the rest of us will be forgiven from having to endure His wrathful, although well-deserved judgment." Months later, he observes three full weeks of mourning and fasting using a regimen that excluded tasty food or wine or any meat that might bring pleasure to his body. Daniel's actions are rewarded once again with a new vision that temporarily drains his vigor.

As the vision unfolds, Daniel is overcome by a deep slumber and finds himself prostrated on the ground. While in this altered state of consciousness he feels a hand grabbing him and a dreamy voice saying, "Have no fear, Daniel, because from the first day you set yourself to gain understanding and practiced abstinence before your God, your prayers were heard, and I am here with you because of it." "But how can God's servant speak with my Lord, seeing that my strength has failed me and no spirit is left in me?" Daniel replies. Feeling the touch of a humanlike figure again, he hears it say, "Have no fear, precious man, all will be well with you; be strong, be strong!" (Dan. 10:12, 17–19).

A short time later, strength does indeed return to his body, and his mind becomes a bit clearer. Now able to accept the countless battles and acts of cruelty, strife, instability, and uncertainty the human community must still endure to attain its lofty ends, he finally comprehends why things will need to get worse before they get better. His desire for things to turn around fast and the community to thrive again will have to be patient for they need first to hit rock bottom before transformative changes can have a chance to take hold. And when they do, they will usher in an era of peace and happiness. Then the righteous will be recognized and valued by others, the blessings of eternal life bestowed upon those who have suffered undeservedly and on those whose lives ended prematurely; those who have lived wickedly will be condemned to everlasting misery. General knowledge will also increase, leading to the establishment of a significantly more educated, wiser human community, one better able to care for itself and live harmoniously, cooperatively, and in peace.

Able to see this glorious future, Daniel yearns to know precisely when such a wonderful time will arrive. The answer he receives from heaven, however, is cryptic, prompting him to press on for further clarification, which turns out to be fruitless. The most he is able to discern is that this glorious time will happen after his death because he is to be among those who would be resurrected and raised to their destiny—although what that destiny was remained shrouded in mystery. Knowing that at the end of time people would better understand what happened to them and would feel their lives more meaningful and balanced assuages Daniel. The wicked, as expected, would remain ignorant and blind to what caused their downfall, and while this saddened him it was also fitting and just, for ignorance is terribly damaging in this complex world of ours.

Daniel's bewildering vision gives expression to his developing awareness that to experience redemption from suffering one has to reach the nadir of one's descent into despair. Only then can one begin to peel off the thicker layers of denial and rejection of reality one has carried and learn to see the world in broader, more realistic terms. From this emerging perspective, the misery that Daniel and others still needed to endure was precisely what was required for redemption to set in. A part of Daniel knows that what was presaged for humanity was incredibly painful but also healing, and thus he was encouraged to stay strong and faithful to the process for ultimately it would lead him and his people to the outcome he so wishes for.

While Daniel's prophesies came to him in the form of visions and dreams, it is quite possible that a good part of their content may have been historical; in other words, they described events that had taken place during the three hundred years between the time in which the Book of Daniel was written and the time in which Daniel presumably lived. The prophecy addressing events to take place at the end of time, however, was a novel addition to the biblical narrative, affirming in the strongest of terms that regardless of how much power kings may amass over time, how strong their armies may become, how much land they may conquer, or how much fear they may sow in people's hearts, these were unsustainable gains. Eventually, these oppressors and destroyers would be vanquished, and an era in which love, cooperation, and friendship prevailed would be ushered in, an era in which suffering would be nothing more than an unwelcome memory.

Daniel's utopian vision may have helped his community maintain hope, but it did not assuage the pain and misery they were experiencing in the here and now. Their lives continued to be dominated by a God who seemed to judge them severely and from a distance. His compassionate side, while revealing itself at times, still did not express itself often enough to make a significant impact on the quality of their lives. Feeling uncared for, disenfranchised, and forgotten, a sizable segment of the population clamored for more immediate relief.

It took less than two centuries after the appearance of the Book of Daniel—an inordinately long time for suffering individuals, their families, and communities, but a rather short one in evolutionary terms—for new mythical figures to emerge in the Jewish tableau. They embodied forgiveness and compassion, attributes of soul that were now brought to the forefront of man's effort to overcome his despair and hopefully break the hold that those upholding the harsh, legalistic aspects of the tradition had on the social, political, and religious life of Judean society.

CHAPTER 12

The Role of Jeshua/Jesus in
Overcoming Suffering

AS PREDICTED BY THE Prophet Daniel, oppression, violence, and destruction were commonplace during the last two centuries BCE. The seventy years of desolation prophesied for Jerusalem were long gone and the era of everlasting happiness that was supposed to follow had not arrived (Dan. 9:2). Jews continued to live under the yoke of foreign rulers and, while showing courage and a dogged determination to regain their freedom, their successes were costly and short-lived.

During this long stretch of time, the Prophets who spoke in the name of the Israelite God had essentially disappeared (their influence may have waned, given the circumstances facing the people), and His loving and forgiving voice was nowhere to be found. This absence must have created the impression among the citizenry that once again their God had retracted Himself to some distant place, away from earthly things and from caring about their suffering.

This was also a time in which the widening gap in socioeconomic status had increased in Judean society, with the rich becoming richer and the poor and downtrodden ever more destitute. To further compound this terrible situation, tensions were flaring up between Judahites who had embraced the Greek culture and become Hellenized and those who felt horrified by what this foreign culture was doing to their tradition. The result was violence between brethren, triggering an equally violent crackdown on the Judean population by their Greek and later on their Roman masters. The loss of life this brought forth further rent the already fractionalized community.

From the perspective of Israel's ever-evolving and complex relationship with their created God, the citizens of Judea must have been at least vaguely aware of the calamities their supposedly "just" God had inflicted upon men of unblemished character, such as was the case with a man like Job. Unable to discern the affirmative, healing message embedded in Job's saga, the actions attributed to God must have seemed outrageous and unconscionable. In his book *Answer to Job*, Carl Jung suggested that a divine debt against humanity was incurred, one that the suffering Judeans expected their God to pay back in full.[1]

In the last century BCE the Judean community consisted of an amalgam of more than twenty-four different religious sects, the major ones being the Pharisees, the Sadducees, and the Essenes, each with their unique set of beliefs and practices. The Pharisees were the largest group and, while socially conservative, were religiously liberal, tending to embrace the more lenient interpretations of Torah Law. The Sadducees, on the other hand, were a rather small but highly influential group, both politically and religiously. They included members of the aristocracy and the religious and political elite. Socially liberal, they embraced Hellenistic culture freely, but their religious practices were Orthodox and strict. The Essenes, on the other hand, were a community of men and women who had withdrawn from political life, establishing themselves in small communes where they lived a more contemplative, ascetic kind of existence. Essenes believed in a divinely sent Messiah, in the resurrection, in the afterlife, and in the ultimate punishment of the wicked. They had also introduced rituals of purification, such as baptism, into religious practice, as a way to symbolically wash away people's sins. John the Baptist (Johanan in Hebrew) was thought to be a member of this sect.

These complex socioeconomic and psycho-spiritual conditions constituted the matrix on which the numinous figure of Jeshua of Nazareth appeared. The life of historical Jeshua is shrouded in mystery, and we may never be able to decipher it with any empirical accuracy. What is clear, though, is that the authors of the Gospels perceived him as the incarnation of God in a human body for the purpose of serving as a sacrificial lamb for the expiation of Israel's sins.

According to Jung, each of us lives in two complementary realities (or truths): a physical one, based on empirically derived information, and a second, subjective one, based on belief and faith. This second category of truth is psychical and can neither be explained, proved, nor contested on empirical grounds.[2] From such a perspective we can unequivocally say that regardless of who Jeshua might have been objectively—that is to say, historically—subjectively he was, and still is, a psychic truth, a product of human imagination and, more importantly, of human need. The fact that his numinous image has endured for millennia attests to the critical need it fulfilled then and continues to fulfill now for the more than one billion people who embrace him as their savior.

Jeshua according to the Gospels

The picture painted of Jeshua by the Gospels is inspirational; it must have felt highly reassuring to those hungering for someone capable of turning their miserable lives around. According to the Gospel of John, Jeshua was not only the Son of God but also a figure exuding *grace and truth* (John 1:14). His coming was not simply fortuitous, it was announced in advance by Johanan (John) the Baptist, a charismatic Jewish teacher who proclaimed to all those ready to listen that among the Israelites stood "the one" who was the Lamb of God and who had come to take away the sins of the world (John 1:15, 29). The lamb was a valued possession in the Israelite tradition and was given as a sin offering to substitute for the real sinner and pay for his transgression (Lev. 16:9, 10).

Centuries earlier someone writing in the name of the Prophet Isaiah described a man raised by God to serve as a sacrificial lamb for the sins of others. The man so described by Isaiah had been grown by God "like a tree trunk out of arid ground" and represented the prototypical antihero: "despised, shunned by men, a man of suffering, of sorrows, familiar with disease and misery" (Isa. 53:3). And even though he had done no injustice against men and had spoken no falsehood against God, he was to carry the people's sickness and their suffering in his being. He was a man God had smote not because he deserved it but rather as a way—perhaps the only way—to atone for the sinfulness and iniquities of all his evildoing brethren. While the chastisement God had levied against this man of sorrows caused him to suffer profoundly, it had beneficial effects on the community for it promoted the healing of their bodily wounds and the attainment of their spiritual calmness (Isa. 53:4–10).

Isaiah's prophesy, motivated perhaps by the state of mental oppression and desperation prevalent in his community, gave voice to a growing feeling that man had reached an irremediable impasse in his efforts to overcome suffering: he was simply incapable of attaining redemption through his personal efforts. A credible alternative was needed, one sanctioned by God and dependent on His powers and not on those of fallible man.

Imagining God favoring the appearance of a man of sorrows who was ready to sacrifice his well-being and his life for the sake of his brethren, especially if this was a preamble for the coming of an era of everlasting peace and happiness, must have been highly comforting and reassuring to some members of the Judean community.

Echoes of the same kind of mythical idea can be found in the writings of the Prophet Malachi, who lived presumably during the time of Ezra and Nehemiah and the Persian rule over Judea, a later time than Isaiah. In the concluding verses of his book, Malachi said: "Lo, I will send the Prophet Elijah to you before the coming of the awesome, fearful day of the Lord. He shall reconcile parents with children and children with their parents, so that when I come, I do not strike the whole land with utter destruction" (Mal. 3:23, 24). Elijah is thus portrayed as someone who brings healing to the soul of people before the dawn of the kingdom of heaven. So the idea of a man of sorrows both willing to carry the community's sins and capable of healing personal and interpersonal wounds was already in the collective consciousness centuries before the arrival of Jeshua. It is not surprising, therefore, that the authors of the Gospels used those writings as proof of the soundness of their assertion that Jeshua of Nazareth was indeed the man of sorrows announced so much earlier by Isaiah; he was the expected redeemer of the people's misery, the Christ (the anointed, in ancient Greek).

Given that he was God incarnate, the writers of the Gospels portray Jeshua as a man of power, able to perform acts defying explanation, as one would expect of a God. These acts included feeding thousands of hungry people with a few loaves of bread and a fish, walking on water, restoring sight to the blind and health to dying children and grown men who had been sick for decades, exorcising demons, and even resurrecting a man from his death. All the terrible, unwelcome, frightening things Judean society had been wrestling with for centuries and would do anything to avoid—incurable illnesses, hunger, poverty, violence, permanent disabilities, and death—Jeshua was able to conquer just through his faith. He had no need for medicines, medical procedures, or any of the methods used by ordinary human beings to deal with such insurmountable challenges. He had been granted the authority to perform miracles by his Father in heaven, proving beyond reasonable doubt that he was the anointed one, the one sent by God to redeem all those who would have faith in Him.

Jeshua is also portrayed in these books as a profoundly compassionate and just being. So when an adulterous woman is brought to him by scribes and Pharisees asking him to stone her according to Mosaic Law, he responds by saying, "If there is one of you who has not sinned, let him be the first to throw a stone at her" (John 8:7).

Confirming to his disciples and followers that he is the anointed one, he forewarns them of the danger they face if they do not accept him as their savior: "You are from below and I am from above," he tells them. "You are of this world; I am not of this world. I have told you already: you will die in your sins. Yes, if you do not believe that I am He, you will die in your sins" (John 8:23, 24).

The path to salvation offered by Jeshua was not only inclusive but one that, by and large, relieved the people of the burden of having to fulfill difficult commandments and precepts to gain it. To be rewarded with everlasting life in a blissful tomorrow no longer required being part of the people God had chosen originally. All that was required now was embracing the belief that the same God that once entered into a sacred covenant with the people of Israel had now sent His son to earth to offer salvation to all those willing to recognize him as Messiah. However, this did not exempt the people from having to fulfill the Law and behave in moral ways. For example, in the Gospel according to Matthew we hear Jeshua state, "Do not imagine I have come to abolish the Law and the Prophets. I tell you solemnly, till heaven and earth disappear, not one dot, not one little stroke, shall disappear from the law until its purpose is achieved" (Matt. 5:17, 18). Even Paul, who gave birth to a new religious paradigm, recognized the value of the Law. Nonetheless, the emphasis placed by the new religious tradition had shifted from fulfilling the commandments and precepts in the Torah to having faith in Jeshua.

The Transfer of Power

The God worshiped by Abraham, Isaac, and Jacob and then the people of Israel was abstract, distant, and at times aloof. And while the people of Israel believed fervently that their God intervened actively in their lives, His actions—reflected in the suffering and/or joyfulness experienced by the people—were unpredictable and at times incomprehensible. Their God had secured Israel's sovereignty by fighting its enemies. He had also performed remarkable miracles in Egypt, broke the Pharaoh's steel heart, thus freeing the Israelites from bondage, and when threatened by a pursuing determined Egyptian army, He drowned them in the sea of reeds. He was a God who, when offended, swallowed thousands of people by causing the earth to open, but He was also a God able to pardon and forgive His people when they showed remorse for their sins.

This same, all-powerful God, however, could not prevent the Israelite nation from being under occupation for centuries, from having its people dispersed, and from having His majestic Temple ransacked. There were no images of this God; furthermore, making them was strictly prohibited. He was the Word, as John describes Him in his Gospel, a God to be known in one's heart and mind rather than one that could be apprehended through our senses.

This was also a God who, after being in communication with Israel through His Prophets, had not spoken to His people since he spoke to Daniel a few centuries before. The Jewish people and their leaders had prayed to Him, exhorted Him to act, to intervene, to help, but He had remained silent, uninvolved, and seemingly oblivious to what was going on with them. The new myth spun by the Gospels changed this terribly distressing, hopeless situation forever by bringing forth the good news of the return of the absent God to the world of man through His incarnation in the body of Jeshua, thus offering man a viable solution to his seemingly unsolvable predicament: how to regain the paradisiacal life he once enjoyed and make suffering a forgotten ill.

As the incarnation of the Divine, Jeshua provided people a divine being to whom they could attach themselves with conviction. He was an emanation of God whose actions and thoughts were known and, later on, were accessible to his followers through the Gospels. Being a palpable, human reality, it was easier for some people to have and maintain faith in him, the Son, and thus trust the commitment of his Father to their welfare. Having established a new covenant with the followers of His Son, Jeshua, God the Father (a sometimes irascible and unpredictable Yahweh) now took on the image of a loving parent, one ready to take responsibility for ensuring that the promises made to the people in His name by His Son were always fulfilled, because this time around their fulfillment depended on His grace rather than upon some essential action the people would surely fail to enact to satisfaction.

According to the Gospels, a transfer of power and authority took place between the distant God the Father and the compassionate Jeshua, His Son. Instead of authority residing in some unknown heaven, as it had since Noah entered into a sacred covenant with God, it was now going to be held by a flesh-and-blood representative of Him on earth. Jeshua confirms this monumental happening when repeatedly proclaiming that all his doings are at the instigation of his Father, that whatever he proposes is what his Father asked him to propose. He and the Father are in complete alignment—in essence, they are one and the same: "I tell you most solemnly, the Son can do nothing by himself; he can only do what he sees the Father doing: and whatever the Father does the Son does too. Thus, as the Father raises the dead and gives them life, so the Son gives life to anyone he chooses; for the Father judges no one for He has entrusted all judgment to the Son; whoever refuses honor to the Son refuses honor to the Father as well . . . The father and I are one" (John 5:19, 21–23; 10:30).

For those in need, Jeshua's formula for the redemption of man's enduring misery was difficult to refuse: "Whoever listens to my words, and believes in the one who sent me, has *eternal life* . . . I am the bread of life. He who comes to me will never be hungry; he who believes in me will never be thirsty. I have come from heaven, not to do my own will, but to do the will of the one who sent me, to hear the teaching of the Father, and learn from it, is to come to me" (John 5:24; 6:35, 38, 45).

These verses suggest an important shift in God's assumed responsibility to the people of Israel and humanity in general. Having lived for centuries under foreign occupation (most recently under the yoke of Rome, the strongest and most powerful of the empires that ever ruled them), the continued belief in a religious mythology based on the power and prowess of a warrior God capable of liberating them from foreign oppressors was a recipe for disillusionment and depression. As a result, a new image of God was born, one steeped in compassion and loving-kindness and the promise of everlasting life and bliss for all those who had faith in Him through having faith in His Son, albeit this future glory was not to be attained in this world, but rather in the world to come.

Given the state of psychological development of the Israelite community during the first century CE, the authors of the Gospels may have intuited that living according to the high standards the imagined God of the old covenant had demanded of His people was unattainable. So after more than one thousand years of persistent efforts by the Israelites to live according to such lofty standards, it became clear to the primordial artists living in the recesses of the Jewish collective mind that this pathway was not doable for many, if not most, and therefore could not serve as the blueprint to be used by humanity in the future. A new, less burdensome blueprint was needed, one with a higher chance of leading to collective success. The idea of a redeemer coming down to earth to free people from the fear of punishment for sins and who demanded primarily that, in order to gain entrance into the kingdom of heaven, they simply have faith in him, was a highly persuasive one.

A Psychological Perspective on Jeshua

That a man like Jeshua of Nazareth emerged from the depth of Israel's soul is not unexpected, given the need within the Israelite community for a figure capable of relieving the people of the guilt of sin, and of the belief that they would continue to be punished severely for it.

We will never know why, of all people, it was Jeshua of Nazareth who took on the mantle of redeemer/savior. What is clear, though, is that whenever the need for a heroic figure constellates within a human collective, he or she will eventually emerge: Abraham, Jacob, Joseph, Moses, David, Job, Jesus, Mohammed, Joan of Arc, Siddhartha Gautama, Gandhi, Martin Luther King, Mother Theresa, Nelson Mandela, and so many others are examples of such numinous figures emerging at the right time and place, as if Providence provided us with exactly what was needed. People like these are ardent defenders of justice—social, political, and economic—have great integrity and honesty, and exhibit compassionate hearts. They are people of broad vision, ready to fight, even give up their lives if necessary, in support of the causes they have embraced. They are transcendental figures able to rekindle in people the belief that things will turn out well for them, that unmitigated suffering does not have to be their ultimate fate.

While the image of Jeshua painted in the Gospels is mythical—God incarnate, the Son of God, Christ, Messiah Ben David—approached psychologically, it describes with great accuracy what one expects to see when the archetypal Self erupts into consciousness and becomes embodied.[3] This psychic force has such supernatural power that once emerged it will tend to overtake the person's psyche and become the dominant mental force for the duration of his life. The Self, God, our Inner Higher Wisdom are different denominations for a psychic force that generally operates below conscious awareness but that, on occasion, perhaps responding to pressing collective and/or individual needs, will burst forth, giving the impression the person has been possessed by a mysterious, extraordinary being, God himself incarnating in a human being, a human mind. The Self I am referring to, however, is constitutional and hard-wired, the repository of vast experiential knowledge, wisdom, and insight accumulated by our ancestors over the millennia. Some people like Abraham, Jacob, Moses, and the Major and Minor Prophets seem to have been in intimate relationship with it; fewer actually get to embody and live it out, as it seems Jeshua did.

The energy that Jeshua expressed was not novel. Many biblical figures preceding him invoked this energy and drew it into the human community when praying to God on behalf of the people of Israel. They may even have embodied it for short periods of time. But in all these cases the locus of the energy was still in the heavens (i.e., in the deeper layers of the unconscious) in a state of noncorporeal existence. In Jeshua's case, however, this energy was immanent, flowing continuously from his inner mystery into his ego-self and out into the physical world. That is why in the Gospels he is not described as conversing with God the Father, imploring or asking Him to forgive, save, or heal the people of Israel. He did not need to do so for it was he who did the forgiving, the healing, the saving, and the redeeming. Only when he is hanging from the cross, moribund, about to breathe his last breath, does he address God in heaven, crying out to Him in a loud voice, "My God, My God, why have you deserted me" (Matt. 27:46).

Jeshua was also a man who instead of threatening sinners with banishment from divine love, as other Prophets were wont to do, offered them consolation, support, and encouragement. And to those who judged their fallible brethren harshly he reminded them they were fallible too. Instilling the fear of God into the people's broken hearts was offensive to him for he represented love, compassion, and kindness, not judgment and punishment. Opening the eyes and ears of the people to what went on in their daily lives, however, was an important part of his calling. A mender of bodies and minds, his energy and voice were exactly what a segment of the Judean community needed to relieve its mounting distress.

There is little evidence to suggest that Jeshua's main intention was to become a political leader for it is not what redeemer/savior archetypes are meant or want to do. Instead, his mission was to serve as a teacher of wisdom and a purveyor of loving-kindness, guiding people to everlasting goodness in the kingdom of heaven. But as such he was also a teacher of truth who was intent on exposing corruption and deviation from moral living, and in this way, he became involved as a political actor. So, as the time for the celebration of Passover approached, he went to the Temple in Jerusalem, which was at the center of both religious and political power, and made a big scene there; he turned over the tables of the moneychangers, scattering their coins, and told the dove sellers to get their things out of there. He was disgusted and irate that they had turned his Father's house into a marketplace.

Despite this being his first public act, it sealed his fate. Rather than being perceived as a repudiation of the way the sacred Temple was being used, his actions were seen as politically motivated, threatening the power and privilege of the religious and civil authorities of his time.

Archetypes of the psyche are unyielding psychic forces that do not easily adjust when conditions unfavorable to their vision and action develop. So when the political and religious authorities decided to target Jeshua, he did not back down. Instead, he pushed forward seemingly unconcerned with the consequences. Accomplishing his mission was his calling, his duty, not the preservation of his life and freedom—after all, archetypes are immortal, so why worry? As a result, he is charged with sedition, judged, and sentenced to an excruciatingly painful and slow death by crucifixion.

The eruption (or incarnation) of "the self"—the divine archetype—in the body of a member of the Judean citizenry was of transcendental import to communal life. It offered the potential of fostering wellness and harmony to that part of the citizenry for whom the covenantal agreement with God had not ushered relief of the pain and misery hoped for either by the collective or individuals. And while faith, compassion, and divine love were parts of Israelite culture, they did not have the preeminent position given them by Jeshua. By questioning the value of blind submission to the Law, performing deeds based on duty rather than heart, and by exposing the inflexible, judgmental, punitive attitude of the religious elite of his time, Jeshua highlighted the danger of the Judean religious tradition becoming a harsh, castigatory, and oppressive one based on strict adherence to law, instead of a tradition promoting a way of life that was not only ethically principled but also compassionate and caring toward its members.

Jeshua's teachings, his actions, and his ministry were meant to enhance the health and well-being of the Judean community—if not immediately then in the long run. By advocating a more spiritual and humane approach to human life, he showed, in fact, how critical these attributes were for the attainment of the lofty ethical goals his compatriots strived for. There is no evidence that his questioning, his teachings, and/or his actions were intended to destroy the foundational principles of his religious tradition or to repudiate the essence of the covenant with God. His energy and ministry should have been welcome developments in the evolutionary unfolding of the Israelite understanding of life and world and its relationship with the Divine. However, it was not to be. Other critical developments in the decades following his death precluded the integration of his contributions to the Jewish canon and the life of the majority of the followers of the Jewish tradition, both in Judea and abroad.

How Jeshua of Nazareth Became Jesus Christ

The mythical idea of the people of Israel having been chosen by God to be His holy people had created an unforeseen and unsustainable psychic conflict that caused grievous distress, not only in Israel but whenever other seekers of religious redemption appeared. It is not inconceivable that, gradually, in the deeper layers of the Jewish collective mind, it became clear that something needed to be done to correct this unfortunate psychic disequilibrium. After all, the potential for redeeming suffering had to be accessible to all human beings, regardless of their ethnicity, race, religion, or nationality, and not just to a selected group. So from the depth of the Jewish soul, a new mythical idea emanated ensuring that the rest of humanity would also have a secure path to the redemption of its angst.

To understand how and why Jeshua became Jesus Christ and gave rise to a new orthodoxy, a new religion that split away from its Jewish roots, we must first understand the psychological and spiritual challenges facing humanity during the first century of the Common Era. It was a time in which substantial segments of both the Judean and, more importantly, the Gentile community of the Roman Empire suffered grievously. On first impression, Jeshua seemed to have emerged to alleviate the pain and distress of the poor, the disenfranchised, the orphans, and the widows among the people of Israel. But from a broader perspective, the emergence of a redeemer/savior in Judean society may not have been meant exclusively for the benefit of Jews but rather for the benefit of a much larger constituency of sufferers for whom spiritual healing and a defined pathway for the redemption of their suffering had heretofore been neither available nor possible. Vulnerable to the vicissitudes of daily living, and faced with the knowledge of an omnipotent, omniscient, and omnipresent God with whom they had no relationship whatsoever, their condition seemed indeed perilous. This large community yearned for a mythical figure that could offer them salvation and hope, one they could willingly embrace as their God. The appearance of a man like Jeshua, embodying the savior energy, created an excellent opportunity for the fulfillment of a collective human need that had been building up for centuries. But for Jeshua of Nazareth to transform himself from the embodiment of love, compassion, and healing into Jesus, God's anointed son, purveyor of good tidings and redeemer of humanity's sins, something dramatic and transcendental had to happen, and indeed it did.

I am referring specifically to the miraculous transformation experienced by another devoted Jewish man, Saul of Tarsus. This mystical transformation caused him to evolve from being a pursuer of Christian Jews—a new sect within Judaism, which, believing they were to be resisted and punished, he viewed with great hostility—to a man that elevated Jeshua/Jesus to the position of Messiah, the Lamb of God, a man who had descended to earth to usher in an era of everlasting life and peace for all of humanity and not just for those calling themselves "the chosen."

A Covenant of Law Becomes a Covenant of Faith

Saul of Tarsus (5–66 CE) was an educated, Diaspora-living Jew, highly versed in the nuances of Jewish Law. A committed Pharisee, he was terribly opposed to the Jews who followed Jesus and his apostles. In the Book of Acts in the New Testament, he describes how, while on his way to Damascus in pursuit of Christian Jews, he experienced a vision that changed forever his understanding of Jesus and the nature of his mission: "At midday as I was on my way I saw a light brighter than the sun come down from heaven. It shone brilliantly around me, and my fellow travelers. We all fell to the ground, and I heard a voice saying to me in *Hebrew*, 'Saul, Saul, why are you persecuting me?' Then I said, 'who are you, Lord?' And the Lord answered, 'I am Jesus, and you are persecuting me. But get up and stand on your feet, for I have appeared to you for this reason: to appoint you as my servant and as witness to this vision in which you have seen me, and of others in which I shall appear to you. I shall deliver you from the people and from the pagans, to whom I am sending you to open their eyes, so that they may turn from darkness to light'" (Acts 26:9–18).

Hearing a voice claiming to be that of a man resurrected from death by God stopped Saul's crusade against Christian Jews in its tracks. A call from God's begotten had been received, and it had to be heeded. Saul had experienced a transformative encounter; with it, the course of humanity's history was changed forever.

The impact this psychic event had on Saul was so overwhelming that it left him blind. Only a few days later, after a disciple of Jesus laid hands on him, did his sight return. Emboldened by the calling from a resurrected man/god, he made it his sacred duty to spread the good news of Jesus's coming. Just as divine grace had opened his eyes and ears, he now considered it his sacred duty to do the same for all sufferers seeking salvation. Saul's consciousness had been heightened;

feeling the love and guidance of the divine presence within himself he was now ready to preach the coming of love, compassion, and healing to the world.

Analyzed in the light of contemporary psychological knowledge it is infinitely more likely that what Saul heard came from within, from his archetypal self, more precisely, from his suppressed compassionate, loving, and healing side. This was a part of his Self that he had perceived as weak and unacceptable, given his previous polarization around authority and law. To Saul's utter bewilderment, the encounter with the voice revealed the presence in him of a force carrying the same kind of energy as the one embodied by those he was persecuting. Having lived a good part of his life compartmentalized, reflecting a state of internal fragmentation and disownment from his more humane aspects, his consciousness was pried open by these disowned energies, demanding actualization and proper expression.

Saul's transformation into a champion of the Jesus Christ religious movement and his later repudiation of Jewish Law (the same law that he had zealously defended) exemplifies what happens to people who, having lived polarized around a particular archetypal configuration, become terribly vulnerable to its polar opposite. Just like the historical Jesus seems to have been polarized around the energy of love, compassion, and healing, Saul of Tarsus had been polarized around an energy invested in justice and the rule of law, which mistrusted and was repulsed by the energy embodied by Jesus and his followers, thus explaining Saul's crusade against Christian Jews. Unbeknownst to him, though, this state of psychic existence concealed the presence of aspects of his till-then censored Self, causing the formation of a large psychic shadow within Saul's psyche. The more he despised and persecuted Christian Jews, the more this shadow grew in stature, accelerating its inevitable eruption into consciousness, thus his "miraculous" and befuddling transformation. Having lived in strict adherence to the Law and ferociously battling those who dared to deviate from its orthodoxy, Saul was about to succumb precisely to the energies and beliefs of those he had been trying to extricate from his community and, more importantly, from his own life. A staunch upholder of

Moses's Law on the outside, inwardly, in the recesses of his soul, parts of Saul were yearning to emerge and offer love, compassion, and healing to all, in particular, those he fiercely opposed.

Psychic shadows are often viewed as aspects of our personalities that we want to hide from ourselves, such as greed, enviousness, competitiveness, cruelty, cowardice, malice, and selfishness. In fact, our psychic shadow also contains inborn, innate, archetypal forces belonging to the transpersonal realm of human existence. I am referring here to our inner gods and goddesses, great mothers and fathers, saviors and redeemers, magicians, mystics, and healers, all of which are concerned with realities larger than those our personal, ego-centered selves care and worry about. Transordinary realities operate outside of chronological time and space; they are concerned with the collective good, need, and resolution of issues of general import. When aspects belonging to this second category of shadow erupt into consciousness they tend to create disarray and confusion for they invariably encourage us—"compel" may be a better term—to override ordinary concerns and priorities and undertake pursuits that disrupt our day-to-day living.

When God, speaking out of a burning bush, asked Moses to go to the Pharaoh and request he let the Israelites go, Moses initially resisted the command, trying to avoid the responsibility. Similarly, Jonah, when commanded by God to go to Nineveh and alert the people of their impending doom, fled as far away from the city as possible. In the cases of Daniel and Saul the encounter with the inner voice so overwhelmed them that, for a period of time, it caused Daniel to lose consciousness and Saul to go blind. In the end, though, the emergence of transpersonal forces into consciousness cannot be denied indefinitely. Sooner or later they must be heeded and their commands fulfilled, as with Saul, who changed his name to Paul and gave birth to a new religious vision for the redemption of humanity's suffering: Christianity, to which he devoted the rest of his life.

For Saul of Tarsus/Paul the Apostle, the encounter with the inner voice did not so much lead to the healing of his psychic wounds and the attainment of psycho-spiritual wholeness, as it had done for Job, for example. Instead, it was the spark that unleashed a collective healing through the formulation of a new religious mythos based on the life and ministry of Jeshua of Nazareth. The collective redemption I am referring to, however, was neither immediate nor easy. In fact, after the death of Jeshua, control over the budding church passed into the hands of James, "Lord and Bishop of the Holy Church," whom Jesus himself had named as his successor, according to The Gospel of Thomas (12), which was presumably written toward the end of the first or the beginning of the second century of the Common Era. In fact, in his Epistle, James insisted on the importance of maintaining a proper balance between devotion to Torah study, fulfillment of the Law, and faith in Jesus as Messiah.

James's Epistle may have been construed as a corrective of Paul's preaching. The hostility it displays toward Paul is unmistakable: whereas Paul dismisses the Law of Moses as a "ministry of death, chiseled in letters on a tablet of stone," James celebrates it as "the law of liberty." Moreover, James dismisses Paul's notion that only through faith can one receive salvation, stating, "Faith apart from works of the Law is death" (James 2:26).

While James was alive, and even after his death, the authority of the Jerusalem assembly headed by James remained, and Paul's teachings were discredited, causing him to lose followers from many of his congregations. In Luke's Book of Acts, a rendering of the final meeting between James and Paul presents Paul silently acquiescing to the Temple rite demanded of him. This, however, is highly disingenuous. Considering the disdain Paul had developed for the Law of Moses, the rite at the Temple was intended to prove to the Jerusalem assembly that he did not believe or abide anymore by what he had been preaching to others, a humiliating act for Paul, to say the least.

But Paul was a man driven by a numinous image not to be denied. After Jerusalem was ransacked and its people expulsed from Judea by the Romans in 138 CE, Paul's understanding of Jesus created a revival that gradually became widely accepted in many of the Christian congregations of the time. In founding and giving shape to Christianity, Paul expressed why humanity at large needed to transition from a mythology that offered salvation through the fulfillment of Torah Law to one in which salvation was obtained through faith. In his letter to the Romans, he wrote: "God's justice that was made known through the Law and the Prophets has now been revealed outside the Law, since it is the same justice of God that comes through faith to everyone—Jew and pagan alike, who believe and have faith in Jesus Christ" (Rom. 3:21–24). Later on, he emphasized this point even further when stating, "Is God the God of the Jews alone, and not of the pagans too? Of the pagans too, most certainly, for there is only one God, and He is the one who will justify the circumcised because of their faith and the uncircumcised through their own faith" (Rom. 3:29–31). Further, he asserted, "The Law, however, was not pointless, but rather an important component of service that needed to be given its proper standing and value" (Rom. 3:31). This understanding and valuing of Jewish Law may have changed for him later on for in James's Epistles he purportedly described the Law as a ministry of death.

Like later Jewish sages and exegetes, Paul attempted to ground his novel interpretation of Jesus's teachings in scriptural precedents. He argued, for example, that God justified Abraham, the ancestor of all people, whether Jews or Gentiles, because he put his *faith* in Him (Gen. 15:6). Moreover, this justification was granted to Abraham before he was circumcised, thus transforming him into the ancestor of all *uncircumcised believers* as well as those who, while circumcised, did not rely on that fact alone for their justification but followed God along the path of faith (Rom. 4:1–3, 10–12). In this same letter, Paul claims as well that the promise God made to Abraham and his descendants about the world they would inherit was not made to Abraham on account of any set of laws he had fulfilled but rather on account of his righteousness, which was rooted in his faith in God. If the world God promised was to be inherited only by those who submitted to the Law, then faith was pointless, he argued, and redemption through faith worth nothing. Moreover, redemption through obedience to the Law involves the possibility of punishment for breaking it—which had happened innumerable times to the people of Israel; only where there is no law can this threat be completely avoided. That is why what fulfills the promise is faith, so that whatever one gets is received as a gift available to all of Abraham's descendants, not only to those who belong to the Law but also to those belonging to the faith of Abraham (Rom. 4:13–17).

Had Jeshua been alive at the time that Paul's letters and the synoptic Gospels were written, he might have questioned, contested, and refuted some or perhaps most of their assertions and conclusions about him. But for those authoring them and for those embracing the message of the Gospels, he was precisely what they said he was: a redeemer of humanity's sinful past, present, and future and the man/god who promised humanity the kingdom of heaven.

In summary, the emergence of two polarizing figures during the first century of the Common Era, responding in all likelihood to powerful individual and societal needs, resulted in the birth of Christianity, which in time became the religion with the highest number of devotees. The first figure in question was that of Jeshua/Jesus of Nazareth, a man who offered a pathway to the redemption of suffering that combined respect for Jewish Law with love and compassion for man's foibles. The second one was that of Saul/Paul of Tarsus who, after experiencing a transformative vision, became a man driven to spread the good news of God's commitment to the redemption of all of humanity's sins through faith and faith alone in God's begotten son.

Why Did the Majority of Jews Not Embrace Paul's Religion?

Despite the attractiveness of the message contained in the Gospels and in Paul's letters and the relief from the burden of guilt that Christianity seems to offer, the citizens of Judea did not convert en masse to the new religious views and in fact rejected its foundational premises altogether. For one, the fact of Jesus's death refuted the image of a Messiah that would usher in an era of everlasting peace and happiness and bring forth the resurrection of the dead, as offered by their sacred writings. Additionally, these people were descendants of Abraham and Moses, the beneficiaries of a pathway for the redemption of suffering that despite being terribly difficult felt fundamentally right—live a principled and moral life and you will suffer less or not at all.

Let us also not forget that Judean citizens were the holders of a millenary tradition that not only explained how the world worked but also offered them a sophisticated system of jurisprudence, social organization, political and religious governance, and an advanced code of ethics and moral values that had served them fairly well. Their religion and the way of life it fostered gave them the ability to maintain a level of self-rule even when under foreign occupation. As Max Dimont states so lucidly in his book *Jews, God, and History*, the Jews might have lost their independence and lived for centuries under the rule of Babylonians, Greeks, and Romans, but their religious organization prevented them from losing their religious and spiritual freedom and identity.[4] Able to regulate the behavior of the citizenry, the religious and spiritual leaders were given latitude by their oppressors to govern their people, which significantly reduced concern for the possible eruption of social unrest.

Additionally, during the later part of the first century BCE a revival of the spiritual life of the Judean population was taking root. Promoted by another charismatic teacher in Jerusalem who favored a more liberal, lenient, and compassionate interpretation of Jewish Law, this revival shared basic qualities with the later teachings of Jeshua. This teacher and his ministry had been very well received by the people of his time. I am referring to Hillel the Elder, who, having acquired a prodigious Torah knowledge under the tutelage of the greatest sages in Jerusalem, held the office of Nasi—president of the Great Assembly of the Judean religious community—from around 30 BCE to 10 CE, a period that coincided with the reign of Herod the Great. As Nasi, Hillel offered rulings and created new laws in cases where the Torah gave no explicit instruction or where there was no previous oral tradition.[5]

Hillel was a charismatic, wise leader known for promoting an ethic of reciprocity, respect, empathy, brotherly love, humbleness, and cooperation between human beings, regardless of their social status and means. He taught, for example, that a person must love and pursue peace and never judge a fellow man until having been in his shoes for a reasonable period of time (Pirkei Avot 2:5). Having been very poor himself, he enacted laws to improve social justice and the lot of the poor. He excelled as a leader not only because of his vast knowledge of the sacred texts and his intelligence but also because he lived according to what he preached. He was humble and caring and loved people. Asked once by someone who wanted to convert to Judaism to define the Torah while standing on one foot, he said: "Do not do to others that which is hateful to you. This is the whole Torah, now go and learn." This principle applied to all people, Jewish or not, observant or not. He also promoted an ethic of self-care and altruistic care of others. He is famous for saying: "If I am not for myself who will be for me, and if I am only for myself, then what am I? And if not now then when?" (Pirkei Avot 1.14). These wise principles of behavior were anything but legalistic, offering most of the citizenry respite and relief from the oppression they may have been experiencing at the time.

All these factors worked together in making most of the citizens of Judea somewhat immune to the promises offered by the new religion, especially in Paul's version. It is also noteworthy that despite its inherent appeal, Christians were heavily persecuted and oppressed by the Romans for more than three centuries, making their lives perilous and miserable. By contrast, Rome neither persecuted nor oppressed Jews for practicing their religion, and their souls were afflicted by their rulers' actions only when they rebelled against Rome and caused social unrest and violence. It was not until the fourth century CE, when Constantine made Christianity the official religion of the Roman Empire, that it disseminated like wildfire among Rome's Gentile population.

The Aftermath

Under the leadership of James the Just, the first community of Christian Jews in Jerusalem remained faithful to their Jewish heritage and tradition. They considered themselves Jews, honoring Jewish Law and the covenant, but also believed in Jesus as Messiah and, more importantly, in his message of love and compassion for the poor and the downtrodden. James's leadership over this emerging community came to an end in 62 CE following his execution by a former high priest under the guise that he had broken the Law but more realistically as a result of the former priest feeling threatened by James's populist "inflammatory rhetoric."[6] The years that followed James's death were full of strife, violence, and chaos for the Judean community. On several occasions the Jews rebelled against their Roman oppressors, inflicting significant pain and losses on them, which in turn caused further pain and misery for the Jewish population. In the year 70 CE, despite the valiant efforts of the Jewish rebels, Jerusalem and the second Temple were ransacked and burned and the Jews massacred in the most brutal of ways. A profound institutional and spiritual crisis ensued within the high priesthood and the Israeli assembly, or Sanhedrin, the latter becoming temporarily nonfunctional. Nonetheless, a new religious attitude emerged intent on rebuilding the spiritual life of the nation, one spearheaded by sages who embraced Hillel's perspective and approach to the legalistic aspects of the tradition. Steeped in Torah knowledge, these religious leaders were able to integrate the various strands of Judaism then in existence and establish a religious practice centered on Torah study, fulfillment of the commandments, and the performance of good deeds.

Coincidentally, it was during this time of Jewish national decline and loss that Paul's version of Christianity gained wide acceptance within the community of Jews that had embraced Jeshua as the Messiah and, more importantly, among the increasing number of Gentiles converting to the new creed. The ruined sanctuary where God used to dwell and the terrible calamities afflicting the Israelite nation were taken by the promoters and the followers of the new religion as definitive proof that their God had abandoned Israel; otherwise, what would explain their misery?

Since Paul's Christianity was directed primarily toward the vast Gentile population of the Roman Empire, it needed to be shaped as a religion for the Gentiles rather than as a strand within Judaism. And so the new religion made sure to emphasize a new covenantal relationship between God and Jesus's followers—the Christians—intended to replace the one He had established so much earlier with the Jews.

228

Following the failure of the Bar Kokhba revolt in 135 CE, Jews were persecuted, killed, sold as slaves, and dispersed throughout the Roman Empire. But a small population was still left in Judea that would eventually recover its bearings and strive again. After Judea had fallen to the Arab invaders, however, around the year 620 CE, the majority of Jews left, spending centuries living among the nations of the world, yearning to return to the land God had promised their ancestors and once again live there as sovereign people. Their yearning was not just for a homeland, but for a place where they could serve God in the way He had commanded them, which could only happen in the Promised Land.

For most Jews, Jeshua's death proved he was not the redeemer that would bring forth the resurrection of the dead and an era of everlasting peace and wellness for the people of Israel. They could have benefited from his teachings, his parables, his social concerns, and more importantly his loving energy, but given the schism that took place between Judaism and Paul's Christianity, Jeshua's teachings were lost to the Jewish people, treated by their sages and religious leaders as if they were never given.

As a result, a growing need seemed to have developed within the Jewish community for a figure capable of embodying a similar presence and message. This critical need was eventually fulfilled by the emergence of a mythologized version of the life and ministry of the Prophet Elijah. According to what the Hebrew Bible tells us about him, Elijah was a man who knew no peace in his heart, but the fact that he was not known to have died but instead taken to heaven on a chariot considerably enhanced his aura among Jews in the centuries that followed his death. This allowed his image to gradually morph into a softer, more caring and gentler one that was kind, supportive, and compassionate toward his fellowmen. Eventually, he came to personify the champion of the poor, the weak, the oppressed, and the downtrodden. He was the spirit that would show up when the people needed support and succor. For the Jews living in the Diaspora, the presence of his soul among them made their lives more bearable, even while enduring the rigors of living in exile and suffering the frustration of not being able to self-determine and self-rule.

The emergence of love and compassion as critical components of healing and the attainment of individual and collective spiritual well-being was of transcendent importance, complementing the role that knowledge, understanding, morality, the Rule of Law, ethical principles, and an effective constitution had on helping man redeem his suffering.

Underneath the mythological underpinnings of the Israelite tradition, however, lay the understanding held by most Jews that the covenant with God symbolized a yearning for a just, moral, ethically principled society that would bring happiness and peace to all its citizens. And while the Israelite nation had been unable to attain such lofty goals collectively, they were still not ready to give up the hope that one day, perhaps through much effort, they would. Convinced that the path to achieving their goals required persistent dedication to developing the psychological and spiritual resources required to overcome suffering, they came to know that love and compassion were indispensable and needed to be integrated into the fabric of their religious tradition.

From the time of their dispersion from their homeland, to the time of their return in large numbers in the mid-twentieth century to create the modern State of Israel, to this very day, all communications from God to the Jewish people ceased. There were no more instances of God expressing dissatisfaction and displeasure with His chosen people or any additional mythical emanation that better explained why life was unfolding the way it did for the Jews the world over. During the Middle Ages, mystical schools and interpretations of the Creation emerged, like the Jewish Kabala: these schools provided an interpretation of the origin, the architecture, and the functioning of the universe rather than a new revelation about it received by man from God. The harsh, punitive, unpredictable God of old disappeared as a communicating being—even God gets tired of repeating the same things over and again. And while life was hard and Jews were often persecuted, oppressed, and murdered, no new explanation or redemptive stories appeared.

Jews were too geographically dispersed and fragmented to be able to function as a cohesive whole. Instead of Prophets or priests, Jews now had rabbis and rebbes—teachers and wise sages who attended to the religious, spiritual, and emotional needs of the people in their congregations. Temple worship, which could only take place in Jerusalem where the two Temples had existed, was now substituted with synagogue worship in sanctuaries erected wherever Jewish communities existed; and the great Jewish sages who lived during the first centuries of the Common Era developed a way of Jewish life rooted in the teachings of the Torah and Moses's Law. This way of life, or Halakah, provided an organizing framework for how Jewish people were to comport themselves in their daily lives, leaving little to chance. It guided them as to how to behave when waking up and when going to sleep; how to dress, eat, pray, celebrate holidays, sanctify the Sabbath and the seasons, interact socially, conduct business, even who and when to marry; and, most importantly, how to treat God, other people, and animals. Halakah also taught what was commendable and righteous to do in life, and what was prohibited and forbidden, as well as what was true and untrue, thus providing a moral framework for living a harmonious and well-structured life.

Halakah provided excellent guidelines for day-to-day living regardless of geography or the cultural and religious environment in which Jews lived. It spelled out effectively the people's duties and responsibilities and encouraged the creation of important systems of social support to assist others in times of need, but it did not, and does not, provide a reliable path for the resolution of the people's existential angst. In short, Halakah tells people how to follow God's path but not how to be enduringly happy.

Not surprisingly, Jews, more particularly observant ones, have continued to carry a deep yearning and an unshakable belief in the coming of the Messiah and, more importantly, of a Messianic era, as prognosticated in their sacred texts. For them, it is not a matter of whether but rather when such a time will come. But once it arrives, their troubles will cease, their efforts to attain happiness will be fulfilled, and all those whose behavior merits it will live forever in a restored earthly paradise.

Having become the central authority on which Jewish life was founded, the Jewish Bible and its multiplex stories, laws, precepts, and recommended practices remained in force for millennia, providing the framework for the survival and prosperity of the Israelite people wherever they lived. But to accomplish and ensure this, refinements in the methods of understanding and interpretations of Mosaic Law were needed. Reason and logic were applied to what had been derived from revelation, giving rise to what Jews called the *Mishna*. The intent of these additions and interpretations of Divine Law was to mine the depth of the Torah and identify what the Divine intended to teach us through His revelations and apply these teachings to daily life. The multiple interpretations and perspectives on Torah Law, however, were meant to be memorized rather than written, thus becoming what was referred to as the Oral Law, a complement to the Torah and later to the whole Bible.

Over the subsequent centuries, a great deal was added to the laws, rules, rituals, and practices recommended by the Torah as a result of new legal precedents, procedures, and rites, as well as novel interpretations of contradictory or ambiguous passages in the Bible. Somewhere during the first two centuries of the Common Era the Mishna was canonized, thus closing the door to further interpretations of Torah Law. Despite its canonization, the Mishna remained an oral tradition, leaving the Hebrew Bible as the only written sacred text. As one may expect, the closure of the Mishna to potentially new insights promoted a new type of commentary, this one centered on the observations that make up the Mishna: it is known as *Gemara*—or supplement, in Hebrew.

The Gemara grew significantly in importance and size between the third and sixth centuries CE. Finally, over a period of more than two hundred years Mishna and Gemara were compiled and codified into a series of texts known collectively as the *Talmud*. Intertwined throughout the Talmud is the Halakah, which observant Jews attempt to fulfill to the best of their ability.

Despite the many benefits that Halakah brought to Jewish wellness, a modern, new explanatory vision of man's origins, one capable of restoring dignity and hopefulness into the heart of the Jewish and human community, was still needed. This vision would be based not on the fulfillment of difficult laws and precepts or on accepting fate through faith but rather on the coming of an era of unprecedented goodness for humanity at large. This would come about through a healing of the terrible distortion of human nature that had pervaded human life for thousands of years; it would usher in a time of celebration of all that evolution has uniquely gifted upon us to make us human, its unintended consequences notwithstanding.

CHAPTER 13

Coming Full Circle
Paradise Regained

IN REVIEWING MAN'S EXPLANATION for why he lost the happy life he once had in Eden, we notice that his first inclination was to blame himself for it. Burdened with the bad feelings that resulted from this knowing, he defended himself by projecting culpability for his actions and for the feelings they evoked onto others. An example of this type of psychological maneuver can be found as early as Adam's response to God when the first man is queried about having eaten from the tree of the knowledge of good and bad. Instead of assuming responsibility for what he did and for the bad feelings this evoked in him, he blamed Eve and even God for it: "The woman *You* put at my side—she gave me of the tree, and I ate" (Gen. 3:12).

Projecting responsibility for bad feelings onto others is commonplace among all people, whatever their ethnic, religious, cultural, socioeconomic, or racial group; it allows them the illusion of having freed themselves from the stigma of being bad. In reality, when a projection of psychological material occurs, all that is accomplished is a displacement onto others of that which belongs individually or collectively to us. While in some situations the responsibility for our distressing feelings can be squarely placed on the actions of others—cases of physical, sexual, or mental abuse, enslavement, oppression—on many occasions, feeling enraged, offended, wronged, demeaned, or belittled gives expression to underlying psychological conditions in us rather than these feelings being provoked by the actions perpetrated by others. Psychological displacement builds up prejudice, mistrust, condemnation, racism, and many other "isms" between people, nations, religious groups, families, and individuals, and thus it pro-motes unrest, violence, oppression, and repression between brethren, a condition bedeviling humanity from time immemorial.

Why humanity believes in its constitutive badness and has accepted a mythology that affirms this categorically is because it could not—and still cannot—understand why suffering is so prevalent in life. Unable to blame their principled God for this nefarious reality, the only reasonable explanation left is that it is man's fault. Implied in this convoluted explanation of what in effect is unavoidable in us is a rejec-tion of aspects of our nature and the life and world we live in, which cannot lead to positive outcomes.

To this very day, suffering, especially when perceived as undeserved, challenges our sense of fairness and our emotional stability and com-fort. It makes us feel that things are not right in the world, that they should be better, that man should suffer less, and that enduring happi-ness should be an attainable goal. While religious ritual and practice, science and technology, and mind-regulating techniques have helped ameliorate our day-to-day suffering they have not succeeded in help-ing us get rid of it altogether. The happy world we once presumably enjoyed in Eden has not yet been regained, and the one an author like Aldous Huxley describes in his book *Brave New World* was only attained by the use of drugs and mind control procedures rather than through the development of a genuine sense of being good.[1]

Paradise Regained

There is a pathway, however, sketched out thousands of years ago in the pages of the Book of Job, that can and does lead to the eventual resolution of the suffering man experiences as a result of his misguided beliefs and interpretations of what is physiological in him. It is a path that welcomes and celebrates self-reflective consciousness and all it implies for the life of man and encourages us to expand this wonderful human attribute to the farthest reaches possible.

Healing humanity's enduring state of unpleasantness—its primor-dial illness—by expanding consciousness is a paradoxical approach to the resolution of suffering for it demands we experience a great deal of misery before gaining access to the joyfulness and deep sense of harmony and well-being this approach offers. The experience is akin to traversing a dark and lengthy tunnel—at times pitch black, scary, foreboding, and disorienting—before reaching the radiant light that surrounds, nourishes, and heightens us and makes us feel at home.

In chapter 5 of the Book of Job, one of his friends makes allusion to this paradoxical pathway when responding to Job's violent diatribe against God and the ills He had thrust on him. The friend, Eliphaz, says admonishingly, "Happy indeed is the man whom God corrects! Then do not refuse this lesson from Shaddai, for He who wounds is He who soothes the sore, and the hand that hurts is the hand that heals" (Job 5:17, 18). In making this puzzling statement, Eliphaz is acknowledging God as both an injuring and healing force. For the contemporaries of Eliphaz and Job, as for most of us today, this assertion is hard to comprehend and even harder to integrate, particularly when experiencing God's injuring hand leaning heavily upon one's flesh. Taken at face value, the statement seems to suggest the existence of forces in nature and the world capable of affecting our lives in arbitrary, capricious ways. But when instead of God we consider that it is an expanding human consciousness that Eliphaz was symbolically referring to then these intriguing verses take on a very different meaning. For we know from direct experience that the dawn of self-reflective consciousness and its subsequent expansion is injurious to the soul of man. If proof is needed, all we have to do is remember the fear and shame felt by Adam and Eve after their minds were awakened to the truth of their nakedness and their disobedience, so much like our own fear, shame, and guilt when we become aware that we have disobeyed authority or done harm to another, whether purposely or unwittingly.

Conscious awareness of our vulnerabilities—from knowing we do not have enough food to feed ourselves and our families to knowing about the dangers posed by natural forces and other living creatures, or knowing we are getting old and our bodies don't function as well as they once did—is indeed anxiety provoking. As a result, being self-conscious may cause us to live in a state of fearful vigilance; defended, imagining calamities will strike any moment. But when we are able to glimpse the enormous rewards that an awakened and expanded consciousness offers and develop the determination to allow ourselves to pursue it, then we can—better yet, we will—arrive at a state of happy existence that is enduring. Of course, suffering will still be part of our experience, but we will be able to appreciate it as an integral part of our lives, the price we must pay for all the wonderful gifts that being self-conscious affords us—knowing our pleasures, boosting our chances to survive and live well, allowing us to promote justice and morality in our personal and communal lives, and so much more.

By expanding our consciousness through a diversity of experiential approaches—meditation, ritual, dream work, prayer, creative works, body movement, and dance—and more importantly by taking advantage of those transformational life events that awaken us by challenging our systems of belief, we are able to tap into the secrets of animate and inanimate nature and perceive our world and life more accurately. From a state of habitual fearfulness, shame, guilt and psycho-spiritual contraction we can transition into one in which we see ourselves growing, developing, and maturing in an ever-deepening communion with others, with our environment, and with our world.

Unfortunately, most of us have not enjoyed the freedom and enduring happiness that an expanded consciousness can provide. Furthermore, having experienced the suffering that self-consciousness imposes on us, we tend to view this awesome gift as something we would gladly shy away from—the less conscious we are, the less we will suffer. As Koheleth so beautifully stated in his book, "To increase learning is to increase heartache" (Koheleth 1:18). So for thousands of years, we have denigrated our endowment, perceived it as a curse, and hoped to find a way—through belief in a transcendental reality responsible for all that happens to us—to return to some paradisiacal life we once enjoyed as adults. Such a misguided approach, however, can never take us home.

To attain this freedom and the state of blissfulness, tranquility, and inner and outer harmony associated with it, we must first learn to face and overcome our personal, familial, and cultural shadows—all those aspects of self and world that have been unacceptable and intolerable to us: our weaknesses, enviousness, competitiveness, greedi-ness, and aggressiveness, as well as our fears of death, aging, and becom-ing physically and/or emotionally dependent—not a small undertaking to say the least. We also need to learn both by ourselves and with the assistance of others to reign over our anxieties and worries and stop imagining negative outcomes for our lives and the lives of our families, community, and the world. By doing so, we will avoid the amplifi-cation of distressful feelings these imaginings provoke. Additionally, we must engage in a process of deconditioning ourselves from beliefs we acquired early on, during childhood and adolescence, beliefs that while useful may lead to a distorted understanding of our reality dur-ing adulthood, which may then lead to making bad choices at impor-tant times in our lives.

As consciousness expands during the initial stages of our journey to health and healing, we may feel more frightened, vulnerable, ashamed, and emotionally unsafe than we had previously. This can readily be seen in children when they transition from the innocence of infancy and early childhood to the distress and angst of their teens and early adulthood. Suddenly, they are more cautious, more tentative, and more restrained in their actions than they had been. The world does not appear as safe and happy anymore.

It takes courage and vision, effective guidance, and a great deal of emotional fortitude for people to undertake this pathway for the redemption of suffering. Once having done so, however, they will enjoy the privilege of being part of something grand, beautiful, exhila-rating, and deeply humbling.

My Own Journey to Healing and Wholeness

On a personal note, after being diagnosed with a life-threatening ill-ness at the age of 37, I too felt overwhelmed with fear and foreboding and had a sense that something was defective in me; otherwise, why illness? Like Job centuries earlier, I felt compelled to enter a lengthy process of discovery and healing that, while initially focused on my physical health, ultimately became an all-encompassing process that addressed every aspect of my life. Despite my education and training as a physician-scientist, I found myself first seeking for a magician—a shaman perhaps—who could engage the forces of darkness provoking my illness and overtake them. I needed someone with supernatural powers, someone who could access those realms of existence that were beyond my comprehension and help me overcome the illness gripping my body and soul. In retrospect, I realize how regressive and childlike my initial reaction was. Nonetheless, during the beginning sequences of my journey to health, when feeling overwhelmed with alarm and worry, the idea of finding someone like that comforted me best. At that time, just like thousands of years earlier, the world seemed populated by powerful forces able to cause harm and destruction, forces that science and traditional medicine did not know how to control effectively. I did not perceive these forces as gods or evil spirits but rather as part of an unseen, mysterious world I urgently needed to learn to manage.

For months I struggled to find a sage who could help restore my health and my confidence. Eventually, I found a mentor, a physician-healer well versed in contemporary medicine and science who had healed his own illness. And while he did not turn out to be the magician I had hoped for, he did open up for me the idea of consciousness as a remedial force. His ideas on how body energy and mental patterns influence disease confused me at first, but later on I could see how becoming more aware of myself, others, and the world around me could help me restore my confidence and my health.

As my efforts to expand my consciousness proceeded, a day arrived when I became aware of a new presence that had materialized in me. I call this presence my "inner warrior," a resourceful, creative, and sensitive part of myself capable of managing my crisis and promoting the recovery of my physical and spiritual integrity.

Working with this newfound mental resource allowed me to take better charge of my life. Many changes in diet, daily routines, exercise programs, and meditative practices followed. I also learned to connect to my inner world through my dreams and intuitive insights, which I began to address methodically. A renewed sense of strength and directionality came over me. At the same time, I was reconnecting to aspects of my biological, psychological, social, and metaphysical reality that had previously frightened and intimidated me. These aspects informed me that parts of me were flawed, envious, aggressive, and spiteful toward others. Some of these troubling realizations caused me to want to pull back and retreat into oblivion; but other parts of myself, less known to me then, were pushing me forward toward engagement and health. This push-pull condition created a state of inner stress and conflict that was difficult to endure.

For years, as a devoted biological researcher and practicing oncologist, I had seen cancer strictly as a disorder of the cells' maturation and differentiation processes, paying little attention to the role a person's character and lifestyle may have in its development. But as I delved deeper into the nature of the cancerous process afflicting me this first idea was hard to sustain. The physical cancer was mine, it had developed in my body, and it obviously reflected something going awry inside of me. Moreover, as my understanding of health and illness broadened, I began to uncover the roots of more pervasive diseases and unhealthiness in me I had not known before. Unavoidably, my intimate life came up for scrutiny, and I started to feel very vulnerable, frightened, and alone. My former aloofness and habitual anger were challenged, and the damage these paradoxical character traits had inflicted both in me and in those closest to me, those I loved most dearly, became gradually clearer. I, who had pretended to be the epitome of the happy, healthy, always-in-control guy, was being revealed as a deeply troubled, immature, wounded, aggressive boy-man needing lots of guidance, care, love, and, most importantly, maturity.

My goals for healing myself focused initially on my physical health, but as my journey to health continued I realized that curing or preventing the recurrence of cancer was not enough to relieve my enduring distress and angst. Too much darkness pervaded my daily life, darkness that I would need to confront if I hoped to attain my aim. Suddenly, an inner voice began to interrupt my daily activities, a voice that talked about concealment and deception. It was a voice I could not shut off; this, of course, raised my already heightened apprehension. For the life of me I could not figure out what the concealment or deception implied by this mysterious voice was all about.

I reflected hard and persistently, looked for clues, and searched for answers, but my efforts led nowhere. Then, when I least expected it, a nightmarish dream helped clarify the deception and the concealment themes. In the dream, I was able to witness an interior battle being waged between the forces of my conventional ("everything is all right") self and the forces of a ruthless, powerful, unconventional part of myself, a part I came to call "Mr. Murderer." The latter represented a side of me I had managed to conceal and disguise for decades, not only from others but also from myself. Now this force demanded acknowledgment; it would no longer accept being repressed and ignored.

Over time, I learned that the murderer in my dream and the cancer in my body were both parts of my shadow self: the former dark with aspects of personality I did not want to accept, and the latter with aspects of my biological nature I could not accept either. I perceived them both as hateful and bewildering. But it eventually became clear to me that to heal myself I needed to undertake the repair of my personal life and my intimate relationships first, and then work on integrating my larger cultural shadows. In this way, I would become a man capable of affirming his humanity in the fullness of its complexity and beauty.

As my journey toward healing progressed, feelings long buried came to the fore, flooding my consciousness with emotion. The experience was deeply jarring, shaming, and disconsolate but I realized it was a most needed occurrence despite the turmoil and misery it caused. I was learning to understand feelings as language—the way our bodies communicate their needs and wishes—and to respond to its messages attentively and carefully.

Gradually, my deepening connection to feeling helped me overcome much of the emotional reactivity, aggressiveness, shyness, and low self-esteem I had for so long carried, as well as my social ineptitude. The defenses I had formerly used to handle uncomfortable, threatening experiences slowly gave way to the truths embodied in feelings. I could see now that further healing depended on slowly gathering the courage, no matter how long it took, to say yes to my weakness, loneliness, neediness, and fearfulness. Developing the strength to allow myself to be immersed in these powerful emotional states and allowing them free access to my ego/consciousness was the key to learning how to contain them without needing to repress or sublimate them any longer. This precious new skill began to make possible my moving from a place of denying facts, repressing emotions, and patching up psychic wounds toward a richer, more open and encompassing way of living.

To my distress—and later amusement—the complexities of all I had to address and resolve actually increased as my efforts to heal my life expanded and my understanding deepened. Rather than feeling relief when the physical cancer disappeared, I felt frightened and vulnerable to its recurrence. Then, having found plausible resources to forestall a recurrence, the uncertainties surrounding the rest of my existence dejected me. Ultimately, I had to admit the inevitability of my suffering and the abiding possibility of an untimely death. It seemed that resolving one problem had served only to expose others, more complex and demanding. At times, the whole process felt like a cosmic joke being played on me. Gradually, though, I realized it was not a joke but rather the progressive unfolding of a chronic, pernicious state of inner malaise, the result of my inability to accept life, the world, and my human reality the way it is rather than the way I had always wanted—"demanded" may be a more accurate term—it to be. While repairing my personal relationships was wonderfully fulfilling, it did not address the deeper illness I had uncovered. This illness involved the disownment of universal parts of my human nature that, having struck the core of my being, caused me to feel at odds with myself and with the life I had lived.

I needed to continue expanding my awareness of self and world if I was going to acquire the resources needed to overcome the illness pervading me. Finding a path to deeper consciousness and to the eventual acceptance of the larger realities associated with human existence— such as our vulnerability to nature and human nature, the uncertainty surrounding our lives, the wonders of self-healing, the inevitability of death and suffering, our capacity to transform, and more—proved to be erratic and beyond the power of volitional control. I don't know exactly when this critical part of my transformation took place, but once I realized that life—with all of its limitations, compensations, compromises, and possible accomplishments—was an inescapable and incurable condition, I was able to surrender to something wiser and more aware in me, something I now call my "higher-wiser-self"; it is that which eventually led me home. Being aware in each moment of my aliveness (and therefore of what it implied) ceased to be fearful and despised, something to be avoided, and instead became a source of joyful reverence.

Upon further reflection, it became clear that, while curing the physical manifestations of my cancer and using mental approaches to affirm my desire to live and be healthy were all part of my recovery, *healing* revealed itself as being considerably more than those parts. In fact, it was a remarkable process of inner transformation whereby the totality of my being (my body-mind), when faced with a seemingly insurmountable challenge, increased its functional complexity. It was as if a new mutation had taken hold of me and led to an evolutionary leap forward in my psyche.

The increased complexity I speak of reflected nothing less than the actualization of a potential for psycho-spiritual expansion and maturation enfolded in my human matrix from birth—potential that to my delight came to the fore when I most needed it.

Amazingly, what started as an all-out effort to cure my physical illness ended up being a journey of self-discovery and consciousness broadening, engendering significant leaps in understanding and the emergence of new psychological skills and, at long last, the gradual appearance of a new type of human being—one who is resourceful, wholesome, and deeply appreciative of what it means to be human.

Now, after more than three decades since my journey began, the world feels safer and more comprehensible to me, though I am also more aware of my limitations and failings. Knowing more about the workings of my mind has given me confidence. I now appreciate living not as a right but as a privilege, and I make sure to savor it to the max.

It was during the unfolding of this profound experience that a new origin myth took root in my mind. This new iteration of the Edenic myth imagines a God that is truly omniscient, aware of what He is doing and of the long-term consequences of His actions. It is a God that wants man to be conscious and reflective but is also aware that this wonderful attribute will make him a suffering being; hence He reflected deeply before giving way to His wish. I have called this new iteration "The Rightness of Being Human," a myth that honors our humanity by embracing with equal vigor the wonderful gifts as well as the unforeseen burdens that spring from being self-conscious creatures.

The Rightness of Being Human

After molding man and woman from the dust of the earth, God breathed life into their nostrils and turned them into living beings. He then made a garden to appear and from the ground caused the growth of every tree pleasing to the eye and bearing fruit good for eating. In the middle of the garden He grew the tree of life and to its side the tree of the knowledge of good and bad, and He called the garden Eden.

God placed the primordial couple in the garden where He nurtured them by providing all they needed to survive and be well. When they reached the age at which they were able to fend for themselves, God said to them: "Eat now as much as you want from the fruits of every tree in the garden. They are delicious and invigorating. But from the tree of the knowledge of good and bad do not eat yet. Wait until I or one of my angels tells you to. Its fruit is most attractive to the eye, but it is also difficult to digest."

The serpent, which was the shrewdest, wisest, and most conscious of all creatures in the garden, said one day to the woman: "I have watched you grow and develop since you arrived in Eden. You are physically, emotionally, and mentally stronger now. I think you can eat from the tree of the knowledge of good and bad."

The woman, who had in fact yearned to know herself and others better, didn't need much encouragement to take a bite from the luscious-looking apples hanging from the seductive and forbidden tree. For quite some time she had wanted to bite into them but hadn't dared to do so. But now that the wisest of all creatures in the garden enticed her to eat, she grabbed the opportunity and bit into the inviting fruit.

Almost immediately, her mind opened afresh; her ears began to hear sounds she had never heard before; she saw things she had never noticed before; the whole world became suddenly alive to her senses in a new way. "What a glorious sight," she said, and the God who gave her life, listening from His heavenly abode, smiled appreciatively. "Finally," the Divine said, "somebody else, created in my image, values my Creation."

The woman, however, felt something was missing. She too wanted someone else, someone like her, to appreciate the joys she was feeling and share her excitement. To see, hear, and feel what was being revealed to her—the earth and every common sight, appareled in celestial light with the glory and the freshness of a dream—with no one to share it with, felt lonesome, empty, and incomplete. So, turning to her appointed companion, the man, she said: "If you eat from the fruit of this Tree, as I have, you will be able to join me in knowing bliss. Take a bite."

The man hesitated. That the woman had eaten from the Tree made sense to him. After all, the snake had encouraged her to do so. But he had received no such encouragement. Was it possible that he wasn't ready yet to handle this uplifting and enlightening encounter? "I have to exercise discretion and avoid foolishness and hastiness," he reminded himself.

But the invitation of his mate was too strong to resist. She seemed to be having such a good time. So with no further ado, he grabbed the apple and ate.

Suddenly, something strange happened. The man and the woman, who had grown up together and had spent most of their time with each other, began to feel something they had never felt before. It was an uplifting, arousing, and energizing sensation. Their bodies felt lighter and warmer, and they had an urge to touch and caress each other. As these feelings grew, all hesitating thoughts dissolved. They stretched their arms toward each other, embraced for a very long time and, feeling free and vibrant, they stroked each other with gentleness and sensitivity, allowing their bodies to join as they made love for the first time.

When they were done and resting comfortably in each other's arms, the Divine spoke once again to them saying: "You are individuals in your own right, but as you have already seen, to experience your deepest and greatest fulfillment you will often need to depend on each other. So it is for you, Man, to learn about the many needs and complex desires of your woman, and how to help her satisfy them; and it is for you, Woman, to do exactly the same. I know you have already experienced the pleasures of knowing each other sexually. Wasn't that a blissful experience? Nine months from now, as a result of your encounter, a child may be born to you. I'm holding you responsible for the welfare of the child and am entrusting its life to your care and attention.

"Also know that for you to continue to find satisfaction in each other requires thoughtfulness; through trial and error, you will develop skills to do so. You will also need time and above all patience and devotion. I have given you all the mental tools you need to succeed in this most important endeavor. Whether you succeed or fail in your intimacy is in your hands. Happiness or misery, it's up to you."

Then the man and the woman stood before each other and in unison said:

"You are bones of my bones,

"And flesh of my flesh."

And she called him Adam, and he called her Eve.

A few years later, after they had raised two strong and happy children and gained a bit more experience, the Divine revealed Himself again and said: "What have you learned so far about yourselves and your lives?"

"I have learned, Lord," said Adam, "that if I want to eat, short of the few years of infancy and childhood, I have got to work. Nothing is free around here, and while the earth is indeed fertile and grows many nutritious things, for them to be useful to me, I must transform them with my efforts and dedication."

"I, in turn," said Eve, "learned that it is miraculous to give birth to children, but it is also painful, and not just in the physical sense.

Children are blessings, but they are also demanding and dependent, forcing us to postpone many of the other meaningful things we want to do."

"And Lord," they continued, "we have both learned that you made us resourceful and wise and that our imagination and creativity allow us to understand and even change the direction of things. Our powers compel us to approach our actions with great sensitivity and regard, reverence and respect for the world and the life you entrusted us with; otherwise, we might often injure ourselves, and others.

"We have also realized that neither we nor the world will ever be perfect. Gradually, we are learning to accept this fact. We understand that You could not have created a world of living creatures where vulnerability, uncertainty, and impermanence were not integral parts of all existence.

"At first, we were angry and frustrated with You. We thought that our lives were wrong, flawed, and diseased. Perhaps, we thought, we had displeased You and that caused our misery; or perhaps You didn't care about us and made suffering part of our daily lives. But thanks to the special gift You gave us—the gift of reflective consciousness—we realized it is not so.

"Neither are You an uncaring, vindictive, punitive God nor have we done anything wrong to justify our suffering. After much reflection, we came to understand that this was the best and only way human life was possible. You couldn't have made us human—self-conscious; able to speak, think, reason, imagine and plan—and yet be impervious to our distressful feelings. To be human and enjoy this great privilege requires understanding and acceptance of it all. Forgive our ignorance and misguided perceptions. It must have hurt you deeply to see the creatures of Your Creation misunderstand and misrepresent Your work. This, however, will not happen again. We understand better now why You made us this way and we are ready to accept our lot, revere our gift, and be grateful.

"We also want to thank you from the bottom of our hearts for the opportunity to witness and participate in every aspect of our lives. It is such a privilege to be alive in this way. Such an honor."

"I am so pleased to hear this," the Divine said. "I struggled endlessly with this challenging question: Should I give you the gift of reflective consciousness and thus the chance to know me, yourselves, and the world at large but also know suffering, or should I have kept you innocent and pure, like beautiful deer, protected, dependent, but nakedly vulnerable to the mighty forces of nature, including those of your own nature? I am delighted to hear that you both can see and appreciate the wisdom of my choice.

"From here on, I want you to know that you are on your own. Speak to me as much as you want; I will, for the most part, just listen. My responses you will find in your dreams, intuitions, and in those unexpected occurrences you often wonder about. Pay attention to them and remember: Never take life for granted. Seize the day and live in the present because the future, nobody—myself included—can know. That is how I created it, and that is how it is."

Celebrating Our Humanity

In this new iteration of the Eden myth, the primordial couple exhibits qualities of mind similar to those attributed to the God of the Hebrew Bible: reflective, sensitive, insightful, responsible, creative, resourceful, confident, moral, and, most importantly, loving. They appreciate the wondrous gifts God has endowed them with and relish the remarkable opportunities these gifts bestowed on them. They are also grateful and humble human beings, willing and able to follow in God's revealed path not for the purpose of receiving immediate or future rewards but for the purpose of making their lives on earth better, more harmonious, and freer from fear, shame, and distress. Their intention is to create a living environment in which they and their descendants can live and enjoy liberty, prosperity, and psycho-spiritual fulfillment while respecting and loving each other.

The new Adam and Eve are willful human beings endowed with the awesome privilege of knowing themselves, their Creator and others; they are endowed with the ability to distinguish between good and bad, an ability that defines what is quintessentially human in them.

These primordial humans are also able to accept graciously the suffering inexorably woven into who they are.

This new image of man stands in stark contrast to the one offered us in the Hebrew Bible. There, the dawn of our ability to be moral agents is described as a transgression that evokes feelings of shame and fear rather than feelings of wonderment and awe. Moreover, frightened of the punishment they imagined coming their way, Adam and Eve hide from God's presence rather than face Him with confidence and pride.

The Eden myth led our ancestors to believe that most if not all our troubles and sufferings were due to the primordial couple's disobedience and that self-reflective consciousness, which this new version of the myth celebrates and glorifies, was an undesirable, wrong outcome.

Our underlying wish to return to a state of perennial unconsciousness like that experienced by human infants during the first year or two of their lives is a blatant refutation of who we really are and a rejection of our God-given ability to develop mentally. Besides, perennially living the life of infants, unable to speak and think, unconscious of self and others, would be disgraceful. Such human beings would never enjoy the rights and privileges of full-fledged persons who possess free will, imagination, creativity, artistry, language, communications from their interiority via dreams and visions, and so forth. By wishing for that kind of paradisiacal life, man, as the creator of the myth, affirmed a desire for a life in which distressing, unpleasant feelings, and therefore suffering, did not exist. But this would also be a life in which he would remain in a state of vegetative existence, never reaching the height of personhood for which he is encoded, an evolutionary absurdity. By way of contrast, the new myth embodies an understanding of human life that is consistent with what we have learned about our human condition from our sciences, knowledge that continues to unfold as our experiences and efforts deepen. It is this evolving body of knowledge that allowed me to formulate a new narrative about our origins, one that demonstrates that the purpose of our lives is to attempt to unfold all of our awesome capabilities and assume the responsibilities that come along with it.

In the original myth, the snake is seen as an embodiment of deviousness deserving the worst of God's dispensed punishments. An evil adversary intent on subverting God's authority by seducing Eve, and through her, Adam, to eat from the forbidden tree, she is condemned to eat dust all the days of her life (Gen. 3:14). The new myth, however, understands the serpent as the manifestation of a wise aspect of the psyche, capable of appreciating the value that self-reflective consciousness brings into the living and nonliving world. This wise ally, God's angel, encourages us to embrace consciousness, to dedicate our lives to nurture it, and to become ever more aware of our needs, our complexity, and that of the other creatures with which we share our glorious planet. In doing so, the snake, as a representation of wisdom, invites us to celebrate with great joy our emergence from the darkness of unconsciousness to the light of knowing and, more significantly, of knowing that we know.

The God image the new myth paints is also profoundly different. He is not an authoritarian, warrior-like, punitive Father in heaven who at times acts like a tyrannical ruler expecting His charges to demonstrate unconditional obedience to His will. Nor is He a gullible divinity who enters into unholy wagers with His created angels, causing even His most loyal and devoted servants to experience the harshest of calamities. The new Lord is also not a God forced to incarnate in a human body, suffer, and die in order to expiate the sinful acts of other human beings He created. Instead, the God of the new myth is a caring, nourishing Divine Father/Mother who knows that by creating beings endowed with free will He has voluntarily given up control over their lives and, as a result, over the fate of His created world. It is a concession the Divine has made with delight because of the enormous joy He experiences in seeing His children grow up and become independent, autonomous beings, creatures able to act responsibly and morally. This type of human being makes the Divine proud, although, at times—many times—brings deep sorrow to His heart.

And as to the world into which the primordial couple was born, and all of us thereafter, it is one not ruled by a system of retribution in which people who do "good deeds" (as defined by the moral code of the time and region) are rewarded and those who commit "wicked deeds" (defined in similar fashion) are punished. Instead, it is a world in which constructive and destructive forces coexist in a state of dynamic and unstable equilibrium, continuously seeking balance. It is a world in which self-regulating mechanisms maintain homeostasis, and the overall effort of man is to harmonize, blend, and integrate physical, biological, psychical, and metaphysical reality and their complex interconnectedness and interdependence into the fabric of his life. There is in each of us an inner voice, a conscience that guides us and doesn't let us forget when we stray from the healthy, constructive path, and that reminds us, when we commit destructive acts, of our duties and responsibilities, encouraging us to amend our ways.

The type of human being here envisioned is one deeply invested in learning and understanding the meaning of his humanity in the broadest sense of the word. In that regard, Adam acknowledges that while the earth is indeed generous in its offerings—it grows fruit and vegetables without him having to do anything—if he expects to have a stable, reliable food supply he will have to work the earth for it. He understands that there is no free ride but does not feel burdened with a sense of having been cursed. His is a calm acceptance and appreciation of the unvarnished truth of his existence. Similarly, Eve has come to understand that giving birth is a woman's biological privilege, something only she can do, an integral part of her mystery. But this awesome privilege comes with risks and distressing feelings and conditions, which at times can even be life threatening. Together, they are also aware of the duality of joy and pain associated with raising children and how it demands a sacrifice of time and of the freedom to do so many other things they may have otherwise wished to do but now cannot.

Finally, we hear Adam and Eve make remarkable and deeply enlightening confessions about what it means to them to be human and their genuine appreciation of it all. In their meaningful and moving reflections, they acknowledge that God has made them resourceful and wise and that their creativity and imagination confers on them great powers. These powers, however, compel them to approach their actions with great sensitivity and with reverence for the world and life with which they have been entrusted. Having realized that the world is not and will never be perfect, and that life is not necessarily fair, or just, they learn gradually to accept these difficult, often frightening facts. Moreover, they have come to appreciate that whichever way it came about (God, nature, both?) a world populated by self-conscious creatures by definition will also be a world in which vulnerability, injustice, uncertainty, and impermanence will be integral components.

In affirming these painful truths, the newly iterated ancestral couple reveals an understanding of human life that is integrative, realistic, and humane. Instead of seeing their God as a deity sometimes expressing the basest human traits—jealousy, vindictiveness, wrathfulness, and so forth—they perceive God as a caring, supportive, guiding deity immensely pleased by the way humanity has come to understand and embrace the totality of what He intended them to be. This is a God that acknowledges how much He, Himself, agonized over the idea of making human beings conscious creatures for He knew full well the burden this would impose on them. Nonetheless, this is a God willing to allow His children free will, the gift of self-knowledge, and the creative potential to make this world either the most glorious place imaginable or a living hell.

In rewriting the Genesis myth from an evolutionary point of view, I hope to have made some contribution to the soul healing that we must all experience if we expect to find inner peace. It is imperative that we understand the implications of our coming into existence and assume full responsibility for the awesome mental and spiritual attributes with which we have been endowed. The human potential for creative and constructive enterprise is vast and so is its potential for the destructive. It is up to us to reclaim our sacredness and our creative powers and assume our rightful place in the Creation as custodians of life, starting with our own lives and the life of the glorious planet we inhabit.

The time may be nearing for the dawning of a new era in which what is quintessentially human is celebrated and revered, and where we human beings walk humbly and proudly in full recognition of all that we are.

Notes

Chapter 1

1. All biblical quotes are from *Tanakh: The Holy Scriptures; The New JPS Translation according to the Traditional Hebrew Text* by the Jewish Publication Society (Philadelphia: Jewish Publication Society, 1988), except for those pertaining to the Book of Job and the books of the New Testament: those are from *The Jerusalem Bible*, edited by Alexander Jones (Garden City, NY: Doubleday, 1966).

Chapter 2

1. Dean Hamer, *The God Gene: How Faith Is Hardwired into Our Genes* (New York: Doubleday, 2004).

Chapter 3

1. Herman Melville, *Moby-Dick: Or, The Whale* (Berkeley: University of California Press, 2010), 185.
2. John Milton, *Paradise Lost* (Mineola, NY: Dover, 2005), 3.
3. Saint Augustine, *Confessions* (London: Penguin, 1961).
4. David Jolly, "Push for the Right to Die Grows in the Netherlands," *New York Times*, April 2, 2012, http://www.nytimes.com/2012/04/03 /health/push-for-the-right-to-die-grows-in-the-netherlands.html.

Chapter 4

1. *The Decalogue*, dir. Krzysztof Kieślowski, aired 1989–1990 (Chicago: Facets Multimedia, 2003), DVD, 572 min.
2. Søren Kierkegaard, *Fear and Trembling*, trans. Alastair Hannay (London: Penguin, 1986).
3. Nikos Kazantzakis, *The Last Temptation of Christ* (New York: Simon & Schuster, 1960), 1.
4. C. G. Jung, "Answer to Job," *Psychology and Religion: West and East*, vol. 11 of *The Collected Works of C. G. Jung* (Princeton, NJ: Princeton University Press, 1969).

Chapter 6

1. H. H. Ben-Sasson, ed., *A History of the Jewish People* (Cambridge, MA: Harvard University Press, 1976).

Chapter 8

1. "Sheol" means "the place of the dead" or "the place of departed souls/spirits," what today is commonly called Hades.

Chapter 10

1. Nasson Scherman and Meir Zlotowitz, eds., Koheles/Ecclesiastes: *A New Translation with a Commentary Anthologized from Talmudic, Midrashic and Rabbinic Sources*, 2nd ed., ArtScroll Tanach Series (Brooklyn: ArtScroll Mesorah, 1976).
2. Rami Shapiro, *The Way of Solomon: Finding Joy and Contentment in the Wisdom of Ecclesiastes* (New York: HarperCollins, 2000).
3. Robert Gordis, *Koheleth: The Man and His World; A Study of Ecclesiastes* (New York: Schocken, 1968).

Chapter 11

1. *Fiddler on the Roof*, dir. Norman Jewison (West Hollywood: Mirisch Production Company, 1971).

Chapter 12

1. Jung, "Answer to Job."
2. Ibid., xi.
3. C. G. Jung, *The Archetypes and the Collective Unconscious*, vol. 9, pt. 1 of *Collected Works of C. G. Jung*.
4. Max I. Dimont, *Jews, God and History* (New York: Simon & Schuster, 1962).
5. Yitzhak Buxbaum, *The Life and Teachings of Hillel* (Lanham, MD: Jason Aronson, 2000).
6. Flavius Josephus, *The Antiquities of the Jews*, in *Josephus: The Complete Works.*, trans. William Whiston (Nashville: Thomas Nelson, 2003).

Chapter 13

1. Aldous Huxley, *Brave New World* (New York: Harper Perennial, 2006).

Index

Diaspora, 200, 229

Dimont, Max, *Jews, God, and History*, 138, 221, 226

disasters
ability to overcome, 33–34
as betrayals, 72–73
fear of, 37
Job's experiences of, 151
Noah and the ark story, 64
reign over natural, 70
vulnerability to, 26–27
worrying about, 17–18

diseases. *See* health issues

disillusionment, 180

disobedience, 42–46, 46–48, 62, 67

disorder, introduction of, 63

displacement, psychological, 235–236

distress, 136–138, 144, 184–185

Divine, the. *See* God; Jeshua of Nazareth (Jesus); Jesus Christ

Divine command, 42–46

divine debt against humanity, 208

divine grace, 220–221

Divine Law, 232. *See also* Mosaic Law; Torah

Divine Order, 109

Divine Voice, 77

dread, 21, 153

dreams, 87–89, 198–199, 201

E

Ecclesiastes, 35
1:2, 3, 180
1:10, 181
2:13, 188
2:17, 180
3:11, 186
3:17, 19, 20, 187
4:1, 188
5:3, 4, 190
5:9, 11, 190
7:1, 191
7:2–4, 191

Ecclesiastes (*continued*)
7:11, 12, 188
7:15, 187
7:16, 188
7:20, 188
8:1, 183
8:9, 188
8:11–14, 187–188
11:5, 189–192
first appearance of, 179
Koheleth's pursuit of happiness, 179–183
overcoming despair in, 149
See also Koheleth

Eden myth of creation, 174
acquired suffering, 50–52
Adam and Eve's curse in, 199–200
ambivalence in, 52–56
birth of/reason for, 44–45
disobedience to the Divine, 42–46
effects on ancestors of, 250
efforts to return to Eden, 56
expulsion from Eden, 46–49, 64–65
God's creation of man in His image, 39–42
new iteration of (*see* Rightness of Being Human)
shame of Adam and Eve, 236
submission of the feminine principle, 49–50
symbolism of snake in, 251
as voice of contradictions, 42–43

ego
in collective psychological functioning, 38
development of, 4–5, 5–10
as driver of self, 186
emergence of "I," 6–7
immaturity of, 82
during sleep, 6–7
ego-self, 9, 138–139

James the Apostle, 223
James the Just, 227–228
jealousy/envy, 188
Jephthah, 113
Jeremiah, Book of
  2:28–29, 134
  30:10, 136
  44:11–19, 139
  defiance of the Covenant,
    139–140
Jeremiah the Prophet, 134, 136
Jerusalem
  Christian Jewish community in,
    227–228
  desolation of, 201
  Hezekiah's reign in, 135
  Kingdom of Judea in, 179
  pestilence sent by God to,
    142–143
  rebuilding of, 173
  socioeconomic differences in,
    176–177
Jeshua of Nazareth (Jesus)
  according to Gospels, 209–212
  acts performed by, 211
  contribution to Jewish canon of,
    218
  death of, to Jews, 229
  as the Divine, 213
  energy of, 216–217
  intentions of, 217
  life of, 208
  as man of sorrows, 210–211
  psychological perspective on,
    215–218
  as Son of God, 209
Jesse, 136
Jesus Christ
  change of Jeshua of Nazareth to,
    218–220
  as Messiah, 225, 227
  Paul's interpretation of teachings
    of, 224

Jesus Christ (*continued*)
  truth of Gospels on, 225
  See also Jeshua of Nazareth (Jesus)
Jewish canon. *See* Jews/Judaism
Jewish Law. *See* Jews/Judaism;
    laws/rules; Mosaic Law; Ten
    Commandments; Torah
Jews, God, and History (Dimont), 226
Jews/Judaism, 34–35
  Christian Jews, 219, 220, 221,
    227–228
  coming of Messiah in, 200
  Covenantal agreement with God
    and, 140–141
  development of way of life, 231
  emergence of rabbis and rebbes,
    230–231
  establishment of religious practice,
    228
  feelings toward Paul's new religion
    in, 225
  feminine presence in, 50
  under foreign rulers, 207
  geographic dispersal of, 230–231
  God of, 224
  on Jesus as Messiah, 225–226
  Jewish canon, 178, 218
  Jewish Law (*see* Mosaic Law;
    Torah)
  Jews as chosen people, 103–104,
    218–219
  Kabbalists, 123
  management of world in Kabbala,
    23
  narratives of (*see* Hebrew Bible)
  need for mythologized version of
    life by, 229
  oppression of, 227–228
  orthodox, 179, 200
  Passover Seder, 99–100
  and Paul's new religion, 225–227
  persecution of, 109, 220, 229
  sacred stories in, 35

About the Author

Jacob Zighelboim, MD, is a physician/scientist who has authored some eighty peer-reviewed scientific research papers and coauthored ten scientific books, most of them having to do with the immunology of cancer and the application of immunological principles to the treatment of human cancer.

Formerly a professor at the medical school at UCLA, his discovery of his own cancer led to a philosophical, spiritual, and professional search for knowledge and understanding and a renewal of his own ideas about health, illness, suffering, and the healing process.

In the late '80s, he established a program of humanistic oncology, a type of medical practice that explores the experience of illness and how to help people with cancer reach the highest potential for recovery and well-being. Later, in the context of his own journey to health and healing as well as the journeys of his patients, he discovered deep correlations between the human themes addressed in some of the books of the Hebrew Bible and the themes he and his patients were addressing in their efforts to reduce suffering and attain healing.

During the last fourteen years, he has been teaching the art of medicine to medical students and since 2003 has been on the faculty of the Academy for Jewish Religion California, where he teaches Jewish Wisdom, Bioethics, and the Biblical Roadmap to the Eradication of Suffering.

Jacob welcomes your comments and invites you to contact him:
Website: http://www.jacobzmd.com/
E-mail: Jacob@JacobZMD.com

Made in the USA
Middletown, DE
07 January 2019